WORLD OF WELLNESS
Health Education Series

Physical Activity and Nutrition for Health

Chris Hopper, PhD

Bruce Fisher

Kathy D. Munoz, EdD, RD

Humboldt State University

Human Kinetics

Library of Congress Cataloging-in-Publication Data

Hopper, Christopher A., 1952-
  Physical activity and nutrition for health / Chris A. Hopper, Bruce Fisher, Kathy D. Munoz.
       p. cm.
   ISBN-13: 978-0-7360-6538-2 (soft cover)
   ISBN-10: 0-7360-6538-5 (soft cover)
  1. Physical education for children--United States.   2. Physical fitness for children--Study and teaching--United States.   3. Children--Nutrition--United States.   I. Fisher, Bruce, 1949-   II. Munoz, Kathy D., 1951-   III. Title
   GV443.H657 2008
   613.7'042--dc22

                                                      2008015476

ISBN-10: 0-7360-6538-5
ISBN-13: 978-0-7360-6538-2

Acquisitions Editors: Bonnie Pettifor Vreeman and Scott Wikgren; **Developmental Editor:** Amy Stahl; **Assistant Editors:** Anne Rumery and Lauren B. Morenz; **Copyeditor:** Patrick Connolly; **Proofreader:** Julie Marx Goodreau; **Permission Manager:** Martha Gullo; **Graphic Designer:** Bob Reuther; **Graphic Artist:** Kathleen Boudreau-Fuoss; **Cover Designer:** Keith Blomberg; **Illustrator (cover):** Jenny Parum; **Photographer (interior):** © Human Kinetics/Kelly Huff; **Art Manager:** Kelly Hendren; **Associate Art Manager:** Alan L. Wilborn; **Illustrator:** Tim Offenstein; **Printer:** Versa Press

Printed in the United States of America   10   9   8   7   6   5   4   3   2   1

Human Kinetics
Web site: www.HumanKinetics.com

United States: Human Kinetics
P.O. Box 5076, Champaign, IL 61825-5076
800-747-4457
e-mail: humank@hkusa.com

Canada: Human Kinetics
475 Devonshire Road Unit 100, Windsor, ON N8Y 2L5
800-465-7301 (in Canada only)
e-mail: info@hkcanada.com

Europe: Human Kinetics
107 Bradford Road, Stanningley, Leeds LS28 6AT, United Kingdom
+44 (0) 113 255 5665
e-mail: hk@hkeurope.com

Australia: Human Kinetics
57A Price Avenue, Lower Mitcham, South Australia 5062
08 8372 0999
e-mail: info@hkaustralia.com

New Zealand: Human Kinetics
Division of Sports Distributors NZ Ltd.
P.O. Box 300 226 Albany, North Shore City, Auckland
0064 9 448 1207
e-mail: info@humankinetics.co.nz

Contents

Section 2   Food for a Workout 109

Preface

Physical activity and nutrition are interrelated concepts, and presenting these two concepts together will enable teachers to be more effective in dealing with the obesity epidemic. *Physical Activity and Nutrition for Health* provides lesson plans for elementary teachers (K-6) working in self-contained classrooms. These lesson plans are designed to teach students ages 5 to 12 to incorporate more physical activity and healthy eating habits into their daily living patterns. This book focuses on helping teachers plan and implement programs in physical education and nutrition education to significantly improve the health of their students. At the same time, the lessons support learning in other subject areas, such as health education, mathematics, and science. For example, in section 1, students learn about the science concepts related to the structure and function of the heart. In section 3, students learn about the muscles in the body, and they also learn how eating quality protein will fuel and provide the building blocks for muscle synthesis. Throughout the book, nutrition lessons cover topics from health and science, including reading food labels, calculating calories in food, and choosing products containing healthy fat.

The lesson plans in this book expand on those in the *WOW! Health Education Series* by including more options for physical activity. In addition, this book provides nutrition lessons that include even greater depth and detail. The lessons also include modifications for younger and older students, adding greater flexibility for teaching across ages 5 to 12.

The main goals for this book include the following:

- To supplement the *WOW! Health Education Series* by serving as a companion guide to the series and a resource for physical activity and nutrition
- To provide user-friendly lesson plans that enable teachers to improve their students' health, specifically aimed at reducing obesity
- To provide lessons that are adaptable across elementary grade levels
- To enhance the expertise of teachers in a variety of school settings

Physical Activity and Nutrition for Health provides the following benefits for students and teachers:

- Ready-to-go lessons that are easy to understand
- Cross-curricular information to support other subject areas
- Lessons that promote the development of critical thinking and analytical skills
- Multiple assessment techniques
- Lessons that present fitness and nutrition as part of a lifestyle
- Physical activity lessons that include easy transitions between the warm-up, the main activity, and the cool-down
- Family and community activities that students can do outside of school

This book includes several unique features:

- Detailed descriptions and diagrams to accompany each lesson

- ▸ Lessons designed to be completed in a 30-minute time frame
- ▸ Lessons that require simple, easy-to-obtain, and inexpensive materials
- ▸ Adaptations that enable teachers to include students with disabilities
- ▸ Challenges for higher-level and higher-skilled students
- ▸ Lessons that effectively integrate physical activity and nutrition concepts as they relate to healthy lifestyles
- ▸ Lessons that provide students with a conceptual understanding of the components of a healthy lifestyle by helping them learn the connection between physical activity and nutrition

Because this book is connected to the *WOW! Health Education Series,* it can be easily incorporated into your current curriculum. The lessons in the book are designed to reinforce standards in health, physical education, mathematics, and science. These standards are referred to throughout the book. More information on the standards related to health, physical education, and science can be found at www.education-world.com/standards/state/toc/index.shtml.

Mathematics standards can be found at http://standards.nctm.org/document/chapter3/numb.htm and www.education-world.com/standards/national/math/index.shtml.

This book is made up of four sections, with 60 specific lesson plans. We begin in section 1 by presenting the concept of the energy equation. This includes lessons about how people must consume calories for energy. Other lessons cover the role of the heart and cardiorespiratory system in providing energy during exercise. Section 2 introduces the concept of aerobic activity. This section presents the FIT principle and covers the function of carbohydrate and fat as fuel sources for aerobic activities. The lessons in section 3 focus on improving strength, endurance, and flexibility. These lessons are also designed to broaden students' knowledge about nutrition as it relates to weight management and obesity. Section 4 emphasizes physi-

cal activity and nutrition as a part of a healthy lifestyle.

Each section is divided into parts that include a concept or nutrition lesson followed by interactive, engaging activities that reinforce the subject matter in the corresponding lesson. This consistent lesson structure makes the book more reader-friendly. For teachers who don't want to use the entire set of lessons, each lesson can also stand alone, providing flexibility in lesson planning. Icons have been placed by each lesson in the table of contents and throughout the book to make it easy for teachers to identify each type of lesson:

- ▸ Lessons that focus on nutrition can be found by the 🍎 icon.
- ▸ Concept lessons correspond to the 💡 icon.
- ▸ The 💗 icon denotes lessons relating to physical activity and movement.

The overall goal of *Physical Activity and Nutrition for Health* is to change the attitudes and behaviors of students so they embrace a lifetime commitment to health and fitness. When students develop this commitment, they will be better able to maintain a healthy weight throughout their lives. This book presents an easy-to-use and comprehensive curriculum for teaching physical activity and nutrition. These lesson plans provide quality, ready-made units for busy classroom teachers. The descriptions of activities are straightforward and manageable for teachers who have multiple preparation tasks. Lessons include content from a variety of subject areas, such as mathematics and science, which reinforces learning of topics throughout the entire elementary school curriculum.

To learn more about nutrition, students are involved in problem-solving activities while they learn to communicate, explore, and collaborate. Innovative lessons are used to teach concepts and provide fun activities that promote physical activity as a part of everyday life. This standards-based curriculum is realistic for classroom teachers and does not require extensive amounts of equipment. The book is versatile enough to be used across grade levels and curriculum areas. It provides essential knowledge for teachers who are focusing on standards-based programs in health and physical education. The lesson plan format is designed to provide essential information for planning, organizing, and teaching the lesson. Each lesson includes key vocabulary words that can be introduced in class ahead of time. Specific details about the needed equipment are provided to assist with planning. Each lesson also includes modifications for older and younger students, along with assessment strategies. Adaptations and suggestions for teaching students with disabilities are also included.

Getting started is often the hardest part in developing a physical fitness and nutrition program. This book makes getting started easy.

Warm-ups, cool-downs, and stretching are described in the introduction. Then select a lesson to meet your teaching needs from a variety of topics. Use family activities to help reinforce what your students learn in the classroom. Plan to use the assessments to track the progress of your students.

Additionally, a bound-in CD-ROM is located at the back of this book. The CD-ROM includes every card, family activity, transparency, and worksheet appearing in the book for a total of 124 easy-to-print and easy-to-use reproducibles. All reproducibles included on the CD-ROM are highlighted in the book with a ⊙ icon appearing next to them in the each lesson plan's "Get Ready to WOW! 'Em" section.

Introduction

Warm-Up, Cool-Down, and Stretching Exercises

Warm-ups and cool-downs should be part of any exercise routine. Warm-ups allow the body to gradually adjust to more intense exercise, and cool-downs allow the body to return safely to a preexercise level. Warm-ups prepare the body for exercise by increasing body temperature and providing an increased supply of blood to the muscles. In this way, the muscles are prepared for stretching and other activity in a systematic way that prevents injury. In a reverse manner, the cool-down enables the body to gradually recover from the fitness activity. A proper cool-down aids in the prevention of soreness and injury and allows a return to normal breathing levels.

Warm-Up and Cool-Down Activities

The activities in this section can be used at the beginning of the lesson to prepare students for physical movement. They can also be adjusted to serve as cool-downs. When using an activity as a warm-up, the intensity of the activity should gradually build. When using an activity as a cool-down, students should gradually decrease their activity level. Some activities can serve as warm-ups and cool-downs in the same lesson. Initially, each warm-up or cool-down activity should be thoroughly explained to students to ensure understanding.

Warm-up and cool-down activities should be repeated on a frequent basis. This will help students recognize the activities by name. It will also help ensure that students execute the activities correctly.

Select warm-ups that allow an easy transition to the main activity of the lesson. For example, the jump rope and stretch warm-up would be ideal if the main focus of the lesson is jumping rope. The equipment is already available. Also, select cool-downs that allow an easy transition. For example, if students are already in pairs, the partner greet activity may be appropriate.

1. Jump rope and stretch: Each student has a jump rope and slowly starts jumping. On a signal, students perform a stretch using the jump rope. An example would be to fold the rope in half and hold it overhead while bending from side to side.

2. Ready, draw!: In pairs, players start with their hands behind their backs. On the "Draw" command, the players show either one or two fingers. If the players show different numbers, they do 10 repetitions of an exercise (e.g., jumping jacks). If they show the same numbers, they do nothing and "draw" again.

3. Skier: Students stand next to a line on the playground or in the gym. They jump from side to side without touching the line for 30 seconds. Ask students, *How many times did you cross the line?* Then tell them to try again to see if their scores improve.

4. Triangle tag: Students are in groups of four. Two students face each other and hold hands. The other two stand on either side of the students holding hands. One person is "it" and chases the other. The two holding hands act as a shield for the one being chased.

5. 15-second gusto: After some light running, students complete a series of exercises as follows:
   - 15 seconds of jumping jacks
   - 15 seconds of squat thrusts
   - 15 seconds of skiers
   - 15 seconds of jogging on the spot, bringing the knees up high
   - 15 seconds of modified push-ups

   As a cool-down, students perform two to three exercises with fewer repetitions (five) and in a slow manner with a walk between each exercise. All of these exercises are described in detail in lesson 6.

6. Partner greet: Begin the activity with the students walking around the gym in a scattered formation. On command, each student finds a partner to face and shakes that person's hand. This person is designated as the student's "handshake" partner. Again, the students scatter throughout the gym. On command, they must find their handshake partners and shake hands. They then find a second partner and create a different handshake. The activity continues with students finding different partners and doing a different action with each partner, such as standing back to back or giving each other a high five. During the time between locating partners, the students walk or jog.

7. Weave run: The entire class starts walking counterclockwise in a circle around a designated area (e.g., track, gym, softball diamond) with at least two yards (183 cm) of space between each student. One student is the lead runner, and one is the back runner. On a signal, the back runner weaves in and out of the runners until reaching the front. Then each of the other runners in turn weave their way to the front. When each runner has weaved through the line while the group is walking, students progress to a jog and repeat the activity while the line runs.

8. Leader: Students form groups of four to six students. Designate a leader for each group. The other students form a line behind the leader. The leader runs, and the line follows.

The leader determines the movement pattern and is allowed to jog, run slowly, skip, hop, or run sideways or backward. You can permit other movements after the students become familiar with the task. Every 30 seconds, change leaders.

9. Partner jog: Students find a partner and stand side by side, ready to run. On the signal "Go," students run slowly side by side with their partner in the designated area. On the signal "Change," pairs split up and find a new partner. Students greet their new partner.

10. Hexagonal run: Mark out a hexagonal shape with six cones, with the cones 20 yards (18 m) apart from each other. Students jog around the hexagon. Students then complete a walk-jog-skip-run sequence around the hexagon, changing movements at each cone.

11. Rhythm run: Students form pairs and jog side by side around a baseball diamond or basketball court. Instruct them to run so their left and right feet move in rhythm together. When they can do this in pairs, have them progress to groups of four. Encourage students to remind their running partner to use efficient running techniques, with arms moving in opposition to legs, hands held at waist level, and feet pointing forward. Students should slowly change from jogging to walking.

12. Skip progression: Set up four cones in a square (40 by 40 yd [37 by 37 m]). Students start by skipping one circuit around all four cones at a slow rate. On each subsequent circuit, the students speed up a little.

13. Around the group: Arrange students in two lines, side by side. The students jog while keeping the lines side by side. On a signal, the last pair in line runs to the front of the line. Once this pair reaches the front of the line, the next pair runs from the back. This continues until all pairs have run from the back. Then the students slow down to a walk.

14. Grid jog: Mark out four 10-by-10-yard (9 by 9 m) squares with cones. These squares should be arranged in a square format 20

yards (18 m) apart from each other. Divide the class into four groups, with one group in each square. Each group performs an exercise in the square and then walks or jogs in a clockwise manner to the next square to complete a different exercise. After moving to each square in turn, students return to their starting square.

15. Figure 8: Place two cones 30 yards (27 m) apart. Students move single file around the cones in a figure 8 pattern. Call out the movements starting with "jog," "skip," or "gallop," then "walk."

16. Jog and stretch: Set up four stretching stations around the playing area. Explain and demonstrate the stretches for each station. Start by having all students walk or jog two laps around the stretching area. Divide the class into four groups, with one group at each stretching station. After completing 30 seconds at a stretching station, a group jogs two laps around the area and moves to the next station.

17. Run and split: The class jogs single file down the middle of the playing area. At the end of the area, the students split—one person goes to the left, the next to the right, and so on. Runners run around the perimeter of the square. When they return to the starting point, they run side by side down the middle and then split off in opposite directions at the end of the area (with each student going in the same direction as in the previous lap). Finish by having the students walk through the pattern.

18. Jog and jump: Students start by walking or jogging a certain distance and completing jump rope moves. (For this activity, you can use any of the basic jump rope moves in lesson 48, "Jump for Life.") Students continue with light jogging and jump roping.

19. Hopscotch drill: Five circles are placed on the floor. A five-inch (13 cm) circle or floor spot is recommended. The distance between the squares is shown in figure I.1 and should be adjusted to suit the size or ability of the student, 18 inches (45.7 cm) is a good start-

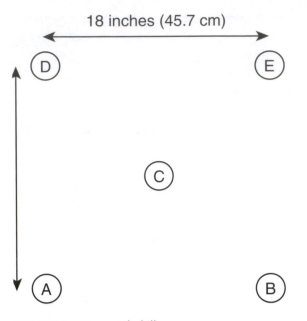

FIGURE I.1   Hopscotch drill.

ing point for the distance. Many variations in jumping patterns can be used:

- Start at one end with feet on A and B. With both feet, jump to C and then to D and E. Come back the same way.
- Both feet are on C. Jump with both feet to D and E and back to C. Jump with both feet to A and B and back to C.
- Use right or left foot only and jump in a pattern going to each square.

20. Come friend, come over: Divide the class into groups of four. Each group further divides into pairs, with one student behind the other. The two pairs should be positioned 20 yards (18 m) apart as shown in figure I.2. The two pairs of students face each other. The first student in one line calls the opposite student over to that side—for example, "Francisco, come on over doing a skip." Francisco then skips over and goes to the back of the line. This sequence continues with the first person in line calling the next person over.

Stretching Routines

Different stretching routines can be used after warm-up and cool-down activities. In many cases, the choices for stretching routines are influenced

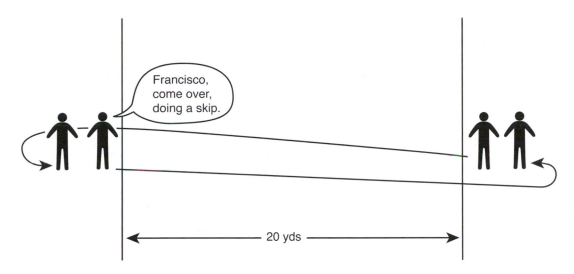

FIGURE I.2   Come friend, come over.

by the facilities available and whether students can sit, kneel, or lie on the ground. Stretching routines 1 and 4 are for outdoors when students are unable to lie on the ground. Stretching routines 2 and 3 can be performed when students are able to sit, lie, or kneel on the floor or the ground (inside or outside). Students can use mats or towels for stretches on the ground.

Stretching Routine 1

Note: Use this routine on the playground (outside) when students are not able to lie on the ground (see figure I.3).

1. Neck stretch: This exercise stretches the neck. Keeping the shoulders back and the spine straight, students slowly roll the head to the right shoulder, straighten, then roll toward the left shoulder, and straighten. They repeat five times. Make sure students *do not* roll the head in a fast, circular manner or roll the head backward.

2. Back and side stretch: This exercise stretches the shoulder and upper arm. Students lift the right arm and reach behind the head and down the spine. With the left hand, they push down on the right elbow and hold. Students then reverse arm positions and repeat.

3. Side bender: This exercise stretches the sides of the body, or the obliques. Students stretch the left arm overhead to the right. They bend

to the right at the waist, reaching as far to the right as possible with the left arm, and then hold. Next, they reach as far as possible to the left with the right arm, and then hold. They repeat on the opposite side.

4. Knee raise: This exercise stretches the back of the legs. While standing, students hold the right leg behind the knee and draw it up toward the chest. They hold for 10 seconds, switch legs, and repeat three times.

5. Heel and toe raise: This exercise stretches the calf muscles. Students stand with the feet close together and the hands on the hips. They rise up on the toes, then on the heels. They repeat three times.

Stretching Routine 2

Note: Use this routine inside a gym, multipurpose room, or classroom where students can lie on the floor to stretch (see figure I.4).

1. Shoulder squeeze: This exercise stretches the back of the arms and shoulders. Students hold both hands behind their back in the standing position. They move the arms back behind their back and join the hands together. They then lift the arms up to stretch the front of the shoulders.

2. Knee to nose touch: This exercise stretches the legs and abdomen. In an all-fours posi-

tion, students lift the knee to touch the nose. They then move the leg back, making sure the leg does not lift higher than the hips (the neck and lower back should not hyper-extend).

3. **Kneeling stretch:** This exercise stretches the ankles and quadriceps. Kneeling on both knees, students turn to the right and press down on the right ankle with the right hand. They hold this position, keeping the hips

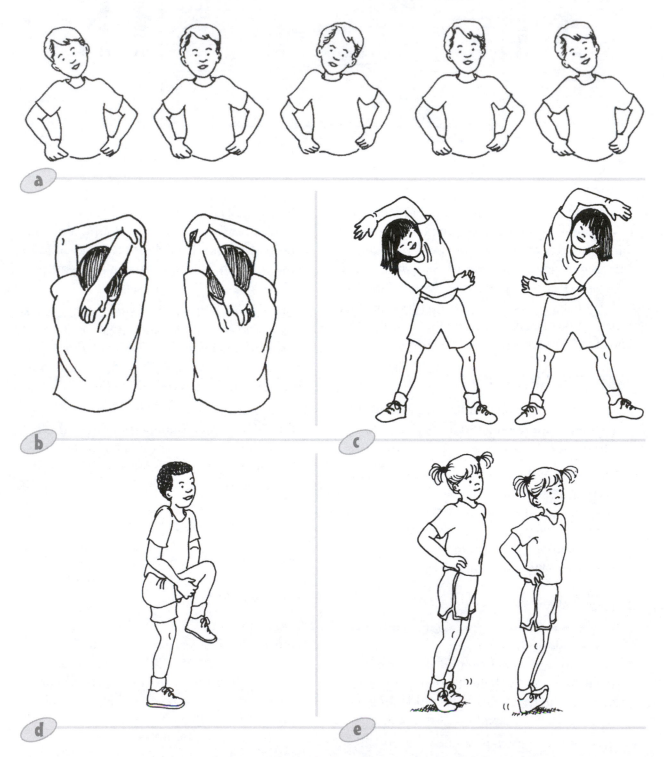

FIGURE I.3   Stretching routine 1: *(a)* neck stretch; *(b)* back and side stretch; *(c)* side bender; *(d)* knee raise; *(e)* heel and toe raise.

Reprinted, by permission, from C.A. Hopper, B.D. Fisher, and K.D. Munoz, 1997, *Health-Related Fitness for Grades 1 & 2* (Champaign, IL: Human Kinetics), 86.

thrust forward to avoid hyperflexing the knees. Make sure students do not sit on the heels. Students repeat on the left side.

4. Single-leg tuck: This exercise stretches the back of the leg and the lower back. Students sit on the floor with the left leg straight and the right foot tucked against the left thigh. Students lower the chest toward the left knee. They repeat the exercise with the right leg.

5. Knees to chest: This exercise stretches the lower back. Students lie on their back and tuck the knees to the chest.

Stretching Routine 3

Use this routine inside a gym, multipurpose room, or classroom where students can lie on the floor to stretch (see figure I.5).

1. Sitting stretch: This exercise stretches the inside of the thighs and the groin. Students sit with the soles of the feet together, place the hands on the knees or ankles, and lean the forearms against the knees. They provide resistance while attempting to raise the knees. Make sure students *do not* bounce their legs up and down.

2. Behind neck grasp: This exercise stretches the back of the arms and shoulders. Students lift the left arm and reach behind the head and down the spine. With the right hand, they reach behind their back and grasp the left hand. Students then reverse hands.

3. One-leg stretcher: This exercise stretches the lower back and the back of the legs. Students stand with one foot on a bench, keeping both legs straight. They press down on the bench with the heel for several seconds; then they relax and bend the trunk forward, trying to touch the head to the knee. They hold this position for a few seconds, then return to the starting position and repeat with the opposite leg. Students should not lock the knees.

FIGURE I.4   Stretching routine 2: *(a)* shoulder squeeze; *(b)* knee to nose touch; *(c)* kneeling stretch; *(d)* single-leg tuck; *(e)* knees to chest.

(a) Reprinted, by permission, from C.A. Hopper, B.D. Fisher, and K.D. Munoz, 1997, *Health-Related Fitness for Grades 1 & 2* (Champaign, IL: Human Kinetics), 63. *(b-e)* Reprinted, by permission, from C.A. Hopper, B.D. Fisher, and K.D. Munoz, 1997, *Health-Related Fitness for Grades 1 & 2* (Champaign, IL: Human Kinetics), 87.

4. Arm stretcher: This exercise stretches the arms and chest. Students cross the arms and turn the palms of the hands together. They raise the arms overhead behind the ears, extending at the elbows. They should reach as high as possible.

5. Trunk twister: This exercise stretches the midsection and waist. Students sit with the right leg extended and the left leg bent and crossed over the right knee. The students place the right arm on the left side of the left leg, and they push against that leg while turning the trunk as far as possible to the left. They place the left hand on the floor behind the buttocks. Students should reverse position and repeat on the opposite side.

Stretching Routine 4

Note: Use this routine on the playground (outside) when students are not able to lie on the ground (see figure I.6).

1. Shoulder shrug: This exercise reduces muscle tension in the neck and shoulders. Students shrug both shoulders up toward the ears. They hold this position for a few seconds and then repeat. Then they shrug the shoulders forward as far as possible, hold, and repeat. Next, they shrug the shoulders backward, hold, and repeat. Finally, they shrug the shoulders in opposite directions (up and down), hold, and repeat. Students complete each move three times.

FIGURE I.5   Stretching routine 3: *(a)* sitting stretch; *(b)* behind neck grasp; *(c)* one-leg stretcher; *(d)* arm stretcher; *(e)* trunk twister.

Reprinted, by permission, from C.A. Hopper, B.D. Fisher, and K.D. Munoz, *Health-Related Fitness for Grades 1 & 2* (Champaign, IL: Human Kinetics), 88.

2. Hip circles: This exercise stretches the core of the body. Keeping the feet and the head still, students slowly rotate the hips in a sweeping circular motion to loosen the midsection. They repeat five times and then change direction.

3. Foot pull: This exercise stretches the thigh. Students stand on one foot. They bend the knee of the other leg and pull the foot upward, holding this position for several seconds. Then they change sides. Students

FIGURE I.6   Stretching routine 4: *(a)* shoulder shrug; *(b)* hip circles; *(c)* foot pull; *(d)* step-out; *(e)* calf stretch.

(a) Reprinted, by permission, from C.A. Hopper, B.D. Fisher, and K.D. Munoz, 1997, *Health-Related Fitness for Grades 1 & 2* (Champaign, IL: Human Kinetics), 63. *(b)* Reprinted, by permission, from C.A. Hopper, B.D. Fisher, and K.D. Munoz, 1997, *Health-Related Fitness for Grades 1 & 2* (Champaign, IL: Human Kinetics), 86. *(c)* Reprinted, by permission, from T. Ratliffe and L.M. Ratliffe, 1994, *Teaching Children Fitness: Becoming a Master Teacher* (Champaign, IL: Human Kinetics), 97. *(d)* Reprinted, by permission, from C.A. Hopper, B.D. Fisher, and K.D. Munoz, 1997, *Health-Related Fitness for Grades 1 & 2* (Champaign, IL: Human Kinetics), 61. *(e)* Reprinted, by permission, from National Association for Sport and Physical Education, 2004, *Physical Best Activity Guide: Elementary Edition,* 2nd ed., CD-ROM (Champaign, IL: Human Kinetics).

can use a wall or a partner to rest against if necessary.

4. Step-out: This exercise stretches the back of the leg. Students step out with one leg and gently rest the hands on the knee. They return to a standing position and step out with the other leg. Make sure students *do not* bend their lead knee past the foot. They should keep the back heel on the ground to stretch the back of the calf and leg.

5. Calf stretch: This exercise stretches the calf and Achilles tendon. Students stand near a wall and lean on it with their forearms. They lean forward with one leg and leave the other leg straight behind. Students press the heel of the back leg to the floor and gently move the hips forward. Both feet are pointing ahead and touching the floor. Students hold the position for 10 seconds and then change legs to repeat the stretch.

SECTION 1

Energy Connection

Maintaining a healthy body weight requires eating enough calories to meet the body's energy needs while at the same time being active enough to burn off excess calories (rather than store those calories as body fat). In section 1, students will learn about the nutrients found in foods and about which nutrients contain calories. They will learn how to balance the calories they eat with calories burned during exercise. In this section, students will also learn that without a strong heart, the calories a person eats cannot be delivered to the muscles for fuel. If the muscles can't use the calories for fuel, the person can't burn off the excess calories to maintain a healthy weight.

At the end of these lessons, students will be able to connect the concept of energy in foods with the role of a strong heart that can deliver oxygen-rich blood to the muscles for energy production.

Calories

This first part of section 1 introduces students to the concept of energy found in food. A calorie is a unit of energy that fuels the body. Different foods contain different levels of calories that people use to fuel their daily activities. These calories also provide the energy that people need to grow taller and stronger. If a person eats more calories than she exerts through exercise and activity, this will cause her to gain weight, even if those calories are from nutritious, healthy foods. When people do not use all the energy contained in the food they eat, they store this energy in their body as fat. Eating fewer calories than a person's body needs to run efficiently can be just as unhealthy. Learning how to balance "calories in" with "calories out" is one of the most important lessons a person can learn to maintain a healthy weight throughout life.

This part begins with lesson 1, "Fueling Up." In this lesson, students will learn about the six types of nutrients a person needs to eat each day and which of those nutrients contain calories. Students will learn to calculate the amount of calories in a variety of foods based on the carbohydrate, protein, and fat content of those foods.

In lesson 2, "Calorie Calculator," students will learn how to read labels on packaged foods to locate the calories per serving.

Lesson 1: Fueling Up

Outcomes

At the end of this lesson, each student will be able to do the following:

▶ Name the six classifications of nutrients found in food.

▶ Define the term *calorie.*

▶ List the three nutrients that contain calories.

Connections to Health Education Standards

▶ Health promotion and disease prevention

▶ Access to valid health information, products, and services

Connections to Other Standards

▶ Science standards: science in personal and social perspectives; life science

▶ Math standards: number and operations; measurement; representation

Connections to WOW! Lessons

▶ Orange level: lesson 13, "A Crunch for Lunch"

▶ Orange level: lesson 15, "Go-Go-Go!"

▶ Yellow level: lesson 15, "Go-Go-Go!"

▶ Green level: lesson 12, "Tacos by Cody"

▶ Blue level: lesson 10, "Cheese Puffs"

▶ Purple level: lesson 9, "The Nutrient–Health Connection"

▶ Purple level: lesson 10, "The Balancing Act"

WOW! Vocabulary

▶ calorie—Unit of measure for the energy in food.

▶ carbohydrate—A nutrient that provides the body's main source of energy.

▶ fat—A nutrient that supplies energy to the body and is the most concentrated source of calories that people consume.

▶ gram—A metric measurement of weight; 1 ounce equals 28 grams.

▶ minerals—Vital nutrients that assist in regulating body functions, such as blood pressure and muscle contractions.

▶ nutrients—Substances in food that enable the body to grow, function, and repair itself.

▶ protein—The nutrient that is necessary to build and repair body tissue.

▶ vitamins—Micronutrients that facilitate many of the body's chemical processes and other functions.

▶ water—A nutrient that keeps the body cool; it has no calories.

Get Ready to WOW! 'Em

You will need the following:

- ▶ Transparency 1.1, Magic Moo (one transparency)
- ▶ Transparency 1.2, Calorie Countdown (one transparency)
- ▶ Overhead projector and transparency pens
- ▶ One orange, one hard-boiled egg, and one slice of whole wheat bread
- ▶ Colored blocks in three colors: You will need 29 of one color to represent carbohydrate, 11 of another color to represent protein, and 7 of a third color to represent fat (math blocks work well for this lesson, but any colored object that you can stack will also work).

Background Information

Food contains chemicals called **nutrients.** The body needs to take in nutrients every day in order to be healthy and active and to have energy to grow. These nutrients can be classified into six different groups, with three of these groups containing **calories** (see table 1.1).

All foods contain some nutrients, and in some cases, highly nutritious foods contain all six nutrient classifications. For example, a glass of low-fat milk contains **carbohydrate, protein,** some **fat, minerals** (such as calcium), **vitamins** (including riboflavin, or vitamin B_2), and **water.** Other foods are not good sources of nutrient value, such as candy and sweetened beverages. As you discuss eating nutritious foods with your students, you should convey the concept that there are no "bad" foods. The idea that things are "bad" or forbidden can make those things more desirable or cause a person to develop feelings of guilt. In the class discussions, make it clear that it is okay to sometimes eat these foods, just not every day (you can refer to these as "sometimes foods").

As noted in table 1.1, three of the nutrients contain calories, which is the form of energy that people get from food. The body needs a certain amount of calories each day, depending on the person's age, body size, and activity level. Knowing how many calories an individual needs and which foods contain calories are important concepts to understand when trying to maintain a healthy weight.

The nutrient that contains the most calories per unit (or **gram**) is fat. Each gram of fat contains nine calories. Carbohydrate and protein contain less than half as many calories as fat does, with only four calories per gram. All three nutrients that contain energy, including fat, are an important part of a person's diet. Learning to balance these three nutrients is one of the keys to healthy eating.

Table 1.1: Nutrients and Calories

Nutrients that contain calories	Nutrients that don't contain calories
Carbohydrate	Vitamins
Protein	Minerals
Fat	Water

Now WOW! 'Em

1. Review the background information presented for this lesson with the class.

2. Place transparency 1.1, Magic Moo, on the overhead projector.

3. Recite each of the six nutrient classifications to students and make sure the students can pronounce each one.

4. Ask the students, *Do you know what a calorie is?* Write the definition of a calorie on the board or directly on the Magic Moo transparency (a calorie is the unit of measure for the energy in food).

5. Next, ask the students, *Do you know which three nutrients contain calories?* As students guess the right ones, write the correct answers on the board or on the Magic Moo transparency under the definition of a calorie.

6. Explain to the students that fat has the most calories per unit or gram. Show transparency 1.2, Calorie Countdown, which contains a picture of an apple and some almonds. Explain to students, *One apple has 0 grams of fat and approximately 60 calories. Almonds are a very nutritious snack, but they contain more fat than an apple. In fact, 72 percent of the calories in almonds are fat, and a quarter cup of almonds* (35 grams) *contains 210 calories. Fat is higher in calories than either carbohydrate or protein.*

7. Next, ask the students to predict the amount of fat in each of three foods. Put the orange, the egg, and the whole wheat bread on the table. Ask the students, *How many grams of fat do you think are in the egg?* Using the blocks that represent fat (each block represents 1 gram of fat), begin placing them next to the egg until the number of blocks equals 7 (7 grams of fat per egg). Next, ask the students to predict how many grams of fat are in a slice of whole wheat bread (1 gram, or 1 block). And finally, ask the students how many grams of fat are in an orange (0 grams of fat).

Wrap It Up!

Finish the demonstration by using the colored blocks to show the number of grams of carbohydrate in each food, and then the number of grams of protein. Here are the correct amounts for each food:

- ▶ Orange: 64 calories, 1 gram of protein, 15 grams of carbohydrate, and 0 grams of fat
- ▶ Whole wheat bread: 73 calories, 3 grams of protein, 13 grams of carbohydrate, and 1 gram of fat
- ▶ Egg: 91 calories, 7 grams of protein, 0 grams of carbohydrate, and 7 grams of fat

Using the following example (the orange), demonstrate to the class how calories in a food can be calculated based on the grams of protein, carbohydrate, and fat. Then ask the students to calculate the total caloric content for the egg and the whole wheat bread.

Orange = (1 gram of protein × 4 calories per gram) + (15 grams of carbohydrate × 4 calories per gram) + (0 grams of fat × 9 calories per gram) = 64 calories

Ask the students, *Why do you think the egg is higher in calories than the orange even though it's smaller?* It's because of the fat content. Finish the lesson by asking the students to think about the foods they eat and how many calories those foods contain.

Teaching Notes

Each lesson has suggested modifications, whenever possible, to adapt the concepts to younger or older students.

Modifications for Younger Students

For younger students who have not yet learned to multiply, have them rank the foods in order from the highest in calories to the lowest in calories. Then explain that the foods that are higher in fat generally have more calories as well.

Modifications for Older Students

None.

Concept Development

Ask students to calculate the calories in other foods, such as their favorite snacks or fast-food meals, based on grams of fat, protein, and carbohydrate. Students should also include fresh fruits, vegetables, crackers, candy, and soda beverages.

Assessment Options

Each lesson includes assessment options for the lesson and may include additional assessment options for the skills performed within a lesson.

For the Lesson

During the class activity, students will demonstrate their ability to define the term *calorie* and to calculate (or rank) the calorie content of foods. They will also name the six classifications of nutrients during the discussion.

Transparency 1.1:
Magic Moo

Transparency 1.2:
Calorie Countdown

Apple: 0 grams of fat
60 calories

Almonds (¼ cup):
17 grams of fat
210 calories

Lesson 2: Calorie Calculator

Outcomes

At the end of this lesson, each student will be able to do the following:

▸ Read a food label and record the calories in each serving.

▸ Calculate the calorie content of various foods.

Connections to Health Education Standards

▸ Health promotion and disease prevention

Connections to Other Standards

▸ Science standards: science in personal and social perspectives; life science

▸ Math standards: number and operations

Connections to WOW! Lessons

▸ Yellow level: lesson 15, "Go-Go-Go!"

▸ Blue level: lesson 12, "The Big Label Discovery"

▸ Purple level: lesson 9, "The Nutrient–Health Connection"

▸ Purple level: lesson 10, "The Balancing Act"

WOW! Vocabulary

None.

Get Ready to WOW! 'Em

You will need the following:

▸ Transparency 2.1, Label Language (one transparency)

▸ Worksheet 2.1, Calorie Calculator (one copy per student)

▸ Overhead projector and transparency pens

▸ Various food labels from packaged foods (one per student)

Background Information

Food labels provide information about the calorie content of a serving of the food in the package. Remember from the previous lesson that foods contain carbohydrate, protein, and fat in various amounts. These three nutrients contain calories that provide people with energy to live and play. Carbohydrate and protein have the same number of calories per gram (4), while fat contains more than double that amount (9 calories per gram). On food labels, two items on the Nutrition Facts Panel indicate how many calories are in the food: the total calories per serving and the number of calories from fat in each serving. Both of these numbers are located at the top of each nutrition label, below the serving size. Learning to read the nutrition section of the food label can help people manage their weight better. Note that the calories listed on the label are just for one serving, not for the entire package. To determine the number of calories for the entire package, you must multiply the number of calories by the number of servings.

Nutrients that contain calories	*Calories per gram*
Carbohydrate	4 calories per gram
Protein	4 calories per gram
Fat	9 calories per gram

Food labels can be used as a guide to determine the caloric content of foods. This enables people to plan the appropriate caloric intake in their diet each day. Each label provides several pieces of helpful information (see worksheet 2.1):

▶ Size of a serving of the food

▶ Total calories in a serving of the food

▶ Total calories in a serving from fat

▶ Total amount of fat per serving (in grams)

▶ Amount of protein per serving (in grams)

▶ Amount of carbohydrate per serving (in grams)

Now WOW! 'Em

1. Review the background information presented for this lesson with the class.

2. Hand out one real food label to each student (or students can work in pairs).

3. Using transparency 2.1, Label Language, explain to the class that some foods come in packages and that the food label identifies how many calories are in each serving of those foods. Ask the students if they can tell you the following from the label illustrated in the transparency:
   - *How many servings are in the package?* (21 servings)
   - *How big is each serving?* (2 crackers)
   - *How many calories per serving?* (60 calories)
   - *How many of those calories are from fat?* (15 calories)
   - *How many grams of protein are in each serving?* (2 grams)
   - *How many total grams of fat are in each serving?* (1.5 grams)
   - *How many total grams of carbohydrate are in each serving?* (10 grams)

4. Tell the students to look at the labels they have. Then ask them, *Can you locate the same information on your label as we just discussed for the transparency label?* Once you think the students can read the label for the information discussed (serving size; calories per serving; calories of fat per serving; and the amount of carbohydrate, fat, and protein in the food), break the students up into small groups to complete worksheet 2.1, Calorie Calculator.

5. Hand out worksheet 2.1 and instruct the students to do the following:
   1. *Based on the information provided for each food, predict the rankings of these foods from the highest in calories to the lowest in calories. Write the food names in the correct order in the blanks provided.*
   2. *Calculate the calorie content of the foods listed. Place the total calories in the blank provided.*

Wrap It Up!

Once everyone has completed the calculations of total calories for each food, tell the students to put the food labels in order from the highest-calorie food item to the lowest-calorie food item based on their calculations. Then tell them to compare these rankings to their predictions. Ask the students the following questions:

1. *Do the foods that are highest in calorie content have something in common?* (higher in fat)

2. *What do the lower-calorie foods have in common?* (little or no fat)

3. *How close were your predictions to the actual rankings of these foods based on calories?*

Teaching Notes

Each lesson has suggested modifications, whenever possible, to adapt the concepts to younger or older students.

Modifications for Younger Students

For younger students who have not yet learned to multiply, have them guess which foods have the highest number of calories and which foods have the lowest number of calories and have them put the foods in order (rank them) from highest to lowest in calories. Tell them whether their predictions are right. Then explain the following: *Foods that are higher in fat have more calories. For example, peanut butter has more fat and more calories than broccoli. They are both nutritious foods, but one has more calories and should be consumed in moderation. Some foods don't have fat and are lower in calories, but they also aren't very nutritious. For example, the cola doesn't have any fat, and it has fewer calories (104 calories) than the yogurt does (211 calories, 3 grams of fat). But the cola doesn't have any vitamins, minerals, or protein in it as the yogurt does and thus is not as nutritious.*

Modifications for Older Students

None.

Concept Development

Using a variety of other food labels, build a classroom bulletin board and have the students put the food labels in order (from highest calories and fat per serving to the lowest amount of calories and fat per serving). Also have the students point out the foods that contain the other important nutrients—such as protein, vitamins, and minerals—in addition to fat and calories.

Assessment Options

Each lesson includes assessment options for the lesson and may include additional assessment options for the skills performed within a lesson.

For the Lesson

During the class activity, students will demonstrate their ability to calculate the calorie content of foods as well as their ability to read a nutrition label. They will correctly complete the worksheet.

Transparency 2.1:
Label Language

Nutrition Facts

Serving size 2 crackers (14 g)
Servings per container about 21

Amount per serving

Calories 60	Calories from fat 15

	% Daily value*
Total fat 1.5g	2%
Saturated fat 0g	0%
Trans fat 0g	
Cholesterol 0mg	0%
Sodium 70mg	3%
Total carbohydrate 10g	3%
Dietary fiber less than 1g	3%
Sugars 0g	
Protein 2g	

Vitamin A 0%	•	Vitamin C 0%
Calcium 0%	•	Iron 2%

*Percent daily values are based on a 2,000 calorie diet. Your daily values may be higher or lower depending on your calorie needs:

	Calories:	2,000	2,500
Total fat	Less than	65g	80g
Sat fat	Less than	20g	25g
Cholesterol	Less than	300mg	300mg
Sodium	Less than	2400mg	2400mg
Total carbohydrate		300g	375g
Dietary fiber		25g	30g

From C. Hopper, B. Fisher, and K.D. Munoz, 2008, *Physical Activity and Nutrition for Health* (Champaign, IL: Human Kinetics).

Worksheet 2.1: Calorie Calculator

Instructions: Look at each food pictured on this worksheet. Working as a group, predict which food has the most calories per serving and write it in the first blank. Continue with your predictions, ranking the foods from the highest-calorie food item to the lowest-calorie food item, until all the foods have been listed.

1. _____

2. _____

3. _____

4. _____

5. _____

6. _____

7. _____

After predicting the order of these foods based on highest to lowest calories per serving, calculate the total calories for each one using this formula: (grams of carbohydrate × 4) + (grams of protein × 4) + (grams of fat × 9) = total calories. Write the total calories per serving for each food in the blank provided. Did your group predict correctly?

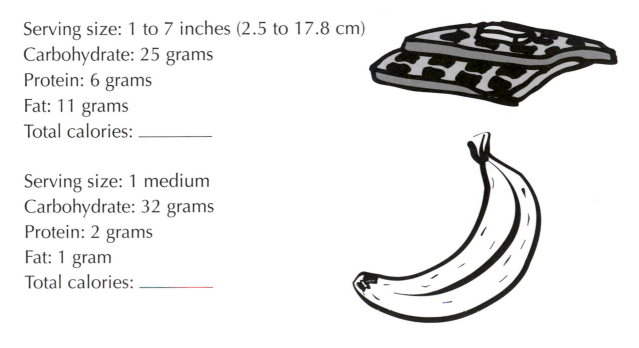

Serving size: 1 to 7 inches (2.5 to 17.8 cm)
Carbohydrate: 25 grams
Protein: 6 grams
Fat: 11 grams
Total calories: _____

Serving size: 1 medium
Carbohydrate: 32 grams
Protein: 2 grams
Fat: 1 gram
Total calories: _____

From C. Hopper, B. Fisher, and K.D. Munoz, 2008, *Physical Activity and Nutrition for Health* (Champaign, IL: Human Kinetics).

(continued)

(continued)

Serving size: 1 cup raw (88 g)
Carbohydrate: 4 g
Protein: 2 grams
Fat: 0 grams
Total calories: _____

Serving size: 1 cup (245 g)
Carbohydrate: 34 grams
Protein: 12 grams
Fat: 3 grams
Total calories: _____

Serving size: 1 medium
Carbohydrate: 20 grams
Protein: 4 grams
Fat: 4 grams
Total calories: _____

Serving size: 2 tablespoons
Carbohydrate: 6 grams
Protein: 8 grams
Fat: 15 grams
Total calories: _____

Serving size: 1 cup (240 ml)
Carbohydrate: 26 grams
Protein: 0 grams
Fat: 0 grams
Total calories: _____

From C. Hopper, B. Fisher, and K.D. Munoz, 2008, *Physical Activity and Nutrition for Health* (Champaign, IL: Human Kinetics).

Energy Balance

Calories provide fuel for physical activity and exercise as well as for growth and well-being. In part 1, students learned about which foods provide energy to the body. In part 2, students will learn how those calories provide energy in the Energy Balance lessons.

We begin the lessons by learning which foods are carbohydrate rich and which foods contain fat. Students practice categorizing foods into each type and learn how much to eat to balance physical activity.

In these two lessons, students will calculate the amount of aerobic activity they would have to do to burn the calories in a variety of different foods.

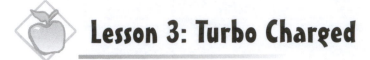

Lesson 3: Turbo Charged

Outcomes

At the end of this lesson, each student will be able to do the following:

▶ Describe the relationship of calories to food and aerobic fitness.

▶ Recognize the amount of exercise required to burn off calories consumed.

▶ Distinguish between foods that are high in fat versus foods high in carbohydrate.

Connections to Health Education Standards

▶ Health promotion and disease prevention

Connections to Other Standards

▶ Science standards: science in personal and social perspectives

▶ Math standards: number and operations

Connections to WOW! Lessons

▶ Red level: lesson 15, "Go-Go-Go!"

▶ Orange level: lesson 13, "A Crunch for Lunch"

▶ Orange level: lesson 14, "Tacos by Cody"

▶ Orange level: lesson 15, "Go-Go-Go!"

▶ Yellow level: lesson 15, "Go-Go-Go!"

▶ Blue level: lesson 14, "Fuel for Thought"

▶ Purple level: lesson 8, "What Do You Eat?"

▶ Purple level: lesson 9, "The Nutrient–Health Connection"

▶ Purple level: lesson 10, "The Balancing Act"

WOW! Vocabulary

aerobic fitness—The ability of the heart and lungs to take in, transport, and use oxygen.

Get Ready to WOW! 'Em

You will need the following:

▶ A felt board with two titles across the top: "Foods Higher in Fat" and "Foods Higher in Carbohydrate"

▶ Food cards (see figure 3.1) that can be placed on the felt board under each title. On the back of each food card is information related to the serving size and the amount of calories in a serving. This information will be used for part 2 of the lesson. A list of potential food cards is included in this lesson.

• Card 1: Fried egg (92 calories)

• Card 2: Serving of strawberries (50 calories)

- Card 3: Waffle (200 calories)
- Card 4: One cup of grapes (60 calories)
- Card 5: Spaghetti (100 calories)
- Card 6: Bowl of rice (100 calories)
- Card 7: Can of soda (150 calories)
- Card 8: Banana (100 calories)
- Card 9: Two homemade chocolate chip cookies (350 calories)
- Card 10: A container of low-fat yogurt (200 calories)
- Card 11: Small box of apple juice (100 calories)
- Card 12: A serving of cereal (100 calories)
- Card 13: Bowl of ice cream (130 calories)
- Card 14: String cheese (60 calories)
- Card 15: Handful of carrots (30 calories)
- Card 16: Serving of pudding (150 calories)
- Card 17: Chicken leg (200 calories)
- Card 18: Cheeseburger with bun (350 calories)
- Card 19: Slice of cheese pizza (220 calories)
- Card 20: Orange (60 calories)
- Card 21: Hot dog (no bun) (175 calories)
- Card 22: Piece of toast (60 calories)
- Card 23: Serving of broccoli (30 calories)
- Card 24: Serving of French fries (400 calories)

▶ Strips of paper with an activity written on them. Each strip should identify one activity and the amount of calories burned in 15 minutes of this activity for a 100-pound (45 kg) person. These strips of paper should be placed in a container. Samples of exercises are included in the lesson (see figure 3.2), or you can use examples from www.MyPyramid.gov.

- Card 1: Hiking (71 calories)
- Card 2: Swimming (91 calories)
- Card 3: Watching TV (12 calories)
- Card 4: Walking to school (28 calories)
- Card 5: Riding a bike (45 calories)
- Card 6: Jumping rope (114 calories)
- Card 7: Playing computer games (15 calories)
- Card 8: Playing soccer (114 calories)

▶ Stopwatch or a clock with seconds

▶ Worksheet 3.1, Turbo Balance (one copy per group of students)

▶ Worksheet 3.2, Exercise Log (one copy per student)

▶ Family Activity for Section 1, Superstar Veggies and Dip (one copy per student)

Background Information

Three of the nutrients found in food contain calories: carbohydrate, fat, and protein. When a person eats food that contains any or all of these nutrients, the person is consuming calories that can either be used for energy (and thus burned off) or be stored for later use. If a person eats too many calories, the extra calories will be stored mostly as fat. If a person eats too few calories, the person will burn the calories consumed as well as some stored calories—this person will lose weight. If a person eats the same number of calories as he burns off, the person will maintain his weight.

Fat is much higher in calories than either carbohydrate or protein. In fact, fat contains 9 calories per gram, while both carbohydrate and protein contain 4 calories per gram. It doesn't matter what type of fat a person eats when it comes to calories; all types of fat contain the same number of calories per gram. Thus, foods that are high in fat will usually have more calories and can lead to weight gain. However, eating an excess of carbohydrate and protein can also lead to weight gain. It's the calories that count. For example, if a person eats 100 calories more than that individual burns off each day, this will result in one pound of weight gain in five weeks. If a person eats 500 extra calories per day, that person will gain a pound in one week.

One of the best fuel sources for **aerobic fitness** is fat. Individuals who exercise at least 30 minutes per day most days of the week have a lower risk of obesity. Carbohydrate is also used for energy. However, carbohydrate is not as high in calories compared to fat, and a limited amount of carbohydrate is stored in the body. Therefore, stored body fat becomes the body's preferred fuel source during aerobic exercise. Protein is rarely the best source of fuel for aerobic fitness, unless the person eats a very low-calorie or low-carbohydrate diet.

Now WOW! 'Em

This lesson contains two parts.

Part 1

1. Review the background information presented for this lesson with the class.

2. Explain to students that there are three nutrients in food that contain calories:
   - Fat = 9 calories per gram
   - Carbohydrate = 4 calories per gram
   - Protein = 4 calories per gram

   Tell the students, *A calorie is a unit of measure for food energy. Calories are used as a fuel for your muscles to move and contract.* Use the analogy of gas in a car to explain this concept to the students.

3. Tell the students, *Remember that when you eat too many calories, or more calories than you burn, you store them mostly as body fat and you gain weight. When you exercise your heart, you burn the calories you eat and don't store them or gain weight. To avoid becoming overweight, you need to balance the calories you eat with enough exercise.*

4. After discussing the three nutrients that contain calories (fat, carbohydrate, and protein), ask the students, Which nutrient do you think has the most calories? Tell the students, *Fat has the most calories, and therefore people need to learn to eat a diet that is low in fat. We're going to do two activities today in class that will begin to explain this relationship.*

5. Ask for a volunteer from the class to participate in a timed activity. Ask the volunteer to come forward to the felt board where you have the two titles posted: "Foods Higher in Fat" and "Foods Higher in Carbohydrate." Also show the student the food

cards you've already prepared. Explain that she will have 20 seconds to correctly place the food cards under the correct heading. Tell the student, *Ready, set, go.*

6. After the 20 seconds, ask the student to stop. If there are still cards remaining, ask for another volunteer from the class. Tell the second volunteer that he will have 20 seconds to place the remaining cards under the correct category. Follow this procedure until all the cards have been categorized.

7. Ask the class, Do you agree with the card placement? If they don't, change the cards until the class is satisfied. If there are any mistakes, ask the students to reconsider and move the cards to the correct position.

8. Ask the students, Can you see a pattern in the card placement? They should see that fruits, vegetables, breads, and cereals are low in fat and high in carbohydrate. They should also see that snack foods such as cookies, muffins, and chocolate—as well as meats and fried foods—tend to be higher in fat.

Part 2

1. Break the class into groups of two or three students each. Ask each group to choose three activity slips out of the container you prepared before the lesson. Each slip of paper should list an activity along with the amount of calories burned in one hour of this activity for a 100-pound (45 kg) person.

2. Randomly distribute the food cards you used in part 1 of this lesson. Ask the students to write the names of the foods from the cards on worksheet 3.1, Turbo Balance. Tell them to list the number of calories in a serving of each food.

3. Instruct the students to calculate to the nearest 10 minutes how many minutes they would need to do each activity listed on the slips of paper to burn off the food listed on their handout. Go through an example on the board and then ask the students to complete their handout on their own.

Wrap It Up!

After the students finish the activity, go over their answers in class. Ask them, *Which foods take more exercise to burn off? Are they foods that are higher in carbohydrate or fat?*

Teaching Notes

Each lesson has suggested modifications, whenever possible, to adapt the concepts to younger or older students.

Modifications for Younger Students

▶ In part 1, instead of asking for a volunteer, have the students participate as a class. Read the food names and ask the class as a whole what heading they think you should place each food under. Then discuss their answers as a class.

▶ If part 2 is too advanced for your younger students, you can adapt this lesson by reading aloud the activity on each slip and the number of calories the activity burns in an hour. Then ask the students to guess which food would provide enough calories to fuel the activity.

Modifications for Older Students

None.

Concept Development

Give the students an aerobic fitness assignment: Using the exercise log on worksheet 3.2, students should record their exercise (in minutes) for one day during the week and one day during the weekend. In class, ask them to calculate the number of calories they burned doing the exercise during the week and on the weekend. Then ask, *Which day did you burn more calories while exercising?*

Assessment Options

Each lesson includes assessment options for the lesson and may include additional assessment options for the skills performed within a lesson.

For the Lesson

Through the activities in the "Now WOW! 'Em" section, students will demonstrate their ability to categorize foods as higher in fat or higher in carbohydrate. By having the students complete the calculations activity in part 2 of this lesson, you'll be able to assess their comprehension of how much they should exercise to burn off calories contained in a specific food.

Section 1: Family Activity 1
Superstar Veggies and Dip

Name: _____

To add color to your diet, try eating fresh vegetables with a low-fat dip.

Ingredients

Fresh vegetables, such as carrots, green peppers, cucumbers, celery, mushrooms, cauliflower, broccoli, and cherry tomatoes

Ingredients for Dip (Makes 2 Cups)

2 cups (490 g) nonfat plain yogurt

2 tbsp dill weed

2 tbsp onion powder

2 tbsp dried parsley leaves

1/2 tsp paprika

1 tsp celery seed

Directions

1. Mix the dip ingredients.

2. Chill the dip in the refrigerator.

3. Clean the veggies.

4. Cut the veggies into small pieces.

5. Serve the dip with the veggies.

From C. Hopper, B. Fisher, and K.D. Munoz, 2008, *Physical Activity and Nutrition for Health* (Champaign, IL: Human Kinetics).

Worksheet 3.1: Turbo Balance

Name: _____

Instructions: Write the name of each food from the food cards on the blank provided. List the number of calories per serving for each food. Using the activities you chose, calculate to the nearest 10 minutes how many minutes you would need to do each exercise to burn off the calories in a serving of each food.

Food	*Calories per serving*	*Minutes of exercise*
1.		
2.		
3.		

From C. Hopper, B. Fisher, and K.D. Munoz, 2008, *Physical Activity and Nutrition for Health* (Champaign, IL: Human Kinetics).

Worksheet 3.2: Exercise Log

Name: _____

Instructions: Enter information to track the exercise you perform on one day during the week and one day during the weekend. Record the date, the activity, and the number of minutes you performed that activity. Then calculate the calories you burned doing that activity.

Date	Activity	Minutes	Calories burned

From C. Hopper, B. Fisher, and K.D. Munoz, 2008, *Physical Activity and Nutrition for Health* (Champaign, IL: Human Kinetics).

FIGURE 3.1   Food cards.

Fried Egg

92 calories

From C. Hopper, B. Fisher, and K.D. Munoz, 2008, *Physical Activity and Nutrition for Health* (Champaign, IL: Human Kinetics).

Strawberries

50 calories

From C. Hopper, B. Fisher, and K.D. Munoz, 2008, *Physical Activity and Nutrition for Health* (Champaign, IL: Human Kinetics).

FIGURE 3.1   Food cards. *(continued)*

Waffle

200 calories

From C. Hopper, B. Fisher, and K.D. Munoz, 2008, *Physical Activity and Nutrition for Health* (Champaign, IL: Human Kinetics).

Grapes

60 calories

From C. Hopper, B. Fisher, and K.D. Munoz, 2008, *Physical Activity and Nutrition for Health* (Champaign, IL: Human Kinetics).

(continued)

FIGURE 3.1 Food cards. *(continued)*

Spaghetti

100 calories

From C. Hopper, B. Fisher, and K.D. Munoz, 2008, *Physical Activity and Nutrition for Health* (Champaign, IL: Human Kinetics).

Rice

100 calories

From C. Hopper, B. Fisher, and K.D. Munoz, 2008, *Physical Activity and Nutrition for Health* (Champaign, IL: Human Kinetics).

FIGURE 3.1 Food cards. *(continued)*

Soda

150 calories

From C. Hopper, B. Fisher, and K.D. Munoz, 2008, *Physical Activity and Nutrition for Health* (Champaign, IL: Human Kinetics).

Banana

100 calories

From C. Hopper, B. Fisher, and K.D. Munoz, 2008, *Physical Activity and Nutrition for Health* (Champaign, IL: Human Kinetics).

(continued)

FIGURE 3.1   Food cards. *(continued)*

Chocolate Chip Cookies

350 calories

From C. Hopper, B. Fisher, and K.D. Munoz, 2008, *Physical Activity and Nutrition for Health* (Champaign, IL: Human Kinetics).

Low-fat Yogurt

LOW–FAT
YOGURT

200 calories

From C. Hopper, B. Fisher, and K.D. Munoz, 2008, *Physical Activity and Nutrition for Health* (Champaign, IL: Human Kinetics).

FIGURE 3.1   Food cards. *(continued)*

Apple Juice

100 calories

From C. Hopper, B. Fisher, and K.D. Munoz, 2008, *Physical Activity and Nutrition for Health* (Champaign, IL: Human Kinetics).

Breakfast Cereal

100 calories

From C. Hopper, B. Fisher, and K.D. Munoz, 2008, *Physical Activity and Nutrition for Health* (Champaign, IL: Human Kinetics).

(continued)

FIGURE 3.1 Food cards. *(continued)*

Ice Cream

130 calories

From C. Hopper, B. Fisher, and K.D. Munoz, 2008, *Physical Activity and Nutrition for Health* (Champaign, IL: Human Kinetics).

String Cheese

60 calories

From C. Hopper, B. Fisher, and K.D. Munoz, 2008, *Physical Activity and Nutrition for Health* (Champaign, IL: Human Kinetics).

FIGURE 3.1   Food cards. *(continued)*

Carrots

30 calories

From C. Hopper, B. Fisher, and K.D. Munoz, 2008, *Physical Activity and Nutrition for Health* (Champaign, IL: Human Kinetics).

Pudding

150 calories

From C. Hopper, B. Fisher, and K.D. Munoz, 2008, *Physical Activity and Nutrition for Health* (Champaign, IL: Human Kinetics).

(continued)

FIGURE 3.1 Food cards. *(continued)*

Chicken Leg

200 calories

From C. Hopper, B. Fisher, and K.D. Munoz, 2008, *Physical Activity and Nutrition for Health* (Champaign, IL: Human Kinetics).

Cheeseburger

350 calories

From C. Hopper, B. Fisher, and K.D. Munoz, 2008, *Physical Activity and Nutrition for Health* (Champaign, IL: Human Kinetics).

FIGURE 3.1 Food cards. *(continued)*

Cheese Pizza

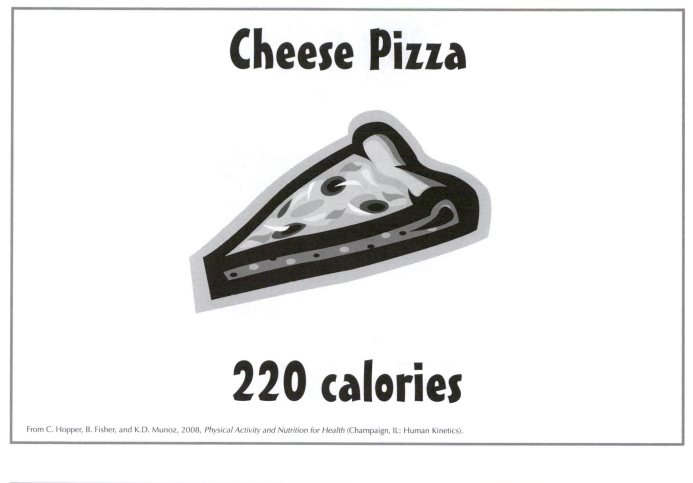

220 calories

From C. Hopper, B. Fisher, and K.D. Munoz, 2008, *Physical Activity and Nutrition for Health* (Champaign, IL: Human Kinetics).

Orange

60 calories

From C. Hopper, B. Fisher, and K.D. Munoz, 2008, *Physical Activity and Nutrition for Health* (Champaign, IL: Human Kinetics).

(continued)

FIGURE 3.1   Food cards. *(continued)*

Hot Dog

175 calories

Toast

60 calories

FIGURE 3.1   Food cards. *(continued)*

Broccoli

30 calories

French Fries

400 calories

FIGURE 3.2   Activity cards.

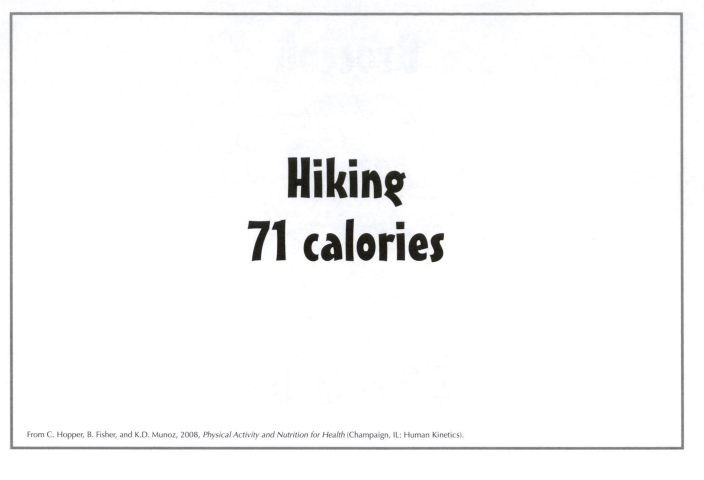

Hiking
71 calories

From C. Hopper, B. Fisher, and K.D. Munoz, 2008, *Physical Activity and Nutrition for Health* (Champaign, IL: Human Kinetics).

Swimming
91 calories

From C. Hopper, B. Fisher, and K.D. Munoz, 2008, *Physical Activity and Nutrition for Health* (Champaign, IL: Human Kinetics).

FIGURE 3.2 Activity cards. *(continued)*

Watching TV
12 calories

Walking to School
28 calories

(continued)

FIGURE 3.2 Activity cards. *(continued)*

Riding a Bike
45 calories

From C. Hopper, B. Fisher, and K.D. Munoz, 2008, *Physical Activity and Nutrition for Health* (Champaign, IL: Human Kinetics).

Jumping Rope
114 calories

From C. Hopper, B. Fisher, and K.D. Munoz, 2008, *Physical Activity and Nutrition for Health* (Champaign, IL: Human Kinetics).

FIGURE 3.2   Activity cards. *(continued)*

Playing Computer Games
15 calories

From C. Hopper, B. Fisher, and K.D. Munoz, 2008, *Physical Activity and Nutrition for Health* (Champaign, IL: Human Kinetics).

Playing Soccer
114 calories

From C. Hopper, B. Fisher, and K.D. Munoz, 2008, *Physical Activity and Nutrition for Health* (Champaign, IL: Human Kinetics).

Lesson 4: In and Out Diner

Outcomes

At the end of this lesson, each student will be able to do the following:

▶ Analyze how many calories are burned during specific exercises compared to how many calories are consumed in a serving of different foods.

▶ Explain the relationship of calories in (consumed) and calories out (burned off) to maintaining a healthy weight.

Connections to Health Education Standards

▶ Health promotion and disease prevention

▶ Decision-making skills

Connections to Other Standards

▶ Science standards: science in personal and social perspectives

▶ Math standards: number and operations; representation

Connections to WOW! Lessons

▶ Red level: lesson 15, "Go-Go-Go!"

▶ Yellow level: lesson 15, "Go-Go-Go!"

▶ Blue level: lesson 11, "Moderation"

▶ Blue level: lesson 14, "Fuel for Thought"

▶ Purple level: lesson 8, "What Do You Eat?"

▶ Purple level: lesson 9, "The Nutrient–Health Connection"

▶ Purple level: lesson 10, "The Balancing Act"

WOW! Vocabulary

▶ healthy weight—The weight at which a person's risk of developing disease (such as cardiovascular disease or diabetes) is the lowest.

Get Ready to WOW! 'Em

You will need the following:

▶ Eight exercise cards. Before class, set up stations around the classroom with exercise cards and food cards on a table. The exercise cards show how many calories are burned by a 100-pound (45 kg) person in 15 minutes of doing this exercise. These cards can be found in figure 3.2.

▶ Food cards that list the calorie content of the specified food (see figure 3.1). At least two food cards should be placed on each table. Students will have to add the calories for all foods together to get the total "calories in."

▸ Worksheet 4.1, In and Out Diner (one copy for every two or three students ⊚

▸ Worksheet 4.2, Activity and Food Log (one copy per student) ⊚

▸ Family Activity 2.1 for Section 1, Vegetable Investigation (one copy per student) ⊚

Background Information

To maintain a **healthy weight,** people need to eat enough calories to (a) grow and mature, (b) fuel physical activity, and (c) digest their food. If the number of calories a person eats is equal to the number of calories the person burns off (through growing, digestion, and physical activity), this person will maintain a healthy weight throughout life.

Whether people want to lose weight or maintain a healthy weight, they need to understand the connection between the calories their body takes in and the calories their body uses. Gaining weight is usually the result of eating too many calories compared to the amount of physical activity the person does each day. The excess calories are stored as fat, which results in weight gain. Children require more calories per pound of body weight than adults do because their bones and muscles are growing longer and becoming denser. Once those growth needs have been met, any excess calories can be used to fuel physical activity rather than be stored for later use. Being physically active prevents the buildup of excess calories and maintains a lean, healthy body. Thus, when calories in equals calories out, the person maintains her body weight. When calories in are less than calories out, the person loses weight. And finally, when calories in are greater than calories out, the person gains weight.

Now WOW! 'Em

1. Review the background information presented for this lesson with the class.

2. Remind the students of the concepts they learned about three nutrients that contain calories. Ask students, *What are the three nutrients that contain calories?* (carbohydrate, protein, and fat)

3. Break the class into small groups of two or three students each. Provide one copy of worksheet 4.1, In and Out Diner, to each group.

4. Explain the following to the students: *You are going to rotate through the stations to determine if the combination of food and exercise at each station would result in weight gain, weight loss, or maintenance of the same weight. To do this, you need to calculate the number of calories in the food and compare it to the calories burned during the exercise. For example, if the two food cards at the table contain a total of 75 calories, and the activity card identifies an activity that burns 100 calories, then the activity would burn more calories than are consumed by eating the food. This means that the food does not contain enough calories to fuel the activity, so you would burn some of your stored energy (such as body fat) to fuel the exercise. This could result in weight loss if you ended the day with fewer calories eaten than you burned off.* Tell the students, *You will have exactly five minutes at each station to determine the outcome.*

5. When all students understand the rules, start the timer. At the end of each five minutes, the groups must shift to the next station.

Wrap It Up!

At the end of the activity, go over the correct answers and see how many groups were correct. Ask the students, *Which activity burned the most calories? Which station had the highest-calorie foods?*

Teaching Notes

Each lesson has suggested modifications, whenever possible, to adapt the concepts to younger or older students.

Modifications for Younger Students

If students are too young to add the calories in the foods at each table, modify the activity by providing the total number of calories taken in. Then ask the students to compare those to the total number of calories burned with the activity.

Modifications for Older Students

For older students, have them subtract the calories in from the calories out, which may result in negative numbers. You can modify the activity by asking the students to determine how many servings of a low-calorie food they could eat to equal the amount of calories burned during the activity.

Concept Development

Have the students keep a journal using worksheet 4.2, Activity and Food Log. Students should record the activities they complete in one hour as well as the amount of food they eat during that hour to see if they burned off the snacks they ate.

Assessment Options

Each lesson includes assessment options for the lesson and may include additional assessment options for the skills performed within a lesson.

For the Lesson

During the group activity, students will demonstrate their ability to calculate the calorie content of foods and compare those calories to the amount of calories burned.

Section 1: Family Activity 2
Vegetable Investigation

Name: _____

The objective in this family activity is to try eating two new vegetables as part of your family's meals. Choose a vegetable that you have never eaten before. Find a recipe and prepare it with your family. After eating the vegetable, write a short description of the vegetable, including its name, color, how you prepared it, and what it tastes like. Under "Comments," indicate whether or not you liked the vegetable.

Vegetable Investigation 1

Description

Comments

Vegetable Investigation 2

Description

Comments

From C. Hopper, B. Fisher, and K.D. Munoz, 2008, *Physical Activity and Nutrition for Health* (Champaign, IL: Human Kinetics).

Worksheet 4.1: In and Out Diner

Instructions: At each station, there are two food cards and one activity card. First, write down the foods and the calories on this worksheet. Then add the calories for the foods together to get the total calories you would ingest if you ate both foods. Write that number in the "Total calories in" column. Next, in the "Calories out" column, write down the activity and the number of calories the activity burns in 15 minutes. If the calories in are greater than the calories out, you would gain weight. If the calories in are less than the calories out, you would lose weight. If both columns have the same number of calories, you would stay the same weight. Write in the column provided whether you would gain weight, lose weight, or stay the same weight. Follow the same procedure until you have completed all the stations.

Calories in (food)	*Total calories in*	*Calories out (activity)*	*Gain/loss/ stay the same*

From C. Hopper, B. Fisher, and K.D. Munoz, 2008, *Physical Activity and Nutrition for Health* (Champaign, IL: Human Kinetics).

Worksheet 4.2: Activity and Food Log

Name: _____

Instructions: Use this form to keep a record of the amount of activity you do in one hour and the amount of food you eat during that same time. Be sure to read the label for the calories in a serving of the food you eat. Did you eat more calories than you burned off with your activity?

Date	Description of the activity	Minutes of activity	Food	Calories in the food

From C. Hopper, B. Fisher, and K.D. Munoz, 2008, *Physical Activity and Nutrition for Health* (Champaign, IL: Human Kinetics).

Heart
Structure

This part introduces students to the general structure of the heart. Because they cannot see their heart, elementary students often have difficulty understanding the important role that the heart plays in daily life and especially during exercise. These lessons are designed to help students identify the basic structure of the heart and to help them understand its role in pumping nutrient-rich blood to the body.

Lesson 5: Heart Facts I

Outcomes

At the end of this lesson, each student will be able to do the following:

▶ Describe the structure of the heart.

▶ Draw and map the basics of the circulatory system.

Connections to Health Education Standards

▶ Health promotion and disease prevention

Connections to Other Standards

▶ Science standards: science in personal and social perspectives; life science

Connections to WOW! Lessons

▶ Red level: lesson 7, "Heart Healthy"

▶ Red level: lesson 18, "Busy Body"

▶ Orange level: lesson 7, "Heart Healthy"

▶ Yellow level: lesson 7, "Heart Healthy"

WOW! Vocabulary

▶ arteries—Blood vessels that carry oxygenated blood away from the heart toward body tissues.

▶ cardiac muscle—The muscle of the heart that contracts and pushes blood through the chambers and vessels.

▶ circulatory system—The heart, lungs, and the blood vessels that circulate blood throughout the body, deliver nutrients and other essential materials to cells, and remove waste products.

▶ veins—Blood vessels that carry oxygen-depleted blood to the heart.

Get Ready to WOW! 'Em

You will need the following:

▶ Transparencies of all four figures contained in this lesson

▶ Overhead projector and transparency pens

▶ Figure 5.1, picture of the human heart (one copy per student)

▶ Standard-size (or 10-inch) softball

▶ Figure 5.2, outline of the human body (one copy per student)

▶ Pint or liter container

▶ Figure 5.3, picture of the cross section of a child's heart (one copy per student)

▶ Red and blue crayons or pens

▶ Family Activity 3 for section 1, Family Favorites Survey (one copy per student)

▶ Figure 5.4, Intensity Guide (one copy per student)

Background Information

The heart is a pump consisting of a special type of muscle called **cardiac** (kar-de-ak) **muscle.** The heart contracts and relaxes about 70 to 80 times a minute, pumping blood that carries oxygen and nutrients from the heart to the body. Blood travels throughout the body in tubes called blood vessels. The **circulatory system** consists of the heart, lungs, and blood vessels. The circulatory system's blood vessels include **arteries** and **veins,** which are small tubes that carry blood. Arteries are blood vessels that transport blood from the heart to body parts and tissues. Veins are blood vessels that transport blood (depleted of oxygen) from the body parts back to the heart.

Now WOW! 'Em

1. Review the background information presented for this lesson with the class.

2. Explain the following: The heart is the strongest muscle in the body. It pumps blood through the arteries to all parts of the body. This blood carries oxygen, which makes it look red. After blood has traveled through the body, it comes back to the heart. The blood looks blue when it returns to the heart because oxygen has been removed. The heart pumps the used blood to the lungs, where the blood receives oxygen. When blood comes back from the lungs, it is bright red. Then the heart pumps the blood to the body. The hard-working heart has to pump blood to the brain cells and millions of other cells in the body—and it must do this night and day without a break.

3. Using the picture of the heart (see figure 5.1), introduce the lesson's topic with a student activity designed to clarify the location, size, and shape of the heart. Tell the students, *Although no larger than your fist, the human heart is probably the most important muscle in the body. Somewhat pear shaped (upside down), the heart has four "rooms"—or chambers—and it weighs about as much as a softball* (show the softball).

4. Describe the purpose and function of the heart. Ask students to draw on the body outline (see figure 5.2) what they think their heart looks like. Instruct them to draw it on the outline where they think it's located. Encourage them to be accurate and to include as much detail as possible.

5. Tell the students, *The heart has a job that never stops. It must squeeze about 10 pints of blood through the body every day.* (Show students the pint or liter container.) *It beats about 70 or 80 times a minute to accomplish this. That's roughly 5,000 times an hour, 120,000 times a day, or over 43 million times a year! The heart is the power source behind the blood flow throughout your entire body. This movement of blood takes place through tubes called arteries and veins. The circulatory process provides nourishment to body cells and removes waste products from the cells.*

6. Using the cross section of the heart (see figure 5.3) that illustrates the internal structure of the heart, explain to students that the heart consists of four chambers—two ventricles and two atria.

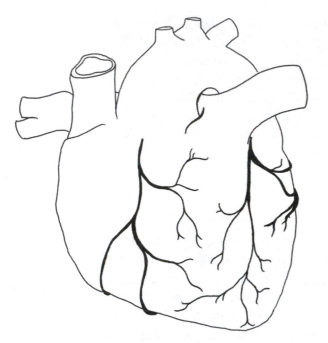

FIGURE 5.1   The human heart.

Reprinted, by permission, from C.A. Hopper, B.D. Fisher, and K.D. Munoz, 1997, *Health-Related Fitness for Grades 1 & 2* (Champaign, IL: Human Kinetics), 4.

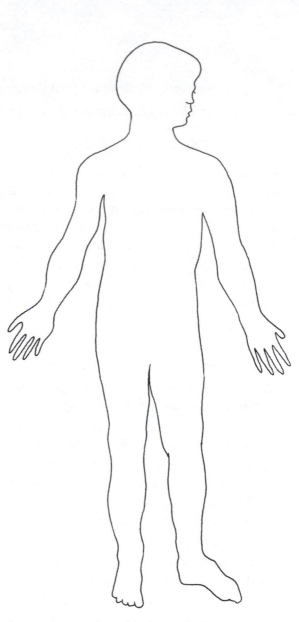

FIGURE 5.2   Outline of the human body.

Reprinted, by permission, from C.A. Hopper, B.D. Fisher, and K.D. Munoz, 1997, *Health-Related Fitness for Grades 5 & 6* (Champaign, IL: Human Kinetics), 5.

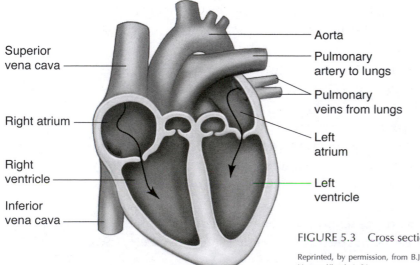

Superior
vena cava

Right atrium

Right
ventricle

Inferior
vena cava

Aorta

Pulmonary
artery to lungs

Pulmonary
veins from lungs

Left
atrium

Left
ventricle

FIGURE 5.3   Cross section of the human heart.

Reprinted, by permission, from B.J. Sharkey, 2001, *Fitness and Health,* 5th ed. (Champaign, IL: Human Kinetics), 91.

Wrap It Up!

Use Family Activity 3, Family Favorites Survey, to collect information about family activity patterns. Use the Intensity Guide (see figure 5.4) to discuss differences between light and vigorous activities and to identify activities that increase the heart rate.

Teaching Notes

Each lesson has suggested modifications, whenever possible, to adapt the concepts to younger or older students.

Modifications for Younger Students

Students can work in pairs to trace a body outline of each other while lying on a piece of butcher paper. Using their outlines, they should then attach a picture of the heart on the body in the correct location. Students can draw a picture of the heart on red paper.

Modifications for Older Students

Invite a school nurse to talk about blood pressure.

Concept Development

Nerves connect to the heart to regulate the speed with which the muscle contracts. During exercise, the heart pumps more quickly to supply the muscles with oxygen and nutrients.

Assessment Options

Each lesson includes assessment options for the lesson and may include additional assessment options for the skills performed within a lesson.

For the Lesson

Students will demonstrate their ability to correctly locate the heart on the body outline and correctly identify the four chambers of the heart.

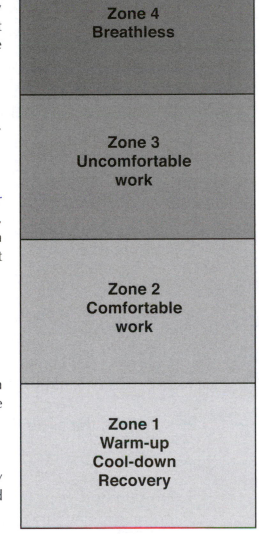

FIGURE 5.4   Intensity Guide.

Section 1: Family Activity 3
Family Favorites Survey

Name: _____

Complete this questionnaire with your family.

1. List the favorite activity or sport of each family member.

Family member	Activity or sport	Intensity (light, moderate, or vigorous)
1.		
2.		
3.		
4.		
5.		
6.		

2. What are the activities that your family participates in together?

3. Do you and your family members do something active every day? If not every day, how often each week?

4. List the physical activities that each of your family members did each day this week.

Family member 1:

Family member 2:

Family member 3:

Family member 4:

Family member 5:

Family member 6:

From C. Hopper, B. Fisher, and K.D. Munoz, 2008, *Physical Activity and Nutrition for Health* (Champaign, IL: Human Kinetics).

Lesson 6: Follow the Red and Blue Road

Outcomes

At the end of this lesson, each student will be able to do the following:

▶ Understand the concept that blood travels in tubes (i.e., arteries and veins) within the body.

▶ Understand that red blood travels in the arteries and blue blood travels in the veins.

Connections to Health Education Standards

▶ Practice of health-enhancing behaviors

Connections to Other Standards

▶ Science standards: science in personal and social perspectives; life science

▶ Physical education standards: regular participation in physical activity; understanding of movement concepts, principles, strategies, and tactics

Connections to WOW! Lessons

▶ Red level: lesson 7, "Heart Healthy"

▶ Orange level: lesson 7, "Heart Healthy"

WOW! Vocabulary

▶ blood—Fluid consisting of plasma, blood cells, and platelets that is circulated by the heart through the vascular system. Blood carries oxygen and nutrients to body tissues and carries waste products away.

▶ heart—Muscular organ that pumps blood to body parts.

▶ laterality—Preference in using one side of the body over the other.

Get Ready to WOW! 'Em

You will need the following:

▶ Playground chalk

▶ Jump ropes (20)

▶ Cones (55 red and 120 blue) to represent arteries and veins (red and blue construction paper can be used to mark cones of different colors)

▶ Fitness exercise cards (use the exercises from the end of this lesson)

Background Information

Arteries and veins are the major blood vessels of the circulatory system. Arteries carry **blood** away from the **heart,** and veins carry blood back to the heart from body organs and body parts.

Now WOW! 'Em

1. Review the background information presented for this lesson with the class.

2. Using playground chalk, jump ropes, or cones, mark areas representing the following parts of the human body: the head, two arms, two legs, and the heart. A large playing area (50 by 50 yards [46 by 46 m]) is desirable, although you can use a smaller area.

3. Join the heart with the body parts using two lines of cones, one being arteries and the other being veins (see figure 6.1). Use red cones for arteries and blue cones for veins indicate red and blue pathways by attaching a piece of construction paper to cones.

4. Divide the class into five teams of equal size.

5. Designate a body part for each team to visit and establish a rotational pattern for all teams to visit all body parts.

6. Each team starts in the heart. On the command "Arteries," each team moves to a designated body part in turn. Students act as blood flowing through the body.

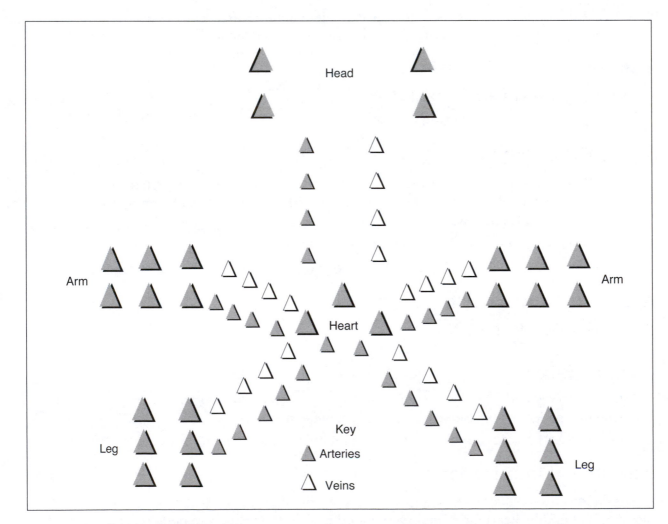

FIGURE 6.1   Follow the red and blue road.

Adapted, by permission, from C.A. Hopper, B.D. Fisher, and K.D. Munoz, 1997, *Health-Related Fitness for Grades 1 & 2* (Champaign, IL: Human Kinetics), 6.

They use the blue and red cones as running and movement pathways. Have the students use different movement patterns—such as skipping, jogging, hopping, or galloping—to move along the pathways. For instance, as a team, the students jog along the line of red cones to the arteries in the arms, legs, or head.

7. Place a fitness exercise card in each body part area and have students complete 5, 10, or 15 repetitions of the exercise at each body part area when they arrive.

8. Tell students, *Visit all five body parts and wait in the heart for further directions; wait in the body parts until all members of the team have arrived. Then begin the exercise specified on the card.* On the command "Veins," students jog back to the heart along the blue line of cones representing veins.

Wrap It Up!

Ask students to explain the differences and similarities between arteries and veins.

Teaching Notes

Each lesson has suggested modifications, whenever possible, to adapt the concepts to younger or older students.

Modifications for Younger Students

Allow students to walk, but encourage constant movement. Ask students if they can identify factors associated with continuous movement, such as breathing harder, a warm face, and a faster heartbeat.

Modifications for Older Students

Increase the size of the playing area as needed. Vary the movements to include skipping and hopping in order to provide a variety of locomotor activities.

Modifications for Students With Disabilities

Use peer tutors. Select students without a disability to assist those with disabilities. These peer tutors can learn how to support, praise, and encourage. They can serve as instructors and provide feedback and overall assistance. In some cases, older students may perform this role, but students in the same class can be equally effective. One of the main contributions of a peer tutor is to help the student with a disability to stay on task and stay safe in the movement. You should provide some basic training for the tutors and explain your expectations. This can include some of the following: reinforcement and repeating of directions as needed, modeling a specific movement for the student with a disability, and providing praise and support for efforts.

Concept Development

1. Encourage continuous movement during the activity in the "Now WOW! 'Em" section. Explain that blood in the body keeps flowing without taking a rest. Allow students to walk if necessary during the activity.

2. You may want to demonstrate the movement used in the movement pathways to illustrate the blood flow pattern; then let students take turns leading their team. Vary the movement pattern and include hopping, skipping, and galloping.

3. Use a hula hoop to teach the concept that blood travels in tubes. Students can move through the hoops.

4. Teach **laterality** by having students hop on their left and right legs.

5. Explain to students that although this activity refers to blue blood, the blood is in fact a darker color of red. Anatomical books refer to blood returning to the lungs as blue.

Assessment Options

Each lesson includes assessment options for the lesson and may include additional assessment options for the skills performed within a lesson.

For the Lesson

Students will demonstrate their knowledge of the color of blood moving to and from the heart by following the correct movement pathway identified by the colored cones.

For Skipping

▶ The student can start the skip with either foot.

▶ The skip includes a rhythmical repetition of the step-hop on alternate feet.

▶ The foot of the nonsupport leg is carried near the surface during the hop phase.

▶ The arms are alternately moving in opposition to the legs at waist level.

Side Leg Raises

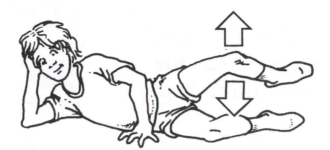

Lie on your right side with your head resting on your right hand. Your left hand is flat on the mat in front of you for support. Raise your upper leg. Repeat, changing sides.

From C. Hopper, B. Fisher, and K.D. Munoz, 2008, *Physical Activity and Nutrition for Health* (Champaign, IL: Human Kinetics).

Mountain Climbers

In front support position, alternate moving your left and right foot forward and backward about 12 to 18 inches (31 to 46 cm). Switch leg positions, keeping a rhythmic movement pattern.

From C. Hopper, B. Fisher, and K.D. Munoz, 2008, *Physical Activity and Nutrition for Health* (Champaign, IL: Human Kinetics).

(continued)

Skiers

With both feet together,
jump from side to side
over a line or jump rope.

From C. Hopper, B. Fisher, and K.D. Munoz, 2008, *Physical Activity and Nutrition for Health* (Champaign, IL: Human Kinetics).

Clappers

Hop on your left foot,
kick your right leg up,
and clap your hands
under your right leg.
Hop on your right foot,
kick your left leg up, and
clap your hands under it.
Land on the ball of your
foot each time.

a

b

From C. Hopper, B. Fisher, and K.D. Munoz, 2008, *Physical Activity and Nutrition for Health* (Champaign, IL: Human Kinetics).

Jumping Jacks

Stand with your arms by your sides. Simultaneously raise your arms above your head and move your legs shoulder-width apart. Then bring your arms to your sides and bring your feet together.

From C. Hopper, B. Fisher, and K.D. Munoz, 2008, *Physical Activity and Nutrition for Health* (Champaign, IL: Human Kinetics).

Cross-Country Skiers

Stand with one foot in front and one foot behind your body. The opposite arm is also in front of your body. Jump and change positions of your feet and arms.

From C. Hopper, B. Fisher, and K.D. Munoz, 2008, *Physical Activity and Nutrition for Health* (Champaign, IL: Human Kinetics).

(continued)

Stride Jumps

Stand with your feet together. Jump off the ground so your feet are spread 3 feet (91 cm) apart. Return to the starting position.

From C. Hopper, B. Fisher, and K.D. Munoz, 2008, *Physical Activity and Nutrition for Health* (Champaign, IL: Human Kinetics).

Squat Thrusts

In push-up position, quickly move your legs toward your hands and jump high into the air.

From C. Hopper, B. Fisher, and K.D. Munoz, 2008, *Physical Activity and Nutrition for Health* (Champaign, IL: Human Kinetics).

Leg Extensions

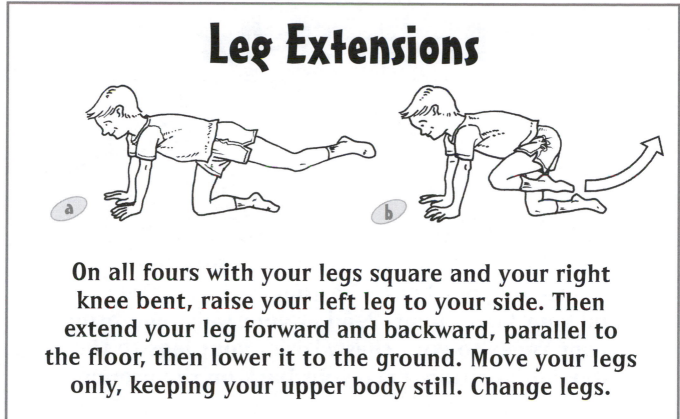

On all fours with your legs square and your right knee bent, raise your left leg to your side. Then extend your leg forward and backward, parallel to the floor, then lower it to the ground. Move your legs only, keeping your upper body still. Change legs.

Jump Twisters

Stand with your feet together, knees slightly bent. Move both arms to your right while moving your legs (from the waist) to the left.

Reverse the action with your arms moving to the left and your legs to the right. Start with small movements of the arms and legs and gradually increase.

(continued)

Reverse Sit-Ups

Lie on your back with your legs together and your knees bent. Bend at your waist and bring your knees to your chest. Lower your legs to the starting position. Keep your back on the ground.

From C. Hopper, B. Fisher, and K.D. Munoz, 2008, *Physical Activity and Nutrition for Health* (Champaign, IL: Human Kinetics).

Crunches

Lie on your back with your legs together and your legs and knees bent, forming a 90-degree angle. Place your hands behind your head. Bring your knees and elbows together directly over your waist area. Do not pull on your head and neck with your hands. Return to the starting position.

From C. Hopper, B. Fisher, and K.D. Munoz, 2008, *Physical Activity and Nutrition for Health* (Champaign, IL: Human Kinetics).

Cross-Body Lifts

Assume an all-fours position with your hands on the floor directly under your shoulders. In this position, raise one arm and the opposite leg simultaneously until they are slightly higher than your lower back. Then lower both simultaneously. Repeat this action with the opposite arm and leg in alternating fashion.

From C. Hopper, B. Fisher, and K.D. Munoz, 2008, *Physical Activity and Nutrition for Health* (Champaign, IL: Human Kinetics).

Curl-Ups

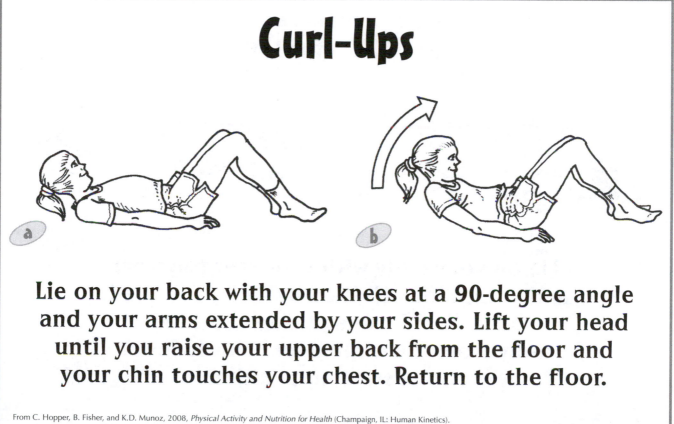

Lie on your back with your knees at a 90-degree angle and your arms extended by your sides. Lift your head until you raise your upper back from the floor and your chin touches your chest. Return to the floor.

From C. Hopper, B. Fisher, and K.D. Munoz, 2008, *Physical Activity and Nutrition for Health* (Champaign, IL: Human Kinetics).

(continued)

Obliques

Lie on your back with your knees bent, your feet on the floor, and your hands held tightly behind your head. Lift your shoulder and upper torso off the floor, twisting one elbow toward the opposite knee. Do not pull on your head and neck with your hands. Return to the starting position and repeat on the other side. Press your spine to the floor so your hips do not roll.

Chest Raises

Lie on your belly with your feet together and your hands clasped behind your head. Raise your head and chest and legs away from the ground and slowly lower to the starting position.

Push-Ups

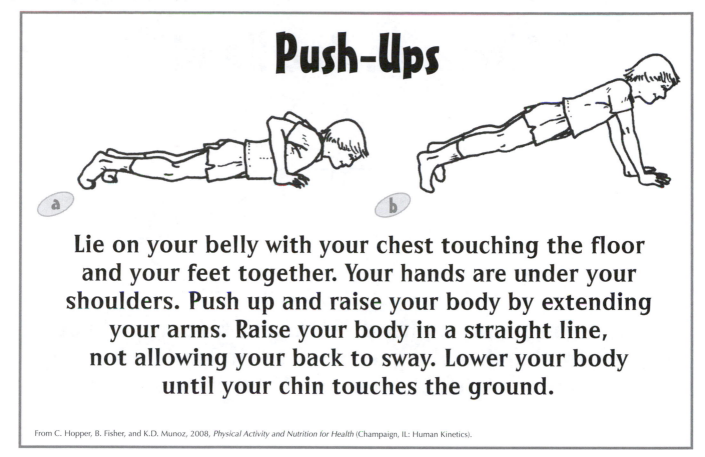

Lie on your belly with your chest touching the floor and your feet together. Your hands are under your shoulders. Push up and raise your body by extending your arms. Raise your body in a straight line, not allowing your back to sway. Lower your body until your chin touches the ground.

From C. Hopper, B. Fisher, and K.D. Munoz, 2008, *Physical Activity and Nutrition for Health* (Champaign, IL: Human Kinetics).

Reverse Push-Ups

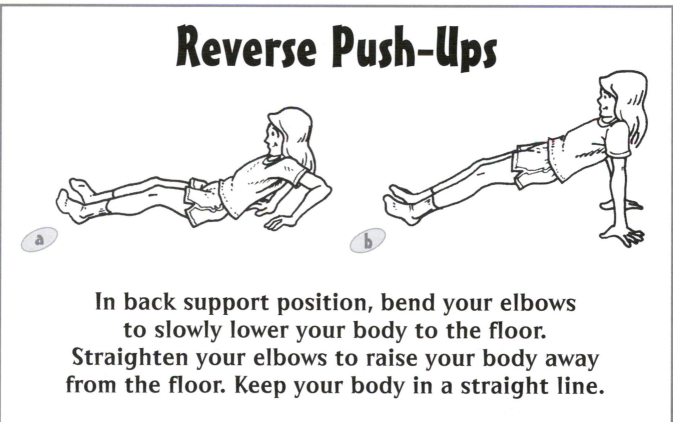

In back support position, bend your elbows to slowly lower your body to the floor. Straighten your elbows to raise your body away from the floor. Keep your body in a straight line.

From C. Hopper, B. Fisher, and K.D. Munoz, 2008, *Physical Activity and Nutrition for Health* (Champaign, IL: Human Kinetics).

(continued)

Circles on One Hand

Pivot on a supporting hand. Work your feet around your supporting hand, making a complete circle while keeping your body straight. Change your hand after one circle.

From C. Hopper, B. Fisher, and K.D. Munoz, 2008, *Physical Activity and Nutrition for Health* (Champaign, IL: Human Kinetics).

Lesson 7: Take It to Heart

Outcomes

At the end of this lesson, each student will be able to do the following:

▶ Understand that the heart has one side with red blood and one side with blue blood.

▶ Explain that the right side of the heart receives blue blood containing carbon dioxide from the body and pumps this blue blood out to the lungs.

▶ Explain that the left side of the heart receives red blood containing oxygen from the lungs and pumps out this red blood to the body.

Connections to Health Education Standards

▶ Health promotion and disease prevention

Connections to Other Standards

▶ Science standards: science in personal and social perspectives; life science

▶ Physical education standards: competency in motor skills and movement patterns

Connections to WOW! Lessons

▶ Red level: lesson 7, "Heart Healthy"

▶ Orange level: lesson 7, "Heart Healthy"

WOW! Vocabulary

▶ atrium—Upper chamber of the heart that receives blood from veins and the lungs.

▶ carbon dioxide—Colorless and odorless gas formed during respiration.

▶ oxygenated—Term used to describe blood that contains oxygen.

▶ septum—Thin partition or membrane that divides the heart into two distinct parts.

▶ ventricle—Lower chamber of the heart that pumps the blood away from the heart to the lungs and body.

Get Ready to WOW! 'Em

You will need the following:

▶ Five large hula hoops

▶ Cones to mark the four chambers of the heart (16 cones)

▶ Red and blue beanbags or red and blue construction paper crunched into a ball shape (two per student)

▶ Family Activity 4 for section 1, Hit the Mark (one copy per student)

Background Information

The left side of the heart contains blood with oxygen, and the right side contains blood with **carbon dioxide.** The left side of the heart receives **oxygenated** blood from the lungs and pumps this blood to body parts. The right side receives blood containing carbon dioxide from the body and sends this blood to the lungs to receive oxygen. The two sides of the heart are separated by the **septum.** An **atrium** and a **ventricle** are located on each side of the heart.

Now WOW! 'Em

1. Review the background information presented for this lesson with the class.
2. Use 16 cones to mark four square areas (10 by 10 yd [9 by 9 m]) to represent the four chambers of the heart, with a right side and a left side (see figure 7.1). Place five hoops to separate the two sides of the heart. These hoops represent the body area. Red and blue beanbags should be equally distributed in the five hoops.

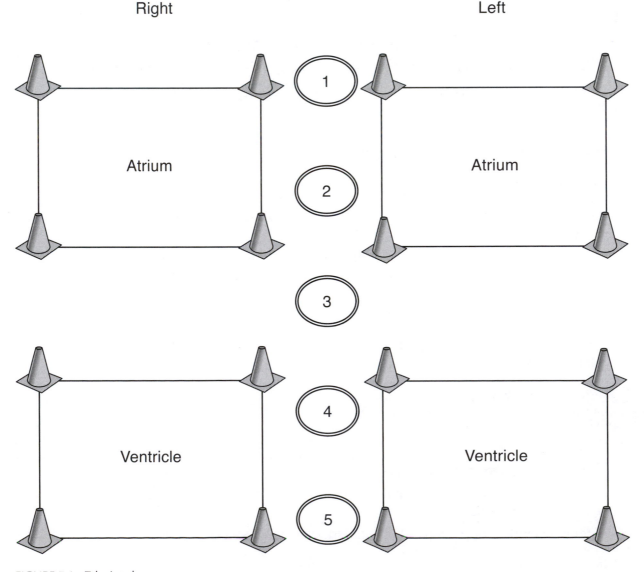

FIGURE 7.1 Take it to heart.

3. Divide the class into four groups. Assign one group to each of the four chambers of the heart. This creates two groups on the right side and two groups on the left side. The two groups on the right are one team, and the two groups on the left are another team.

4. Place the beanbags (2 beanbags per student, with an equal number of red and blue bags) in the five hoops. For example, if you have 30 students, you will need 30 red and 30 blue beanbags.

5. Players represent blood cells. They run to get a beanbag from the five hoops (which represent the body). Players on the left side will get red beanbags. Players on the right side will get blue beanbags. The goal is to try to bring as many beanbags of the correct color to the group's "home" chamber of the heart. Each player may carry only *one* beanbag at a time and must place it in the center of the group's home chamber before trying to get another beanbag.

6. Players may also run to the other side of the heart and take away (steal) a beanbag from those chambers. When doing this, the player returns the beanbag to the hoops that represent the body.

7. Each team tries to secure as many beanbags of the correct color as possible. Some students from each team can be designated to take away beanbags from the other team rather than retrieve their own beanbags from the body area.

8. After two minutes, a signal ends the round, and teams tally their beanbag totals. Students can rotate sides.

9. The hoops representing the body area can be placed in different areas to create a longer running distance.

10. Players can use different locomotor movements, such as running, sliding, and galloping.

Wrap It Up!

Ask students to explain the difference between oxygen and carbon dioxide. Use Family Activity 4, Hit the Mark, to encourage physical activity outside of school.

Teaching Notes

Each lesson has suggested modifications, whenever possible, to adapt the concepts to younger or older students.

Modifications for Younger Students

Younger students can start by retrieving the correct color beanbags and returning them to their chambers without trying to take away beanbags from the other team. Students can be challenged to see how quickly they can do this task. The distances between the chambers and the body area can be gradually increased.

Modifications for Older Students

Require various movement patterns, such as galloping, skipping, and hopping. Upper-grade students can perform the task while dribbling a soccer ball or basketball (one ball per student is needed as additional equipment).

Modifications for Students With Congenital Heart Defects

Check with district personnel (site administrator or nurse) on any health condition that may arise during exercise. Students may have a 504 plan that limits or prescribes certain physical activities. There are a variety of congenital heart defects, many of which are surgically corrected, and students may have no exercise restrictions. These defects include a hole in the septum of the heart and valve problems. In some cases, defects may go undetected. Teach students to recognize symptoms that indicate a need for medical attention, such as chest pain, breathing difficulties, dizziness, swelling of the hands and feet, and a bluish face color that might indicate a heart problem.

Concept Development

Following is a supplemental activity to practice and reinforce the concepts covered in this lesson:

1. Give each student either a blue or red flag (or use pinnies).
2. Students pair up (one with a blue flag and one with a red flag) side to side within an area the size of a basketball court (marked by cones). The two students in each pair represent two sides of a heart.
3. On the command "Body," the pair splits up and jogs.
4. On the command "Heart," students find a new partner with a flag of the opposite color.
5. The partners complete an exercise while side by side. Select exercises such as jumping jacks, mountain climbers, or cross-country skiers (see lesson 6).
6. Any student without a partner keeps jogging. Students can only pair up with a student holding the opposite color.
7. In addition to pairing up, students can form groups of four, with two red and two blue flags. Students then represent the four chambers of the heart. Designate half the students as atria and the other half as ventricles (by color). Each group should consist of two atria and two ventricles.
8. Before calling out the "Body" command, you should name the exercise for that round if you want the students to do something other than jogging.

Assessment Options

Each lesson includes assessment options for the lesson and may include additional assessment options for the skills performed within a lesson.

For the Lesson

By retrieving the appropriate color beanbags, students will demonstrate knowledge of the heart as a pump that has red blood on the left side and blue blood on the right side.

For Sliding

- ▶ The student turns the torso sideways to the desired direction of travel.
- ▶ The student takes a step sideways followed by a slide of the trailing foot next to the lead foot.
- ▶ The movement includes a short period where both feet are off the floor.
- ▶ The student is able to slide to the right and to the left side.

Section 1: Family Activity 4
Hit the Mark

Name: _____

Select any physical activity that you can do with a friend, family member, or neighbor. For every minute that you are active, you score a point. Use the fitness point chart to check off the minutes. Try to reach 100 points this week at home.

Activity   *Time*   *Points*

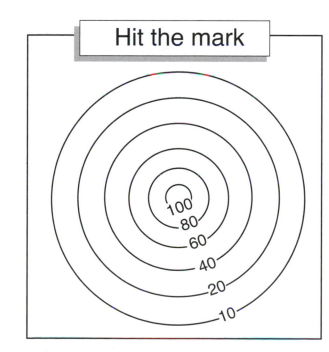

Transfer the points to the figure. Use a different color for each circle as you complete the points.

(continued)

From C. Hopper, B. Fisher, and K.D. Munoz, 2008, *Physical Activity and Nutrition for Health* (Champaign, IL: Human Kinetics). Figure adapted, by permission, from C.A. Hopper, B.D. Fisher, and K.D. Munoz, 1997, *Health-Related Fitness for Grades 3 & 4* (Champaign, IL: Human Kinetics), 12.

(continued)

Bonus Points

Use the following activities to score bonus points and contribute to your goal of 100 points. Each activity is worth 10 points. Write the date that you completed the activities. You can repeat activities to earn more bonus points.

Activity	Points	Date
1. Miss one of your favorite TV shows and go outside to play for 10 minutes.	_____	_____
2. Help a parent with an outside chore.	_____	_____
3. Help sweep or clean a part of the house for 10 minutes.	_____	_____
4. Find someone (friend or family member) to play a ball game.	_____	_____
5. Do 15 curl-ups and 15 push-ups.	_____	_____
6. Wash the car (or assist with washing).	_____	_____
7. Walk to the store instead of riding in a car.	_____	_____
8. Plan a healthy picnic or meal.	_____	_____
9. Take your pulse rate before and after an activity.	_____	_____

From C. Hopper, B. Fisher, and K.D. Munoz, 2008, *Physical Activity and Nutrition for Health* (Champaign, IL: Human Kinetics).

Heart Function

The heart is a pump, a hollow organ consisting of a special muscle. Within the heart are four chambers, a left and right atrium and a left and right ventricle. The atria pump blood into the ventricles, and the ventricles pump blood to the lungs and the whole body. The lessons in this part focus on how the heart and lungs work together to provide oxygen for the body. Contraction of the heart's muscle is involuntary. The heart pumps blood carrying oxygen to all body parts. Oxygen is needed by the muscles as they contract and relax in movement. The heart is the pump that regulates the flow of blood throughout the body. The heart pumps blood to the body with specific contractions that can be measured as the pulse rate. As physical activity increases, the pumping action and the pulse rate also increase.

Lesson 8: Heart Facts II

Outcomes

At the end of this lesson, each student will be able to do the following:

▸ Describe blood flow patterns between the heart, lungs, and body parts.

▸ Explain how the chambers of the heart function and how blood is moved through the heart.

Connections to Health Education Standards

▸ Health promotion and disease prevention

Connections to Other Standards

▸ Science standards: science in personal and social perspectives; life science

▸ Physical education standards: appreciation for the value of physical activity

Connections to WOW! Lessons

▸ Orange level: lesson 7, "Heart Healthy"

▸ Yellow level: lesson 7, "Heart Healthy"

▸ Blue level: lesson 19, "Body Systems"

WOW! Vocabulary

▸ aorta—Main trunk of the artery system carrying blood from the left side of the heart to the arteries of all limbs and organs except the lungs.

▸ inferior vena cava—Large vein that carries deoxygenated blood from the lower half of the body into the heart.

▸ mitral valve—Allows blood to pass from the left atrium into the left ventricle.

▸ pulmonary artery—Artery that carries blood from the heart to the lungs.

▸ superior vena cava—Large vein that carries deoxygenated blood from the upper half of the body to the heart and right atrium.

▸ tricuspid valve—Allows blood to pass from the right atrium into the right ventricle.

Get Ready to WOW! 'Em

You will need the following:

▸ Bicycle pump or hand pump

▸ Figure 8.1, four chambers of the heart (one copy per student)

▸ Figure 8.2, blood flow through the heart, lungs, and body (one copy per student)

▸ Red and blue crayons or pens

▸ Transparencies of figures 8.1 and 8.2

▸ Paper towel tube

▶ Stethoscope (optional)

▶ Tennis balls (you may be able to get old balls from a local tennis club)

▶ Overhead projector and transparency pens

Background Information

The heart is a pump consisting of four chambers. Blood carrying oxygen is pumped from the heart to all the muscles in the body. Oxygen is used by the muscles as they contract and relax to perform movements. As a by-product of the body performing movements, carbon dioxide is produced. Blood returning from body parts carries carbon dioxide back to the heart which in turn pumps the blood to the lungs.

Now WOW! 'Em

1. Review the background information presented for this lesson with the class.

2. Demonstrate the activity of a pump and describe how force is created to generate a pumping action. Explain the following to students: *The heart receives electrical stimulation to create and maintain the pumping action. This electrical message for the heart to contract comes from the brain.*

3. Use the picture of a heart in figure 8.1 to explain the flow of blood through the heart. Students should label the parts of the heart and the blood vessels. Tell the students, *The heart consists of four chambers. The top two chambers are known as the right atrium and left atrium. The bottom two chambers are called the right ventricle and left ventricle. The septum separates the right and left sides of the heart. Blood returning from the body carries carbon dioxide, which the body does not need. Blood from the head or arms enters the right auricle through the* **superior vena cava.** *Blood from the rest of the body comes back to the right auricle from the* **inferior vena cava.**

4. Using figure 8.2, help students trace the flow of blood from the heart to the lungs, from the lungs to the heart, and back to the body. Tell the students, *Inside the heart, blood passes to the right ventricle through the* **tricuspid valve.** *This blue blood is pumped to the lungs through the* **pulmonary artery** *to remove carbon dioxide. After reaching the lungs, blood with a fresh supply of oxygen from the lungs returns to the heart. Oxygenated blood returns to the left atrium and passes through the* **mitral valve** *to the left ventricle. It is then pumped to the head, arms, trunk, and legs through the* **aorta,** *a large artery that branches into many smaller arteries that run throughout the body. The inside layer of the artery is very smooth, allowing the blood to flow quickly. The largest arteries and veins can be 2.5 to 3 centimeters in diameter.*

Wrap It Up!

Explain that one-way valves are important because they prevent any backward flow of blood. Tell students, *The circulatory system is a series of one-way roads.* Family Activity 4, Hit the Mark, on page 73 may be used as needed to encourage students to develop physical activity outside of school.

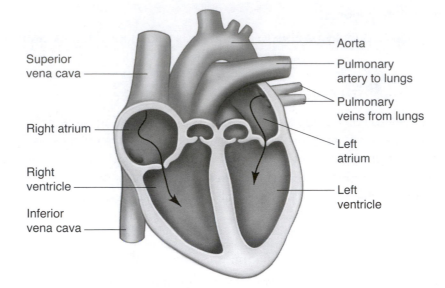

FIGURE 8.1   Four chambers of the heart.

Reprinted, by permission, from B.J. Sharkey, 2001, *Fitness and Health,* 5th ed. (Champaign, IL: Human Kinetics), p.91.

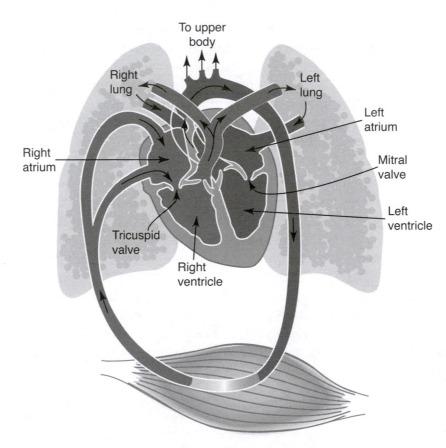

FIGURE 8.2   Blood flow through the heart, lungs, and body.

Adapted, with permission, from M. Flegel, 2004, *Sport First Aid,* 3rd ed. (Champaign, IL: Human Kinetics), 36.

Teaching Notes

Each lesson has suggested modifications, whenever possible, to adapt the concepts to younger or older students.

Modifications for Younger Students

Present the basic information on heart structure, emphasizing the function of the four chambers. Use figure 8.3 to show blood flow pattern.

Modifications for Older Students

Provide some additional background information on blood: Blood transports oxygen from the lungs to body tissue and transports carbon dioxide from body tissue to the lungs. Blood is the fluid of growth and health, providing oxygen and nutrients for the body. Blood contains living cells.

Concept Development

1. Pair off students by the same sex. Tell students, *Use a stethoscope or paper towel tube to hear the sound of the heartbeat. The two sounds—"lub" and "dub"—are the ventricles contracting and the valves closing.*

2. To help students understand the force required for the heart to pump blood, have them repeatedly squeeze a tennis ball. Students should try to squeeze the tennis ball 60 times in a minute.

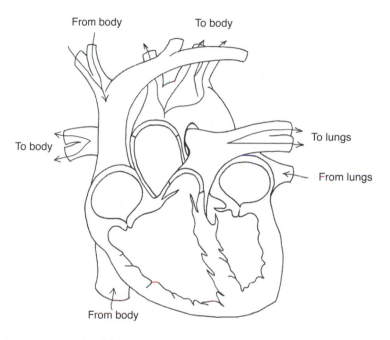

FIGURE 8.3   Blood flow pattern.

Reprinted, by permission, from C.A. Hopper, B.D. Fisher, and K.D. Munoz, 1997, *Health-Related Fitness for Grades 3 & 4* (Champaign, IL: Human Kinetics), 5.

3. Explain to students which parts of the body do not directly receive a blood supply: enamel of teeth, dead layers of skin, parts of the fingernails and toenails.

Assessment Options

Each lesson includes assessment options for the lesson and may include additional assessment options for the skills performed within a lesson.

For the Lesson

Students will demonstrate knowledge of blood flow patterns in the four chambers of the heart and throughout the body.

Lesson 9: Circulation Patterns

Outcomes

At the end of this lesson, each student will be able to do the following:

▸ Demonstrate the pattern of blood flow from the heart to body parts and the lungs by participating in movement activities.

▸ Understand the functions of veins and arteries in relation to the lungs.

Connections to Health Education Standards

▸ Practice of health-enhancing behaviors

Connections to Other Standards

▸ Science standards: science in personal and social perspectives; life science

▸ Physical education standards: competency in motor skills and movement patterns

Connections to WOW! Lessons

▸ Red level: lesson 7, "Heart Healthy"

▸ Orange level: lesson 7, "Heart Healthy"

▸ Yellow level: lesson 7, "Heart Healthy"

WOW! Vocabulary

▸ circulation—Movement of blood through blood vessels as a result of pumping action of the heart.

▸ pulse rate—The number of times a person's heart beats each minute.

▸ supply—To make available for use.

Get Ready to WOW! 'Em

You will need the following:

▸ Playground chalk, 25 cones, or other markers

▸ Color-coded popsicle sticks with the top half red and the bottom half blue (one per pair of students)

▸ Exercise cards (see lesson 6)

▸ Poly spots (one per pair)

▸ Foam balls and selected equipment (see "Concept Development")

Background Information

Blood transports oxygen to the body through the arteries. Blood without oxygen returns from the body parts to the heart through the veins; this blood carries carbon dioxide. The heart pumps oxygenated blood to the muscle cells to provide the energy to do work. The pumping of blood by the heart through the arteries is known as the **pulse rate.** A person's pulse is the throbbing of their arteries as an effect of the heartbeat. During exercise, the body needs a constant **supply** of oxygen.

Now WOW! 'Em

1. Review the background information presented for this lesson with the class.

2. Using playground chalk, jump ropes, or cones, mark out areas representing the heart, lungs, head, arms, and legs (see figure 9.1). Use a playing area of 50 by 50 yards (46 by 46 m). Divide the entire class into pairs. Use Poly spots in the heart area to identify locations for students to move to and from.

3. Designate student A and student B in each pair. Student B is located at a body part (arms, legs, or head, but *not* the lungs), and student A stands on a Poly spot in the heart. Students should be spread equally throughout the body parts.

4. Student A (in the heart) has a popsicle stick with the top half red and the bottom half blue. This student carries the stick in his hand with the red half of the stick showing to represent a molecule of oxygen. Student A runs to meet student B in the body part.

5. Students A and B both perform five repetitions of the exercise designated on the exercise card at the body part (e.g., jumping jacks).

6. Student B then moves to the heart with the blue part of the stick showing in the hand.

7. Students A and B repeat this sequence one more time, with student B now moving from the heart to meet student A in the body part.

8. Student B then moves to a different body part while student A returns to the heart. Student A locates student B, and the exact same movement pattern is repeated. Students must visit all body parts.

9. In the next round of the activity, have the students gallop to the different areas.

10. Introduce the concept of moving faster (run or jog) in the arteries and slower (jog or walk) in the veins.

11. Use the spaces designated as the lungs on either side of the heart. When returning from a body part, the student goes to the heart first and then to the lungs (showing the blue part of the stick) to receive oxygen. Next, the student returns back to the heart and then to the body part (showing the red part of the stick). In each pattern, the correct color on the popsicle stick should be showing in the hand.

Wrap It Up!

Review key points of galloping and compare this skill with other movement skills such as skipping.

Teaching Notes

Each lesson has suggested modifications, whenever possible, to adapt the concepts to younger or older students.

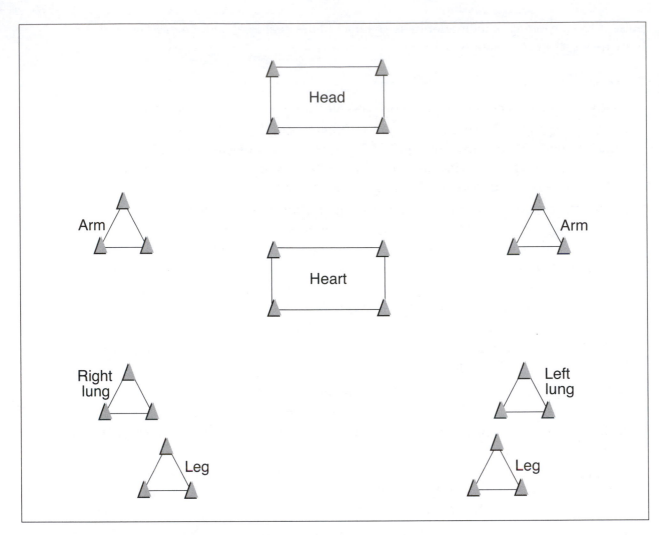

FIGURE 9.1   Circulation patterns.

Adapted, by permission, from C.A. Hopper, B.D. Fisher, and K.D. Munoz, 1997, *Health-Related Fitness for Grades 3 & 4* (Champaign, IL: Human Kinetics), 6.

Modifications for Younger Students

Focus on the first part of the activity, introducing blood flow from the heart to body parts (without including the lungs). In a subsequent class, use this lesson again to introduce the flow of blood to and from the lungs.

Modifications for Older Students

This activity can also be a tag game. Have one person be "it." Students try to move back and forth between the heart and the various body parts. The heart, head, arms, and feet are safe areas. Tagged students become taggers. They should use a foam ball to tag other students. Use a larger playing area to increase the length of the running areas.

Modifications to Reinforce Language Skills

All students, especially those with speech and language problems, can benefit from an emphasis on language concepts that can be reinforced through physical activities.

In teaching **circulation** patterns, specific words can be implemented through movement, such as the following:

- ▸ Directions: forward, sideways, backward, outside, inside, left, right
- ▸ Speed: fast, slow, medium
- ▸ Pathways: straight, narrow, zigzag
- ▸ Qualities: explosive, sustained, rhythmic

Each movement should be explained and demonstrated.

Concept Development

This lesson should be repeated multiple times throughout the year. The following are extensions to develop more advanced concepts.

- ▸ Have students use balls as they move from the heart to the body. For example, students can toss a ball into the air and catch it while running, or they can dribble a ball using their feet.
- ▸ Teach catching and dribbling skills in basketball and soccer.

Assessment Options

Each lesson includes assessment options for the lesson and may include additional assessment options for the skills performed within a lesson.

For the Lesson

By indicating the appropriate color of the stick during this lesson's activity, students will demonstrate their knowledge of the color of the blood moving between the heart, lungs, and body parts.

For Galloping

- ▸ The student steps forward with the lead foot, followed by a step with the trailing foot to a position adjacent to or behind the lead foot.
- ▸ The movement includes a brief period where both feet are off the ground.
- ▸ The arms are bent and lifted to waist level.
- ▸ The student is able to lead with the right and left foot.

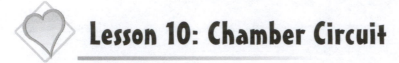

Lesson 10: Chamber Circuit

Outcomes

At the end of this lesson, each student will be able to do the following:

▶ Use movement patterns to simulate the flow of blood through the heart.

▶ Distinguish between ventricles and atria.

Connections to Health Education Standards

▶ Practice of health-enhancing behaviors

Connections to Other Standards

▶ Science standards: science in personal and social perspectives; life science

▶ Physical education standards: competency in motor skills and movement patterns

Connections to WOW! Lessons

▶ Orange level: lesson 7, "Heart Healthy"

▶ Yellow level: lesson 18, "Busy Body"

▶ Blue level: lesson 16, "What Is Asthma?"

WOW! Vocabulary

▶ chamber—A cavity of enclosed space in the heart.

▶ contract—Closing and reducing in size one of the chambers of the heart.

Get Ready to WOW! 'Em

You will need the following:

▶ 40 cones or other markers, such as jump ropes, playground chalk, or Poly spots, that can be used to create body areas (see figure 10.1)

▶ Labels for body parts and for the entry and exit points from the heart: To Body Parts, To Lungs, From Body Parts, and From Lungs (these labels should be taped to cones)

▶ One transparency of figure 10.1 (chamber circuit)

▶ Overhead projector and transparency pens

Background Information

The heart has four major open spaces that fill with blood. The two atria form the curved top of the heart. The two ventricles meet at the bottom to form a pointed base. The left ventricle pumps out blood to the body and **contracts** most forcefully. The walls of the left ventricle **chamber** are three times the thickness of those in the right ventricle. This is because the oxygenated blood that the left ventricle receives from the left atrium has to be pumped throughout the body. A thicker and larger muscle wall provides the strength to pump the blood throughout the entire body.

Now WOW! 'Em

1. Review the background information presented for this lesson with the class.

2. Using a transparency of figure 10.1, explain the pattern of blood flow throughout the body, through the chambers of the heart, and from the heart to the lungs.

3. Mark a large area to represent the heart (25 by 25 yd [23 by 23 m]), and designate an area in the left ventricle for each team. Use different-colored Poly spots to designate the locations where each team should line up.

4. Divide the heart area into four smaller areas to represent the chambers of the heart.

5. Divide the class into five teams of students inside the left ventricle of the heart. Designate a team leader for each team. Teams should change leaders after each circuit (after the team visits each of the body parts, including the head, arms, lungs, and legs). Students stay in line behind the team leader.

6. Assign each team a specific body part (head, arm, lung, or foot) to start with. The team jogs to that body part. Then, they jog back to the right atrium of the heart, through to the right ventricle, and to the lungs. Next, they jog back to the left atrium and then to the left ventricle of the heart. The squad then repeats this pattern, moving in a clockwise fashion to all remaining body parts.

7. Focus on teaching students the running pathway that represents the correct flow of blood between heart, body parts, and lungs. Explain the following: *The heart is a pump that never stops, and blood has to keep flowing to support the functions of the body.* In this activity, encourage students to keep moving to simulate the blood flow. One student from each team can be designated to hold a hula hoop on the pathway to each body part. Team members have to go through the hula hoop; this helps to teach the concept that blood flows through tubes.

8. After students have visited all five body parts, each team waits in the heart for directions.

Wrap It Up!

Students can write a paragraph about blood flow patterns between the heart, lungs, and body. Before they begin writing their paragraphs, ask students to reflect on whether physically completing the movements helped them understand the blood flow patterns.

Teaching Notes

Each lesson has suggested modifications, whenever possible, to adapt the concepts to younger or older students.

Modifications for Younger Students

When teaching the blood flow pattern, have the students walk so that they can become familiar with the sequence of flow between body, heart, and lungs. Then progress to running.

Modifications for Older Students

Students can vary their running or movement speed according to how the blood moves in the body. Blood leaves the heart faster as it is pumped from the left ventricle into

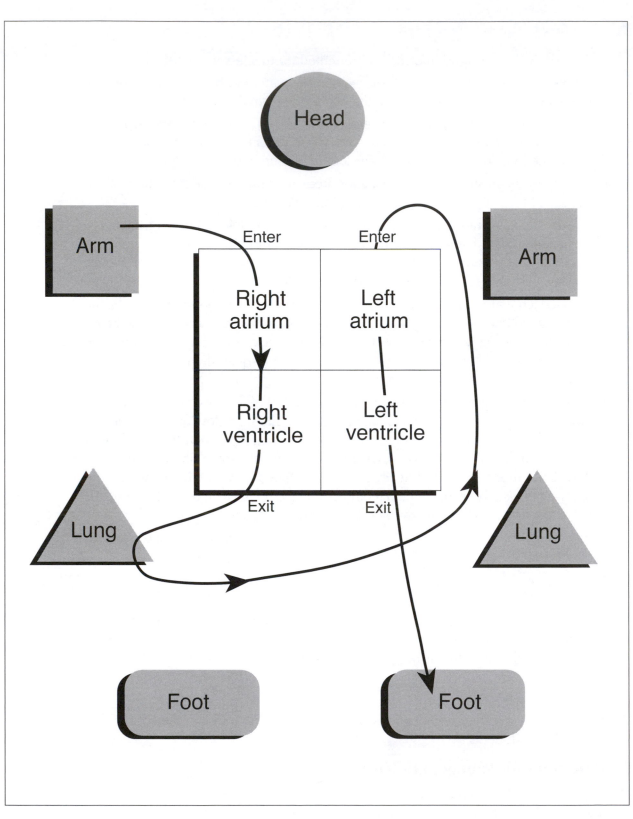

FIGURE 10.1   Chamber circuit.

Adapted, by permission, from C.A. Hopper, B.D. Fisher, and K.D. Munoz, 1997, *Health-Related Fitness for Grades 5 & 6* (Champaign, IL: Human Kinetics), 10.

the aorta. Call out a physical activity that will speed or slow the students' actions. For example, say *Jump rope,* and the team moves faster, or say, *Throw a ball,* and students slow down.

Modifications for Students With Asthma

Each student who has asthma should have an asthma management plan. You should know each individual student's triggers to asthma, and you should make sure the student's prescribed asthma medicines are available for use before physical activity. Students who have been prescribed preexercise treatment should take their medicine 5 to 10 minutes before exercise. Encourage sustained warm-ups before high-energy activities. Cold, dry air may trigger asthma. Very intense, continuous activity is more likely to cause asthma symptoms than intermittent or very light exercise or nonaerobic activities. Most students with asthma should be able to participate most of the time in physical education.

Concept Development

1. Use red and blue cones to mark the pathway taken by blood with and without oxygen. Students run along the correct color of cones—red cones for moving away from the heart and blue cones when moving back to the heart.

2. Tell students, *Identify the names of the major blood vessels that connect to the heart.* The largest of these is the aorta, which is the main artery that carries nutrient-rich blood away from the left ventricle of the heart. The two largest veins that carry blood into the heart are the superior vena cava and the inferior vena cava.

3. Students can vary their running or movement speed according to how the blood moves in the body. Blood leaves the heart faster as it is pumped from the left ventricle into the aorta. Call out a physical activity that will speed or slow the students' actions.

Assessment Options

Each lesson includes assessment options for the lesson and may include additional assessment options for the skills performed within a lesson.

For the Lesson

Students will demonstrate movements that represent how the heart and lungs work together to provide a supply of blood for the body.

For Leaping

▶ The student takes off on one foot and lands on the opposite foot.

▶ The student shows the ability to take off with the right and left foot.

▶ The movement includes a period where both feet are off the ground (longer than running).

▶ The student executes a forward reach with the arm opposite the lead foot.

Heart Rate

A key concept in fitness development is learning to monitor the pulse rate. In the upcoming lessons, students will learn about their pulse rate and how it changes with various levels of physical activity. The students will learn how to determine their resting heart rate, how their favorite physical activities change that resting heart rate, and how fast their heart rate can return to preexercise levels.

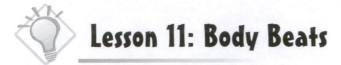

Lesson 11: Body Beats

Outcomes

At the end of this lesson, each student will be able to do the following:

- ▸ Understand that a heartbeat represents the pumping action of the heart.
- ▸ Know the difference between resting and active pulse rates.

Connections to Health Education Standards

- ▸ Practice of health-enhancing behaviors

Connections to Other Standards

- ▸ Science standards: science in personal and social perspectives; life science
- ▸ Physical education standards: appreciation for the value of physical activity

Connections to WOW! Lessons

- ▸ Red level: lesson 7, "Heart Healthy"
- ▸ Yellow level: lesson 7, "Heart Healthy"
- ▸ Blue level: lesson 6, "Crazy Hoops"
- ▸ Blue level: lesson 7, "Four Parts"

WOW! Vocabulary

- ▸ body—The physical structure of a person.
- ▸ carotid artery—Artery in the neck that can be used to find a heart rate.
- ▸ pulse points—Different places on the body to find a heart rate.
- ▸ radial artery—Artery in the wrist area that can be used to find a heart rate.
- ▸ resting heart rate—The number of times the heart beats in a period of time while the person is at rest (sitting down).

Get Ready to WOW! 'Em

You will need the following:

- ▸ Stethoscope or paper towel tube
- ▸ Turkey baster
- ▸ Alcohol wipes (optional)
- ▸ Figure 11.1, taking a pulse rate (one copy per student)
- ▸ Family Activity 5 for section 1, The Beat Goes Home (one copy per student)
- ▸ Two cups or containers, one with a small amount of water and one filled with water (optional)

Background Information

An important part of fitness development is monitoring the pulse rate. A person can do this by finding **pulse points** where arteries are close to the body surface. At these points, the person can feel the heart pushing blood through the **body.** The pulse rate is the number of times the heart beats each minute. This rate changes with activity levels. When people are calm and relaxed, their pulse is slower, and this is their **resting heart rate.** When people are active, scared, or excited, their heart rate accelerates and beats faster, increasing their pulse rate.

Heart rates will vary among students. Most elementary school students have a pulse rate of 75 to 95 beats per minute. Generally, a boy's pulse rate is lower than a girl's. A lower rate usually indicates a more effective cardiovascular system. Heart rates change with age, from 120 beats in infancy to about 70 beats per minute by the age of 18.

Now WOW! 'Em

1. Review the background information presented for this lesson with the class.

2. Demonstrate to students the location of the heart, slightly left of center in the chest area. Students can place their hand on their chest to try to detect a resting pulse rate. In many cases, the resting pulse rate will not be detected through the heart. After exercise, the beating pulse of the heart may be easier to locate in the chest.

3. To demonstrate the pumping action of the heart, use a turkey baster. Tell students, *The heart is a muscle, and muscle contractions force blood out of the heart to the body.* If students are unable to feel their heartbeat, you should have the students complete some exercises to raise their heart rate.

4. Tell students, *You can open and close a hand until fatigue sets in to demonstrate the pumping action of the heart. Note that the heart keeps beating continuously, but opening and closing a hand results in fatigue. Therefore, the heart muscle must be very strong to keep working without stopping to rest.*

5. Tell students, *To find your pulse rate, place your index and middle fingers on your wrist (**radial artery**) or neck (**carotid artery**). Do not use the thumb. The pulse in your thumb may be strong enough to interfere with your count. Hold your fingers in place until you feel the steady beat of your pulse.* (Show the students figure 11.1.) *Pulse rates increase when you are active.*

6. Have students complete some gentle stretching exercises (see "Stretching Routines" in the introduction to this book) for a few minutes and ask the students to find their pulse again. Ask students, *Is your pulse slower by now?*

7. Organize students into pairs of the same sex. Tell students, *We can hear the pumping action of the heart by using a stethoscope or paper towel tube. Press the stethoscope or one end of the cardboard tube against your partner's chest. Put your ear up to the other end and listen to the constant rhythm. The sound "lub-dub" can be heard. Count the heart rate. Every lub-dub equals one beat. Girls and boys should have a heart rate of about 80 beats per minute.*

Wrap It Up!

Ask students to check their pulse rates. Students should use a variety of methods to calculate the pulse rate, including counting for 6 seconds and multiplying by 10, or counting for 15, 30, 45, or 60 seconds.

Give each student a copy of Family Activity 5, The Beat Goes Home. This activity requires students to explain the concept of pulse rate to family members.

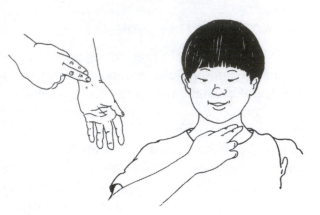

FIGURE 11.1   Taking a pulse rate.

Reprinted, by permission, from C.A. Hopper, B.D. Fisher, and K.D. Munoz, 1997, *Health-Related Fitness for Grades 1 & 2* (Champaign, IL: Human Kinetics), 48.

Teaching Notes

Each lesson has suggested modifications, whenever possible, to adapt the concepts to younger or older students.

Modifications for Younger Students

Younger students may need to complete some light to moderate activity to feel their heartbeat by placing their hand on their chest. Counting a pulse rate can be used to help develop basic mathematics skills.

Modifications for Older Students

Students can calculate their resting and active heart rates by counting their pulse for 6 seconds and multiplying by 10. As a check, ask them to count for 30 seconds and multiply by 2. Use other combinations to help students practice mathematics skills, such as counting for 10, 15, 20, and 30 seconds and using the correct multiplier.

Concept Development

1. Explain to students that a higher pulse rate represents an increase in the amount of blood being pumped by the heart. Use two cups to illustrate the volume of blood being pumped. One cup has just a little water in it (volume at rest), and the other cup is filled full of water (volume during exercise). Explain that during exercise, the amount of blood being pumped increases.

2. Ask students to create a list of sport and physical activities. Encourage students to select activities that are vigorous and will provide 20 minutes of continuous activity. Discuss how some activities may be fun and enjoyable but may not include much physical activity. Discuss ways to increase levels of physical activity in favorite sports and games. For one example, see lesson 21, "Aerobic Kickball" (page 142).

3. Use a model heart or an illustration to show students the structure of the heart. Invite the school nurse into the classroom to demonstrate the use of a stethoscope. Use alcohol wipes to clean ear pieces after each use.

4. Students can then use their heart rate to calculate how many times their heart beats for various time intervals, such as an hour, a day, a week, a month, and a year.

5. Consider with your students the benefit of a well-conditioned heart. Calculate the difference between an individual with 50 beats per minute and a person with 80

beats per minute. The well-conditioned heart beats less often to perform the same task and to pump the same amount of blood to the body.

Assessment Options

Each lesson includes assessment options for the lesson and may include additional assessment options for the skills performed within a lesson.

For the Lesson

Students will demonstrate their ability to find a pulse and to take their heart rates at different times during the day.

Section 1: Family Activity 5
The Beat Goes Home

Name: _____

Teach your family members how to take their pulse rates. In this activity, each family member will take his or her pulse rate while reading or sitting down. Family members then retake their pulse rates during light activity (such as walking), during more moderate activity (such as walking fast), and during vigorous activity (such as running). Students record the pulse rate of each family member in the correct box.

Pulse rates	Family member 1	Family member 2	Family member 3	Family member 4	Family member 5	Family member 6
Resting heart rate						
Light activity: _____						
Moderate activity: _____						
Vigorous activity: _____						

From C. Hopper, B. Fisher, and K.D. Munoz, 2008, *Physical Activity and Nutrition for Health* (Champaign, IL: Human Kinetics).

Lesson 12: Windows of Opportunity

Outcomes

At the end of this lesson, students will be able to do the following:

▶ Improve their cardiorespiratory endurance.

▶ Understand recovery heart rate.

▶ Understand how physical activity sessions can be subdivided into moderate and vigorous segments infused with periods of lighter activity.

Connections to Health Education Standards

▶ Practice of health-enhancing behaviors

Connections to Other Standards

▶ Physical education standards: competency in motor skills and movement patterns; understanding of movement concepts, principles, strategies, and tactics

Connections to WOW! Lessons

▶ Blue level: lesson 8, "The Goliath Beetles"

WOW! Vocabulary

▶ perimeter—The sum of the lengths of the sides of an area.

▶ recovery heart rate—Heart rate after completing exercise.

Get Ready to WOW! 'Em

You will need the following:

▶ Exercise cards (use the cards from lesson 6)

▶ One whistle

▶ Balls (one per pair of students)

▶ Cones or Poly spots (20)

Background Information

Resting heart rates are an indication of levels of cardiorespiratory fitness. Lower heart rates are associated with an active lifestyle, and higher heart rates are associated with sedentary habits. A person's heart rate should decrease after exercise. A faster recovery to a normal heart rate indicates effective functioning of the cardiovascular system. Two minutes after exercising, the **recovery heart rate** should be below 100 beats per minute.

Now WOW! 'Em

1. Review the background information presented for this lesson with the class.
2. For classes with fewer than 20 students, set up a playing area of 40 by 40 yards (37 by 37 m) marked with cones. Use a 50-by-50-yard (46 by 46 m) area for classes with more than 20 students.

3. Pair up students. One member of the pair is inside the playing area. The other partner is stationary on the **perimeter** of the playing area, looking into the middle.

4. Students inside the playing area jog in and out of the cones (or Poly spots). On a whistle cue, they must find their partner outside the perimeter to complete a high five.

5. Students can use the cones to practice changing direction when running. As they approach a cone, they should change direction and move to the left or right.

6. After completing a high five, the outside player does 10 repetitions of an exercise (e.g., mountain climbers, jumping jacks, curl-ups). The players inside keep jogging.

7. After two minutes, the players from the perimeter switch to the inside, and vice versa. The activity continues with different tasks for the players to complete with a partner. Vary the length of the intervals of activity (between one and three minutes) so that students experience shorter and longer periods of activity. Encourage students to work hard during the longer spells of activity.

8. Use balls to provide additional activities (e.g., players dribble a basketball and pass to an outside player, who throws it back to the inside player, who keeps dribbling).

9. Take a break between activities so students can compare pulse rates. Those who have been active should have a higher rate.

Wrap It Up!

After this lesson, use the Intensity Guide from lesson 5 to help students assess their levels of effort in physical activity.

Teaching Notes

Each lesson has suggested modifications, whenever possible, to adapt the concepts to younger or older students.

Modifications for Younger Students

Younger students can carry a basketball (rather than dribble) and hand the ball to the student on the outside. Teach younger students how to change direction when running by bending the knees and shifting the body weight to one side.

Modifications for Older Students

Students can dribble a soccer ball using the feet and following the same pattern as in the basketball dribble. The outside player receives the ball and then passes it back to the inside player.

Modifications for Students With Muscular Weakness

Individuals with muscular dystrophy (resulting in loss of muscle control) and other conditions with muscle weakness require adaptations that accommodate progressive loss of strength. In this lesson's activity, students with muscle weakness can participate on the perimeter. Students who lose the ability to walk through muscle weakness face many challenges in their daily lives. Activities that cause pain or fatigue should be avoided. Students should also avoid activity if aerobic exercise is generally not indicated. Students with muscle weakness expend more energy during exercise than their peers. Short activities followed by rest are essential, and students may need to conserve energy for other daily tasks. Students using canes, crutches, or walkers can still participate (sometimes in a stationary form) in many activities.

Concept Development

1. For a more vigorous activity, the students on the outside could be jogging around the perimeter in the initial phases.

2. When introducing balls into the activity, give specific instructions regarding the types of passes to be used, such as bounce pass or chest pass. Provide teaching tips on each technique.

3. Use this activity as an introduction to specific sports skills that may lead to games.

Assessment Options

Each lesson includes assessment options for the lesson and may include additional assessment options for the skills performed within a lesson.

For the Lesson

Students will practice taking pulse rates during the activity and when in resting roles in an activity.

For the Two-Handed Bounce Pass

▶ The student holds the ball at chest height.

▶ The hands, arms, and chest face the direction of the pass.

▶ The ball is pushed forward and downward by the fingers and hands.

▶ The ball contacts the floor three-fourths of the distance from the passer to the catcher.

▶ The ball rebounds at waist level.

For the Two-Handed Chest Pass

▶ The student holds the ball chest high, with elbows close to the body.

▶ The fingers are spread toward the side of the ball, with thumbs close together behind the ball.

▶ The student steps into the stride stance, with one foot in front of the other, and at the same time extends the arms to release the ball.

▶ The student pushes the ball off with the fingertips and follows through with the hands in the direction of the ball.

Pacing

In this part's lessons, students will learn to calculate a training heart rate that will enable them to improve their cardiorespiratory endurance and strengthen the heart muscle. The "pace, not race" concept is presented so that students can plan their own individual running pace to improve their endurance.

Lesson 13: Training Heart Rate

Outcomes

At the end of this lesson, each student will be able to do the following:

▶ Understand that during exercise the muscles in the body need more oxygen to function effectively.

▶ Know how to calculate a training heart rate.

Connections to Health Education Standards

▶ Health promotion and disease prevention

▶ Practice of health-enhancing behaviors

Connections to Other Standards

▶ Science standards: science in personal and social perspectives; life science

▶ Physical education standards: health-enhancing level of physical fitness

Connections to WOW! Lessons

▶ Red level: lesson 7, "Heart Healthy"

▶ Yellow level: lesson 18, "Busy Body"

WOW! Vocabulary

▶ cardiorespiratory endurance—The ability of the heart, lungs, and blood vessels to deliver oxygen to the muscles of the body.

▶ heart rate training zone—An optimum range for the heart rate to reach in order to improve heart and circulation functions.

▶ maximum heart rate—The number of times the heart beats during intense exercise.

Get Ready to WOW! 'Em

You will need the following:

▶ Worksheet 13.1, Heart Rates Throughout the Day (one copy per student)

Before this lesson, you should review the method for taking a pulse rate described on page 91 in lesson 11.

Background Information

Cardiorespiratory endurance is the ability of the heart, lungs, and blood vessels to deliver oxygen to the muscles of the body. During exercise, muscles—including the heart—have an increased need for oxygen. Regular exercise enables the body to maintain and improve cardiorespiratory fitness. As the students learned in lesson 11, *resting heart rate* refers to the number of times the heart beats per minute while the person is at rest. The **heart rate training zone** refers to the range that an individual needs to reach for cardiorespiratory training to occur.

Now WOW! 'Em

1. Review the background information presented for this lesson with the class.

2. Ask students to calculate their resting heart rate using the method described in lesson 11. The students should use a 6-second period to count their resting heart rate and multiply by 10. In other words, they add a 0 to the end of the score (e.g., 8 beats in 6 seconds equals a pulse rate of 80).

3. Tell students, *To improve fitness, the heart rate needs to increase for an extended period of time into a heart rate training zone.* To help students learn that the heart rate changes with different levels of activity, ask them to take their pulse rate at the following times during the school day: start of school, after recess, after physical education, and after eating lunch. Provide each student with a copy of worksheet 13.1 to complete.

4. Based on a resting heart rate, students can identify a target heart rate using the following list:

Resting heart rate	Target heart rate
<60	150
60-64	151
65-69	152
70-74	153
75-79	155
80-84	159
85-89	161
90+	163

To train the cardiorespiratory system, students should exercise at their target rate for at least 20 minutes, performing activities that use large muscle groups (e.g., running, jumping rope, or bicycling).

Wrap It Up!

Help students make connections between heart rate and the Intensity Guide (see lesson 5).

Teaching Notes

Each lesson has suggested modifications, whenever possible, to adapt the concepts to younger or older students.

Modifications for Younger Students

Younger students can focus on how their heart rate will vary throughout the day and after certain activities. Younger students may be very active at recess; therefore, before and after recess may also be effective reference points.

Modifications for Older Students

Encourage older students to take their pulse rate after school and during the weekend when involved in community physical activities. Encourage them to use their pulse rate as an indicator of their level of effort in physical activity.

Concept Development

1. Use Family Activity 4, Hit the Mark, on page 73 in lesson 7 to enable students to chart their weekly physical activities.

2. Have students use the following formula to calculate a heart rate training zone. Students use their age and resting heart rate to start the calculation.

   220 – age = estimated **maximum heart rate** (MHR)

   MHR – resting HR = heart rate reserve

   heart rate reserve × .60 + resting HR = lower target rate

   heart rate reserve × .90 + resting HR = upper target rate

   Target range for heart rate is _____ to ____ beats per minute.

   Here is an example for a 12-year-old with a resting heart rate of 70:

   220 – 12 = 208 (MHR)

   208 (MHR) – 70 (resting HR) = 138 (heart rate reserve)

   138 (heart rate reserve) × .60 + 70 (resting HR) = 153

   138 (heart rate reserve) × .90 + 70 (resting HR) = 194

   Target range for heart rate is 153 to 194 beats per minute.

Assessment Options

Each lesson includes assessment options for the lesson and may include additional assessment options for the skills performed within a lesson.

For the Lesson

Students will demonstrate an understanding of a target heart rate by calculating a resting heart rate and a target heart rate.

Worksheet 13.1:
Heart Rates Throughout the Day

Name: _____

	Start of school	After recess	After physical education	After lunch
Monday				
Tuesday				
Wednesday				
Thursday				
Friday				

From C. Hopper, B. Fisher, and K.D. Munoz, 2008, *Physical Activity and Nutrition for Health* (Champaign, IL: Human Kinetics).

Lesson 14: Pacing Practice

Outcomes

At the end of this lesson, each student will be able to do the following:

▸ Understand the concept of "pace, not race."

▸ Develop individualized pacing strategies to improve running performance.

▸ Use the Intensity Guide to quantify a level of exertion.

Connections to Health Education Standards

▸ Practice of health-enhancing behaviors

Connections to Other Standards

▸ Math standards: measurement; number and operations

▸ Physical education standards: competency in motor skills and patterns; health-enhancing level of physical fitness

Connections to WOW! Lessons

▸ Red level: lesson 7, "Heart Healthy"

▸ Purple level: lesson 7, "Hockey and Yoga"

▸ Yellow level: lesson 7, "Heart Healthy"

WOW! Vocabulary

▸ estimation—To make an assessment regarding a possible outcome.

▸ pace—To control the rate of speed of movement.

Get Ready to WOW! 'Em

You will need the following:

▸ Whistle

▸ Stopwatch

▸ Eight cones

▸ PACER CD or tape from Fitnessgram

▸ Tape or CD player

▸ Intensity Guide (from lesson 5)

Background Information

In running events such as the one-mile run, students may try to run too fast in the early stages and may be unable to continue at such a fast **pace.** For students to develop a personalized running or exercise schedule, they need to be able to pace themselves and know how much time they will need to run certain distances. To improve running performance—whether running for personal enjoyment or fitness testing—the skill of pacing is essential.

Now WOW! 'Em

1. Review the background information presented for this lesson with the class.

2. A variety of running courses can be used for the activities in this lesson: traditional track, circle, out and back, or rectangular. Use the Intensity Guide on page 53 in lesson 5 to help students determine their levels of effort.

3. Estimation run: In the **estimation** run, all students run the same route, and the goal is for each student to predict her time to run the course. Start with a fairly short distance, such as one lap of a conventional track. Select one or two students to demonstrate the run and time those students. Other students can then estimate their own time and complete the run. Students can keep their estimation to themselves. Ask them to indicate if they met their estimation. After resting, students can then revise their estimation for another attempt. Encourage students to set a realistic time, yet challenge themselves to run as quickly as possible. Challenge them to run at a steady pace and explain how this is the most efficient way of running. Starting off running at a fast pace may not be sustainable over the entire run. Have students identify for themselves a very fast pace, a fast pace, a half-speed pace, and a slow pace.

4. Run and pace: Using a large outdoor area such as a field, create a square 20 by 20 yards (18 by 18 m) to be used as the starting point. Students start by standing in the square. On a signal, such as a whistle, runners identify a destination to run toward (e.g., a corner of the field). They run at a continuous half-speed pace until the next whistle (they stop when the whistle is blown). Start with about 10 to 15 seconds for the length of running time. Runners will be at different locations on the field. On another signal, runners turn around and return to the starting square, running at exactly the same pace. Blow the whistle after the same amount of running time. Students should reach the square at the same time that the whistle is blown. Continue with this activity and vary the amount of time allocated for the run. Students should try to run at an even pace. Increase the amount of time of the run.

5. PACER practice: Set up a 20-meter (22-yard) space for students to run back and forth across as described in the PACER test from Fitnessgram. The following description is from *Fitnessgram/Activitygram Test Administration Manual, Fourth Edition,* by M.D. Meredith and G.J. Welk (Champaign, IL: Human Kinetics, 2007).

   The test is a 20-meter shuttle run with the goal of running back and forth across the 20-meter space to complete as many laps as possible. The pace gets faster every minute. Students run across the 20-meter distance and touch the line with their foot by the time a beep sounds. As the beep sounds students turn around and run back to the other end. If they reach the line before the beep sounds, they wait for the beep to sound before running back. Students continue to run in this format. If they fail to reach the line before the beep sounds they stop and reverse direction to try to get back on pace. After a second time the test is completed. The number of laps completed is the score. This activity provides specific practice for the Progressive Aerobic Cardiorespiratory Endurance Run (PACER).

   - Start with groups of four students, with two students on each side of the 20-meter area (see figure 14.1). Number the students from 1 to 4. Student number 1 runs across the 20-meter space and goes to the back of the line. Student number 3 then runs across to stand behind student number 2. Student number 2 then runs across to join the other

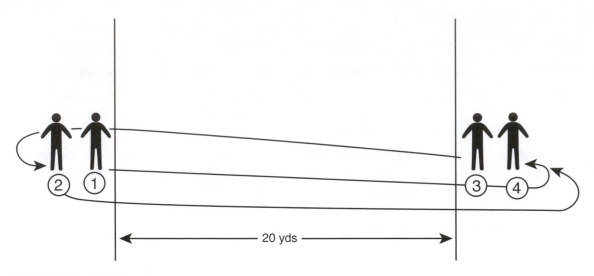

FIGURE 14.1   PACER practice.

line. This pattern continues. Reduce the size of the groups to three and then to two to increase the workload.

- Use the PACER CD or tape, which contains 21 levels (1 level per minute for 21 minutes).

A more detailed description is included in the *Fitnessgram* manual by Meredith and Welk (2007).

6. 40-yard, 100-yard, 800-yard (732 m) and mile run: Students can practice running 40 yards (37 m), 100 yards (91 m), and a mile (1.6 km) at different speeds to determine a comfortable pace for running a mile. Students can select a pace and try to improve their score. Use the students' scores from the Fitnessgram one-mile run to provide a starting point.

7. Ask students to use the Intensity Guide to identify which zone they are working in. For example, if a student runs 800 yards (732 m) in 4 minutes and 32 seconds, that running pace would result in a 10-minute mile time. Students can use the following table to help estimate their running times over certain distances.

40 yards	100 yards	800 yards	1-mile run	Time to run 1 yard*
8.2 sec	20.50 sec	2 min 44 sec	6 min	.20 sec
9.5 sec	23.75 sec	3 min 10 sec	7 min	.24 sec
10.9 sec	27.25 sec	3 min 38 sec	8 min	.27 sec
12.3 sec	30.75 sec	4 min 6 sec	9 min	.31 sec
13.6 sec	34.00 sec	4 min 32 sec	10 min	.34 sec
15.0 sec	37.00 sec	4 min 46 sec	11 min	.37 sec
16.4 sec	41.00 sec	5 min 28 sec	12 min	.41 sec
17.7 sec	44.75 sec	5 min 58 sec	13 min	.44 sec
19.09 sec	47.72 sec	6 min 22 sec	14 min	.48 sec
20.45 sec	51.13 sec	6 min 49 sec	15 min	.51 sec

*Rounded to two decimal places.

Wrap It Up!

Regardless of performance levels, encourage students to try to improve their times. Emphasize that individual improvement should be the goal for each student.

Teaching Notes

Each lesson has suggested modifications, whenever possible, to adapt the concepts to younger or older students.

Modifications for Younger Students

For younger students, the running course can be subdivided into zones with students learning how to run at different speeds: regular walk, fast walk, slow jog, and run.

The major emphasis for younger students (grades K-3) should be on developing effective running techniques and participating in a variety of running activities. The PACER practice activity will help students prepare for the PACER.

Modifications for Older Students

The PACER is highly recommended for students in grades 4 to 6.

Modifications for Students With Learning Disabilities

Students with learning disabilities have difficulties processing information, which may cause problems with understanding spoken or written words. Some of these developmental delays may also affect fundamental movement skills, such as running. Problems with body and spatial awareness can result in awkward movements and an inability to complete oppositional actions, such as using arms and legs in coordination in the running sequence. Students may often add twisting or other uncontrolled movements of the arm or hand as they try to perform a coordinated action. The bilateral coordination required in jumping jacks with upper and lower body sequencing may present some challenges.

Following are specific modifications for this lesson:

1. For students with these characteristics, provide brief but highly specific guidelines and focus on one problem at a time, such as the use of the arms in running.

2. Ask students to repeat back to you the requirements of the task.

Concept Development

1. For the estimation run, use cones to divide the running course into segments (quarters, halves) so that students can identify how far they have run. This provides a reference point as they seek to pace themselves.

2. Students can calculate their running speed for different distances (e.g., 800 yd [732 m]). Students can also calculate their speed per second and per minute over different distances. For example, they can convert their time in the one-mile run to seconds. Then they divide the number of yards (1,760) by seconds to obtain yards per second. As an additional activity, older students can convert yard times to meter times.

Assessment Options

Each lesson includes assessment options for the lesson and may include additional assessment options for the skills performed within a lesson.

For the Lesson

Through a variety of running activities, students will demonstrate an ability to pace themselves.

For Running

- ▶ The student moves the arms in opposition to the legs, bending the elbows.
- ▶ The student holds the head steady, with only a slight body lean.
- ▶ The student lands heel first and pushes off with the ball of the foot.
- ▶ The student swings the legs and feet, landing straight ahead.
- ▶ The stride is longer than when walking.
- ▶ The student bends the elbows (90 degrees), with hands relaxed.
- ▶ The student holds the head so the ears sit over the middle of the shoulders.

SECTION 2

Food for a Workout

When people are aerobically fit, they burn fat and carbohydrate to provide the energy needed to perform aerobic activities. These types of activities, including running and riding a bicycle, need the heart and lungs to work together to deliver oxygen to the muscles. In section 2, the lessons begin with nutrition. Students will learn about hidden sources of fat in food, which foods are rich in carbohydrate, and how animal fat can clog the arteries. Later in this section, students will learn to distinguish between aerobic and anaerobic activities. They will also participate in activities designed to improve their cardiorespiratory fitness. Activities such as aerobic kickball and cardio hoops focus on maximum participation in movement for all students throughout the activity.

Fat

When people know which foods contain fat, they can improve their overall dietary intake and improve their cardiovascular health. In this part of section 2, students will become proficient in recognizing which foods contain animal fat and plant fat, and they will learn how fat tastes and feels to the touch. Students will also learn how animal fat can clog arteries, leading to cardiovascular disease.

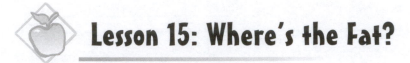

Lesson 15: Where's the Fat?

Outcomes

At the end of this lesson, each student will be able to do the following:

▸ Describe the hidden fat content of common foods.

▸ Identify common properties of sample foods and categorize those foods into food groups.

▸ Record, compare, and interpret data.

Connections to Health Education Standards

▸ Health promotion and disease prevention

▸ Interpersonal communication skills

Connections to Other Standards

▸ Science standards: science in personal and social perspectives

Connections to WOW! Lessons

▸ Red level: lesson 14, "Tacos by Cody"

▸ Yellow level: lesson 14, "Tacos by Cody"

WOW! Vocabulary

▸ food groups—Foods are classified into groups that contain similar nutrient contents; these groups are grains, vegetables, fruits, meats and beans, oils, and dairy.

Get Ready to WOW! 'Em

You will need the following:

▸ Samples of beverages and foods from different **food groups,** with food cut into 1-inch (2.5 cm) pieces and beverages divided into small samples. Examples include milk, soda, bananas, apples, broccoli, peanut butter, butter, mustard, mayonnaise, potato chips, pretzels, bread, cheese, doughnuts, jelly, ketchup, and hot dogs. When choosing foods to include in the samples, be sure that you are aware of any foods that your students are allergic to (such as milk or peanuts).

▸ Brown grocery bags (one per group of students) cut into sheets approximately 12 by 15 inches (31 by 38 cm)

▸ One eyedropper or medicine dropper for each sample liquid

▸ Family Activity 1 for Section 2, Out With the Fat, In With the Lean (one copy per student) 💿

▸ Worksheet 15.1, Where's the Fat? (one copy per group of students) 💿

▸ Plastic wrap

▸ Metal spoon

▸ Overhead transparencies (one per group) and transparency pens (one per group)

▸ Overhead projector

Background Information

In this lesson, students will examine and organize foods into categories, collect information about which foods contain fat, and draw conclusions from their results. Generally, fruits, vegetables, breads, and cereals have very little fat. Furthermore, the fat contained in these foods is usually monounsaturated and polyunsaturated fat, such as the fat in avocados. Dairy foods and meat can be good sources of saturated fat, depending on the choices made within the group. For example, nonfat milk has less than one gram of fat, whereas whole milk has 5 grams of fat per 8-ounce (240 ml) serving.

Learning to recognize which foods contain fat is the first step toward improving overall dietary intake. This knowledge can help people reduce their calorie intake and help them maintain a healthy weight. Remember, calories count when a person is trying to maintain a healthy weight, and all types of fat contain the same number of calories regardless of whether they are monounsaturated, saturated, or polyunsaturated!

Now WOW! 'Em

1. Before the lesson, place the various foods on a table for the class to view.

2. Review the background information presented for this lesson with the class.

3. Have students work in groups of two or three and give each group a transparency to write on. Tell the students, *On your overhead transparency, list all the foods on the table, grouping them in a way that you think makes the most sense.* The goal is to categorize them by food groups.

4. Next, ask the students to label or categorize their groupings. One student from each group will share the group's ideas with the class, displaying their overhead transparency. Ask the students the following questions: *What foods belong to what group? Do any of the categories relate to each other?* (Some may have fat while some may not.) *How might we test the fat content of food?*

5. Ask the students, *What do you think would happen if you were to take one of the foods and rub it on a piece of brown paper?* Tell them to hypothesize about this question. They should respond that food with fat would leave an oily spot.

6. With a small amount of butter on a spoon, demonstrate how to rub the test food on the piece of brown paper and describe what happens to the paper.

7. Ask the students to predict which foods from their list will contain fat and to record their predictions on worksheet 15.1.

8. Provide each group with a piece of brown paper and instruct them to fold the brown paper in half four times to produce 16 blocks. Students should label each block with the name of the test food.

9. Each group will test the food samples by rubbing a small amount of the food in the labeled square. Give students the following instructions:
   - *If the sample is soft like mustard, rub it with a spoon.*
   - *If it is hard like a nut or cracker, place a small piece of plastic wrap over the sample and crush it with a spoon.*
   - *Scrape off any excess sample that sticks to the paper.*
   - *For liquids, use the eyedropper or medicine dropper to place one or two drops on the paper.*

Be sure that students who have food allergies avoid handling those foods that they are allergic to.

10. Tell students to let the paper dry and hold it up to the light. If the food contains fat, it will leave a greasy mark.

11. Students should record the results on the worksheet and compare the results to their predictions.

Wrap It Up!

1. Tell the groups, *Rank the foods based on which ones appear to be higher in fat than the others.*

2. Ask the students to write a summary statement or paragraph about the results of the lesson.

3. Tell the students that they should apply their knowledge to everyday situations. Encourage them to choose foods to eat that are less greasy, which means the foods are lower in fat.

Teaching Notes

Each lesson has suggested modifications, whenever possible, to adapt the concepts to younger or older students.

Modifications for Younger Students

▶ Instead of having students work in groups at the beginning, work as a class and ask the students to name the foods as you hold them up. Then ask them to guess which food group the food belongs in.

▶ Have the brown paper bags already folded with the names of each food written in the 16 blocks before the lesson. Continue to have the students test each food as described in the lesson.

▶ Rather than having the students write a summary statement, discuss the results as a class.

Modifications for Older Students

None.

Concept Development

Ask the students to plan a meal that would be high or low in fat using the concepts learned in this lesson.

Assessment Options

Each lesson includes assessment options for the lesson and may include additional assessment options for the skills performed within a lesson.

For the lesson

By completing worksheet 15.1, students will demonstrate their ability to categorize foods into groups, describe which foods contain fat, and write a concluding statement related to this lesson.

Worksheet 15.1: Where's the Fat?

Name: _____

Food sample	Food group	Prediction (Y/N)	Results (Y/N)

Write a concluding statement or summary:

From C. Hopper, B. Fisher, and K.D. Munoz, 2008, *Physical Activity and Nutrition for Health* (Champaign, IL: Human Kinetics).

Section 2: Family Activity 1
Out With the Fat, In With the Lean

Name: _____

15 Tips to Help You Avoid Too Much Fat

1. Steam, boil, or bake vegetables; or for a change, stir fry them in a small amount of vegetable oil.

2. Season vegetables with herbs and spices rather than with sauces, butter, or margarine.

3. Try lemon juice on salads or use limited amounts of oil-based salad dressing.

4. To reduce saturated fat, use margarine instead of butter in baked products, and when possible, use oil instead of shortening.

5. Try whole grain flours to enhance flavors of baked goods made with fewer fat- and cholesterol-containing ingredients.

6. Replace whole milk with skim or low-fat milk in puddings, soups, and baked products.

7. Substitute plain low-fat yogurt, blender-whipped low-fat cottage cheese, or buttermilk in recipes that call for sour cream or mayonnaise.

8. Choose lean cuts of meat.

9. Trim fat from meat before or after cooking.

10. Roast, bake, broil, or simmer meat, poultry, and fish.

11. Remove skin from poultry before cooking.

12. Cook meat or poultry on a rack so the fat will drain off. Use a non-stick pan for cooking so added fat will be unnecessary.

13. Chill meat or poultry broth until the fat becomes solid. Spoon off the fat before using the broth.

14. Limit egg yolks to one per serving when making scrambled eggs. Use additional egg whites for larger servings.

15. Try substituting egg whites in recipes calling for whole eggs. For example, use two egg whites in place of each whole egg in muffins, cookies, and puddings.

(continued)

From C. Hopper, B. Fisher, and K.D. Munoz, 2008, *Physical Activity and Nutrition for Health* (Champaign, IL: Human Kinetics).

(continued)

Activity

In discussion with your family, choose one of the listed tips that you can accomplish at a meal. Design a short survey that family members can respond to. Use the following two questions as examples, and design a few more questions.

	Strongly agree	Agree	Neutral	Disagree	Strongly disagree
1. The meal tasted as good as when using the old method.	_____	_____	_____	_____	_____
2. I would prefer to use the new method of cooking in the future.	_____	_____	_____	_____	_____
3.	_____	_____	_____	_____	_____
4.	_____	_____	_____	_____	_____
5.	_____	_____	_____	_____	_____

From C. Hopper, B. Fisher, and K.D. Munoz, 2008, *Physical Activity and Nutrition for Health* (Champaign, IL: Human Kinetics).

Lesson 16: Feeling Fats

Outcomes

At the end of this lesson, each student will be able to do the following:

▶ Distinguish between animal and plant fat.

▶ Categorize foods as plant and animal foods.

Connections to Health Education Standards

▶ Health promotion and disease prevention

▶ Interpersonal communication skills

Connections to Other Standards

▶ Science standards: science in personal and social perspectives

Connections to WOW! Lessons

▶ Red level: lesson 12, "Food for Thought"

▶ Red level: lesson 14, "Tacos by Cody"

▶ Yellow level: lesson 12, "Food for Thought"

▶ Yellow level: lesson 14, "Tacos by Cody"

WOW! Vocabulary

▶ animal fat—Fat found in meats and dairy products.

▶ plant fat—Fat found in plant products and in oils such as corn, safflower, and canola oil.

Get Ready to WOW! 'Em

You will need the following:

▶ Paper towel tubing (about 6 in [15 cm] long)

▶ Modeling clay (enough to simulate plaque in the paper towel tube)

▶ Worksheet 16.1, Feeling Fats (one copy per student, plus one overhead transparency)

▶ Samples of foods such as peanut butter, fruits, nuts, vegetables, breads, and cheese. Be sure you are aware of any student allergies to foods such as milk or peanuts.

Background Information

Everybody needs some fat in the food they eat. Fat provides many healthy ingredients, such as vitamins, essential oils, and energy. Fat is also used by the body to make tissues. Most of the fat that people eat each day—such as meat, butter, whole milk, and cheese—comes from animals. Most plants have little, if any, fat. Fat derived from plants includes oils such as corn, canola, and olive oil. A diet that is high in fat (both animal and plant) can make a person gain weight, which will make the heart pump harder and can lead to heart disease. The problem with eating too much **animal fat** is that the body stores it in the fat cells. Animal fat can also block the arteries and possibly result in heart attack or stroke. Although people need a small amount of fat each day, they should eat a diet that is low in both animal and **plant fat.**

Now WOW! 'Em

1. Before class, prepare a model of a simulated blood vessel with a buildup of fat in it. To do this, use a small piece of paper towel tubing with some clay blocking the "artery."

2. Review the background information presented for this lesson with the class.

3. Brainstorm with the students about what foods might contain fat, such as margarine, peanut butter, and meat. As a group, classify several examples of common foods with obvious plant and animal sources. Ask the students, *Which ones contain fat? Is the fat from animal or plant?*

4. Show the students the "blocked blood vessel" and tell them, *Eating too much animal fat can cause a buildup of fat in your arteries, which will block the flow of blood to and from your heart.* Also be sure to emphasize the need to reduce all fat, including plant fat. Say to the students, *Although plant fat doesn't build up in your arteries, all fat is high in calories and can contribute to weight gain.* Be sure to emphasize that people should follow a low-fat diet that includes reducing all types of fat. This is the best approach to healthy eating in order to maintain a healthy weight.

5. After assigning students to groups of two or three, instruct them to use worksheet 16.1, Feeling Fats, to test the samples of foods for fat by using the "feel test." Tell students, *Next to the food name, indicate whether you think the food came from an animal or a plant. Foods that contain fat may feel oily, creamy, or greasy. Indicate with a check mark which foods have fat. Do you see a pattern of food groups without fat?* (Most animal foods have fat.)

6. After the "feel test" has been completed, guide the students through the rest of the foods listed on the worksheet.

Wrap It Up!

When the list is completed, ask the students to write a concluding statement about their favorite foods (other than the foods listed on the worksheet). Students should indicate whether their favorite foods come from animals or plants and whether or not they contain fat.

Teaching Notes

Each lesson has suggested modifications, whenever possible, to adapt the concepts to younger or older students.

Modifications for Younger Students

1. Instead of having students work in small groups, work as a class and ask the students to name the foods as you hold them up. Then ask them to guess whether the food is from an animal or a plant.

2. Have the students touch and feel one food from each food group. Discuss as a class whether the students think each food has fat or not.

Modifications for Older Students

None.

Concept Development

Ask the students to plan a meal that would be high or low in animal fat using the concepts learned in this lesson.

Assessment Options

Each lesson includes assessment options for the lesson and may include additional assessment options for the skills performed within a lesson.

For the Lesson

Students will demonstrate their ability to categorize foods into animal or plant foods, describe which foods contain fat, and write a concluding statement related to this lesson.

Worksheet 16.1: Feeling Fats

Name: _____

Instructions: Which of the following foods do you think contain fat? Use the "feel test" by touching each food to judge whether you think the food has fat in it. Foods that contain fat may feel creamy, oily, or greasy. If you think the food contains fat, put a check mark in the space provided.

Food	Contains fat? Yes	No
Peanut butter	____	____
Tortilla	____	____
Banana	____	____
Processed meat	____	____
Egg yolk	____	____
Egg white	____	____
Chocolate	____	____
Cocoa	____	____
Apple	____	____
Avocado	____	____
Carrot	____	____
Potato	____	____
Oatmeal	____	____
Cheese	____	____

From C. Hopper, B. Fisher, and K.D. Munoz, 2008, *Physical Activity and Nutrition for Health* (Champaign, IL: Human Kinetics).

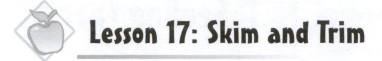

Lesson 17: Skim and Trim

Outcomes

At the end of this lesson, each student will be able to do the following:

- ▶ Describe how fat looks, feels, and tastes in food.
- ▶ Recognize low-fat dairy products.
- ▶ Identify whole milk, 2 percent milk, and skim milk by appearance.
- ▶ Record, compare, and interpret data.

Connections to Health Education Standards

- ▶ Health promotion and disease prevention
- ▶ Interpersonal communication skills

Connections to Other Standards

- ▶ Science standards: science in personal and social perspectives

Connections to WOW! Lessons

- ▶ Yellow level: lesson 14, "Tacos by Cody"

WOW! Vocabulary

- ▶ 2 percent milk—Milk that contains 5 grams of fat per serving.
- ▶ low-fat dairy—Dairy products that contain less than 3 grams of fat per serving.
- ▶ skim milk—Milk that contains 0.5 grams or less of fat per serving.
- ▶ whole milk—Milk that contains 8 or more grams of fat per serving.

Get Ready to WOW! 'Em

You will need the following:

- ▶ Three glass pitchers or jars marked A, B, and C
- ▶ Three types of milk (whole milk, 2 percent milk, and nonfat or skim milk; you can substitute soy milk if you can find three contrasting levels of fat content)
- ▶ Worksheet 17.1, Skim and Trim Taste Test (one copy per group of students)
- ▶ Three paper cups per student (for sampling milk). These cups should be marked A, B, and C.

Background Information

Everyone needs some fat in their diet every day—especially young children. But too much fat can lead to overweight and obesity, as well as cause heart problems later in life. Many foods have low-fat options, including the dairy group. A person can get the same nutritional value out of milk (e.g., calcium) whether it is nonfat milk or whole milk. So, one way for people to reduce fat in their diet is to drink **skim** or **2 percent**

milk instead of **whole milk** and consume other low-fat dairy products. A person can eat less fat and still enjoy the good taste of milk, yogurt, and cheese. Fat in food, whether plant or animal fat, has certain properties that make food taste creamy, oily, greasy, and flavorful. If people can learn to recognize the taste, feel, and smell of foods that contain fat, they can reduce the amount of fat they eat.

Now WOW! 'Em

1. Begin by reviewing the background information presented for this lesson with the class. Tell the students, *Most plant foods are low in fat, and most animal foods are not low in fat.* Ask students the following questions:
   * *Can you describe what the fat in foods tastes like?* (creamy, flavorful)
   * *How does fat feel in your mouth?* (greasy, oily, creamy)
   * *Can you describe how fat smells?*

2. Organize the students into small groups and give them worksheet 17.1, Skim and Trim Taste Test. Explain to the class that three types of milk will be tested.

3. Pour one type of milk into each pitcher.

4. Describe the testing process to the class. First, tell the students, *Observe each of the three types of milk and come up with three terms to describe the appearance of each type.* Have students write or draw these terms on the worksheet, depending on the abilities of your class.

5. Next, have each student sample the milk (if a student is allergic to milk, have just one student in the group do the taste test of the milk). Tell students to write, draw, or discuss three terms to describe the taste of the milk.

6. Then, after all three types have been sampled, tell students, *Predict the rankings of these three types of milk, from the highest to the lowest amount of fat.*

Wrap It Up!

After all groups have finished, discuss the results with the class.

Teaching Notes

Each lesson has suggested modifications, whenever possible, to adapt the concepts to younger or older students.

Modifications for Younger Students

1. Instead of having students work in groups, work as a class with the teacher holding up the pitchers of milk and going through the previously listed steps.

2. Use an overhead transparency of worksheet 17.1 and fill it out as the students discuss each step.

3. Discuss the results as a class.

Modifications for Older Students

Add a fourth milk (1 percent milk) to make the distinction more challenging.

Concept Development

Have students write a summary statement or paragraph about the results of the lesson. Encourage students to apply what they learned about the appearance, taste, and feel of fat when choosing other foods to eat in everyday situations.

Assessment Options

Each lesson includes assessment options for the lesson and may include additional assessment options for the skills performed within a lesson.

For the Lesson

By completing the worksheet and the writing activity, students will demonstrate their ability to identify fat in dairy foods.

Worksheet 17.1:
Skim and Trim Taste Test

Name: _____

Instructions

1. Write the name of the sample in the space provided in the left column.

2. Describe the appearance of samples A, B, and C in the middle column.

3. Describe the taste of samples A, B, and C in the right column.

Sample	Appearance	Taste
A		
B		
C		

From C. Hopper, B. Fisher, and K.D. Munoz, 2008, *Physical Activity and Nutrition for Health* (Champaign, IL: Human Kinetics).

Carbohydrate

Carbohydrate produces energy to fuel the brain, the red blood cells, and the muscles, particularly during aerobic exercise. In this part of section 2, students will learn which foods are rich in both simple and complex carbohydrate, including the complex carbohydrate called dietary fiber. Taking a field trip to the local grocery store will give students experience in reading labels to identify types of carbohydrate, fat, and dietary fiber in processed and packaged foods.

Lesson 18: Carbohydrate Loading

Outcomes

At the end of this lesson, each student will be able to do the following:

▸ Describe the importance of eating carbohydrate as part of a healthy diet.

▸ Differentiate between foods that contain complex carbohydrate and those that contain simple carbohydrate.

Connections to Health Education Standards

▸ Health promotion and disease prevention

▸ Interpersonal communication skills

Connections to Other Standards

▸ Science standards: science in personal and social perspectives; life science

Connections to WOW! Lessons

▸ Yellow level: lesson 14, "Tacos by Cody"

▸ Purple level: lesson 9, "The Nutrient–Health Connection"

WOW! Vocabulary

▸ complex carbohydrate—The type of carbohydrate found in starch and fiber.

▸ simple carbohydrate—The type of carbohydrate found in processed foods and naturally occurring in fruits and dairy.

Get Ready to WOW! 'Em

You will need the following:

▸ Iodine (clear) mixed with water (mix 4 or 5 drops of iodine per 200 milliliters of water and fill each medicine dropper bottle with about 4 tablespoons)

▸ One eyedropper or medicine dropper bottle per group of students

▸ Newspaper (enough to cover the table)

▸ Food samples for each group of students, including saltine crackers, pieces of egg white, small pieces of cheese, bologna or other sandwich meat, pieces of meat such as hamburger or chicken, boiled white rice, cooked pasta, slices of bread, tortillas, and slices of fruit (apples or bananas)

▸ Worksheet 18.1, Carbohydrate Loading (one copy per group of students) 💿

Background Information

To function and grow properly, the human body has certain basic needs that must be met. The most important is the production of energy. Foods that contain carbohydrate provide fuel for the brain, the red blood cells, and the muscles. They are also needed by the digestive tract to process food and provide fiber. Carbohydrate provides the body with energy to meet a student's daily needs for growth and energy.

Foods high in carbohydrate include bread, cereals, dairy, pasta, fruits, and vegetables. Two different types of carbohydrate are found in foods. **Simple carbohydrate** is sugar found in foods such as table sugar, honey, brown sugar, and high-fructose corn syrup. The natural sugars found in fruits and dairy products are also simple carbohydrates. **Complex carbohydrate** is found in foods with starch and fiber, such as whole grain breads and cereals, vegetables, and the peels of fruits (e.g., apples) and vegetables.

Now WOW! 'Em

1. Ask students, *How do you feel after not eating for a long time? Do you feel tired? What foods do you think might provide more energy than others?* Write their answers on the board.

2. Review the background information presented for this lesson with the class. Be sure to explain the different types of foods that contain simple carbohydrate (candy, soda, honey, sugar, fruits, and fruit juices) and complex carbohydrate (starchy foods including pasta, rice, breads, fruits, vegetables, and cereals).

3. Organize the class into small groups. Using the food samples, ask the groups to categorize the foods by food groups and to write them on worksheet 18.1, Carbohydrate Loading.

4. Use a cracker to demonstrate how complex carbohydrate turns blue when you apply a drop of iodine. Ask the students to predict which of the remaining foods contain complex carbohydrate and will turn blue when the students apply a drop of iodine to the food.

5. Give each group a newspaper to spread out on their table, several different samples of foods, and a medicine dropper bottle with the iodine solution. Instruct the students to use the eyedropper to put a drop of iodine solution on each sample. Students should record on their worksheet what happens to the food. Foods with complex carbohydrate in the form of starch will turn blue. Foods with simple carbohydrate will not turn blue.

Wrap It Up!

1. As a class, discuss the groups' findings. Ask students, *How did your results compare to your predictions?*

2. Ask students, *Which food groups contained carbohydrate and which ones didn't?* They should state that meats do not contain any carbohydrate.

Teaching Notes

Each lesson has suggested modifications, whenever possible, to adapt the concepts to younger or older students.

Modifications for Younger Students

Complete the activity as a demonstration by the teacher. Have students predict whether or not the food contains complex carbohydrate before you apply the iodine. Discuss the results with the class.

Modifications for Older Students

None.

Concept Development

Ask the students to keep a food diary for one day and to write down the type of carbohydrate they eat, including simple and complex carbohydrate.

Assessment Options

Each lesson includes assessment options for the lesson and may include additional assessment options for the skills performed within a lesson.

For the Lesson

By completing the laboratory experiment and the worksheet, students will demonstrate their ability to recognize which food groups contain carbohydrate.

Worksheet 18.1: Carbohydrate Loading

Name: _____

Samples	Food group	Prediction (Y/N)	Results (Y/N)

From C. Hopper, B. Fisher, and K.D. Munoz, 2008, *Physical Activity and Nutrition for Health* (Champaign, IL: Human Kinetics).

Lesson 19: Supermarket Sweep

Outcomes

At the end of this lesson, students will be able to do the following:

▶ Read the nutrition labels of packaged foods.

▶ Evaluate packaged foods found in grocery stores for nutritional content.

Connections to Health Education Standards

▶ Health promotion and disease prevention

▶ Interpersonal communication skills

Connections to Other Standards

▶ Science standards: science in personal and social perspectives

Connections to WOW! Lessons

▶ Blue level: lesson 12, "The Big Label Discovery"

▶ Purple level: lesson 9, "The Nutrient–Health Connection"

▶ Purple level: lesson 13, "The Hi-Oc Mission"

WOW! Vocabulary

▶ fiber—A type of carbohydrate found in whole grains, fruits, and vegetables.

▶ nutrition labels—Labels provided on packaged foods to identify nutritional information.

Get Ready to WOW! 'Em

You will need the following:

▶ Worksheet 19.1, Supermarket Sweep (one copy per group)

▶ Pencils (one per group)

▶ Clipboards (one per group)

▶ Family Activity 2 for Section 2, Home Run Cookies

Before this lesson, you should contact the manager of a local grocery store to make arrangements to take your class to the grocery store on a field trip.

Background Information

Processed foods contain varying amounts of fat (total fat, saturated fat, and trans fat), carbohydrate (total carbohydrate, sugars, and fiber), and other nutrients, even within the same category of foods (such as crackers or dairy products). For example, a grocery store might sell crackers ranging from 0 to 6 grams of fat per serving. To help ensure healthy eating, people need to learn to read **nutrition labels** so they can make wise food choices.

Now WOW! 'Em

1. Review the background information presented for this lesson with the class.

2. Explain to the students the importance of reading nutrition labels. Tell them that during the lesson they will be going to a grocery store to learn to read nutrition labels.

3. Discuss your expectations for the students' behavior while on a field trip and for the lesson itself.

4. Organize the class into six investigative groups as follows:
   1. Crackers and chips group
   2. Dairy group (milk, cheese, and yogurt)
   3. Frozen entree group
   4. Processed meats group
   5. Cereal group
   6. Dessert group (cookies, ice cream, and cake)

5. Start with a tour by the store manager so students get an idea of how a grocery store is organized. Once the tour has been completed, instruct the students to find the aisle for their food group and to record the aisle number on their handout (worksheet 19.1).

6. For the activity, instruct each group to read as many labels as possible. Tell them to record the food and the total amount of fat (in grams), the total carbohydrate (in grams), and the total dietary **fiber** (in grams) per serving for this food. Once they have located a variety of food products, they should rank them from the highest to the lowest in fat, carbohydrate, and dietary fiber. Challenge students to find the greatest range of fat and carbohydrate in their food products.

7. Next, tell students to put all the foods in order from the least amount of fiber to the greatest amount of fiber per serving.

Wrap It Up!

Once you've returned to the classroom, ask the students to report their findings and discuss their results with the class.

Teaching Notes

Each lesson has suggested modifications, whenever possible, to adapt the concepts to younger or older students.

Modifications for Younger Students

Modify this lesson by assigning the adults who accompany the groups to read the labels and write the information on the worksheet.

Modifications for Older Students

None.

Concept Development

Develop a class activity by placing students in groups to create a new healthy cereal with a nutrition label to post on the classroom bulletin board. They should include the artwork for the design as well as the nutrition information on the label.

Assessment Options

Each lesson includes assessment options for the lesson and may include additional assessment options for the skills performed within a lesson.

For the Lesson

Students will demonstrate their ability to read food labels by completing the worksheet.

Worksheet 19.1: Supermarket Sweep

Name: _____

Instructions: Write the food category in the blank provided and the number of the aisle in the grocery store where your products are found. Choose a food in your category and write the name of the food in the first blank. Next, read the nutrition label on the product. Write the number of grams of fat, total carbohydrate, and fiber in a serving of the food in the blanks provided. Continue to record at least six different food items in the same food category. When you have finished, rank the foods from highest to lowest in fat by placing a number (1 to 6) in the ranking column next to the food. Rank the foods in carbohydrate and fiber in the same way. Which food do you think is the most nutritious?

Names of group members: _____

Food category: _____ Aisle number: _____

Food	Fat (grams)	Rank	Carbohydrate (grams)	Rank	Fiber (grams)	Rank

From C. Hopper, B. Fisher, and K.D. Munoz, 2008, *Physical Activity and Nutrition for Health* (Champaign, IL: Human Kinetics).

Section 2: Family Activity 2
Home Run Cookies

Name: _____

Try making these cookies for a heart-healthy family snack. By adding high-fiber ingredients and reducing animal fat, we can eat our cookies and be heart healthy too!

Ingredients

3/4 cup (154 g) vegetable shortening

1/2 cup (110 g) brown sugar

1/2 cup (100 g) granulated white sugar

2 egg whites

1/4 cup (60 ml) water

1 tsp vanilla

1/2 cup (60 g) whole wheat flour

1/2 cup (63 g) white flour

1/2 tsp baking soda

1 cup (165 g) raisins

3 cups (243 g) rolled oats, quick cooking or regular

Directions

1. Preheat the oven to 350 degrees.
2. Beat together the shortening, sugars, egg whites, water, and vanilla until creamy.
3. Combine the flours and baking soda. Add to the creamed mixture.
4. Add the raisins and rolled oats. Mix well.
5. Drop by rounded teaspoonfuls onto greased cookie sheets.
6. Bake 12 to 15 minutes.
7. Enjoy! (Makes approximately five dozen cookies.) Keep the recipe for future healthy snacking.
8. With your family, write your reaction to these nutritious treats. Return your responses to the teacher.

From C. Hopper, B. Fisher, and K.D. Munoz, 2008, *Physical Activity and Nutrition for Health* (Champaign, IL: Human Kinetics).

Keep Moving

This part of section 2 focuses on aerobic fitness. Students will learn how to develop the endurance and ability to stay active for a period of time (in a wide variety of activities). Aerobic exercise improves the functioning of the heart and has many other health benefits for the cardiorespiratory system.

Generally, most activities that raise the heart rate and keep the heart working for at least 15 to 20 minutes are aerobic activities. As aerobic fitness increases, the amount of oxygen delivered to the muscles also increases, which allows the muscles to keep working longer. As a person's aerobic fitness increases, the person will be able to do more physical activity without becoming out of breath. Aerobic fitness is related to overall health.

In the upcoming lessons, students will learn about the characteristics of aerobic exercise. They will plan their own personal workouts. They will also participate in physical activities that encourage activity rather than lack of movement. Increased aerobic fitness means the heart and lungs can deliver sufficient oxygen and blood to the muscles during exercise (and return carbon dioxide to the lungs to be expelled). Students will learn the differences between aerobic and anaerobic activity, and they will participate in cardiorespiratory activities that will strengthen their heart and lungs.

Lesson 20: O₂ (Oh-Two)

Outcomes

At the end of this lesson, each student will be able to do the following:

▸ Identify cardiorespiratory activities that are physically demanding and require the body to use oxygen.

▸ Compare and contrast aerobic and anaerobic activities.

Connections to Health Education Standards

▸ Health promotion and disease prevention

Connections to Other Standards

▸ Science standards: science in personal and social perspectives, life science

▸ Physical education standards: health-enhancing level of physical fitness

Connections to WOW! Lessons

▸ Orange level: lesson 8, "Big and Strong"

▸ Yellow level: lesson 17, "Big and Strong"

▸ Blue level: lesson 6, "Crazy Hoops"

▸ Purple level: lesson 7, "Hockey and Yoga"

WOW! Vocabulary

▸ aerobic activity—The ability of the heart and lungs to take in, transport, and use oxygen.

▸ anaerobic activity—The ability to complete short bursts of exercise that do not require the body to use oxygen to produce energy.

Get Ready to WOW! 'Em

You will need the following:

▸ 20 cones

▸ Four stopwatches

▸ Worksheet 20.1, Comparison of Short and Long Runs (one copy per group of students) 💿

Background Information

Aerobic activities, such as running for an extended period of time, require the heart and lungs to work harder and deliver increased amounts of oxygen to the muscles. These are extended activities that make a person breathe hard while using the large muscle groups to move at a regular and even pace. **Aerobic activity** is the most effective form of exercise for developing cardiorespiratory endurance. **Anaerobic activity** can be short and very intense exercises (e.g., running up a short flight of stairs) that do not require the body to use oxygen to produce energy. Anaerobic exercises can also involve activities that last but are not physically demanding (e.g., walking slowly). The terms *aerobic fitness, cardiorespiratory endurance,* and *cardiorespiratory fitness* all refer to the ability of the heart and lungs to take in oxygen and transport it to the muscles of the body.

Now WOW! 'Em

1. Review the background information presented for this lesson with the class.

2. Use cones to set up an extended running course.

3. Use cones to set up four lanes for the 40-yard (37 m) sprint.

4. Tell students, *Cardiorespiratory endurance is defined as the ability of the heart, lungs, and blood vessels to deliver oxygenated blood to the muscles of the body.* Describe some aerobic activities that promote cardiorespiratory endurance, such as walking, running, swimming, bicycling, and jumping rope. Students can describe additional aerobic activities. Tell students, *Many other activities can also provide cardiorespiratory endurance training if they meet the following criteria:*
   - *Requires continuous effort*
   - *Uses large muscles of the body (e.g., leg muscles)*
   - *Increases heart rate*

5. Tell students, *The purpose of this activity is to complete an extended running activity and a very short running activity. You will compare how the body reacts to each activity with regard to effort, heart rate, breathing, and sweating.*

6. Extended running activity: Establish a time period for your class to run based on their grade level. The objective for the class is to keep running for the entire time period. Use the following times as a guide and adjust them as needed:
   - Grades K-1: 3 minutes
   - Grades 2-3: 4 minutes
   - Grades 4-5: 5 minutes
   - Grade 6: 6 minutes

   Students should run at a pace that is consistent and allows each student to run the entire time. For students in grades 4 to 6, you should have them take their heart rate at the end of the run (counting the heartbeat for 6 seconds and multiplying by 10). See lesson 11 for a more detailed description of taking the heart rate. Students rotate through roles as runner, timer, and recorder. Organize students into small groups of four or five.

7. 40-yard sprint activity: Instruct the students to run as fast as they can for the full 40 yards. At the end of the run, students in grades 3 through 6 should take their heart rate for 6 seconds and multiply by 10.

8. Using worksheet 20.1, Comparison of Short and Long Runs, students compare and contrast the extended run and the 40-yard run. After each run, students fill in the chart, recording their observations for each of the criteria. Have students write in the differences between the two running activities.

Wrap It Up!

Ask students to identify the aerobic activities that they participate in most often. Help students select an aerobic exercise that they enjoy participating in.

Teaching Notes

Each lesson has suggested modifications, whenever possible, to adapt the concepts to younger or older students.

Modifications for Younger Students

Shorten the sprint run to 30 yards (27 m). Do the timing and recording for the students or get assistance from older students or other helpers.

Modifications for Older Students

Group students according to similar abilities. This lesson can be repeated with individuals setting goals for improvement. Students can use descriptive terms to describe the differences in effort, heart rate, sweating, and breathing during the two activities.

Concept Development

1. Have the students develop a list of activities that are similar to extended running. They should choose activities based on the following characteristics:
   - Requires continuous effort
   - Uses large muscles of the body (e.g., leg muscles)
   - Increases heart rate

2. Have students classify each of the following activities into one of two categories—aerobic (A) or anaerobic (AN):
   - Table tennis (AN)
   - Playing first base in baseball or softball (AN)
   - Dancing (A)
   - Swimming laps (A)
   - Yoga (AN)
   - Competitive basketball game (A)

   Ask students to add more activities to this list.

3. Ask students to collect pictures of aerobic and anaerobic activities from sports and fitness magazines. Laminate these for use in lesson 30, "Aerobic Voyage."

Assessment Options

Each lesson includes assessment options for the lesson and may include additional assessment options for the skills performed within a lesson.

For the Lesson

Students can write a short paragraph about participating in or watching an aerobic sporting activity.

Worksheet 20.1:
Comparison of Short and Long Runs

Name: _____

Student	Sprint time	Heart rate	Extended run time	Heart rate
1.				
2.				
3.				
4.				
5.				

Use the chart to compare and contrast the characteristics of each running activity.

	Extended run	40-yard run
Effort		
Heart rate		
Sweating		
Breathing		

Indicate which activity required more effort, a higher heart rate, more sweating, and faster breathing.

From C. Hopper, B. Fisher, and K.D. Munoz, 2008, *Physical Activity and Nutrition for Health* (Champaign, IL: Human Kinetics).

Lesson 21: Aerobic Kickball

Outcomes

At the end of this lesson, students will be able to do the following:

▸ Improve their cardiorespiratory endurance.

▸ Practice kicking, catching, and throwing skills.

Connections to Health Education Standards

▸ Practice of health-enhancing behaviors

Connections to Other Standards

▸ Physical education standards: competency in motor skills and movement patterns; regular participation in physical activity; health-enhancing level of physical fitness

Connections to WOW! Lessons

▸ Green level: lesson 3, "Quadriceps"

▸ Blue level: lesson 6, "Crazy Hoops"

WOW! Vocabulary

▸ endurance—Continued use of physical effort to complete a task.

Get Ready to WOW! 'Em

You will need the following:

▸ Four cones for bases

▸ One playground ball

Background Information

Aerobic kickball is a game designed to provide more movement and involvement than in traditional kickball. This active format encourages cooperative and supportive behaviors. Traditional kickball involves a lot of standing around and inactivity for most players. In the aerobic version, all students are constantly moving and engaged with a variety of tasks focusing on **endurance** through continuous movement.

Now WOW! 'Em

1. Review the background information presented for this lesson with the class.

2. Divide the class into two teams: a fielding team and a kicking team.

3. The fielding team spreads out in the field and takes the traditional fielding positions with the exception of pitcher and catcher.

4. The kicking team is divided into three groups (A, B, and C). One member of kicking group A is "up to bat" and kicks a stationary ball (no pitcher) into the field. All

members of kicking group A, including the kicker, run around the bases. Older students can be rolled a ball to kick (from a pitcher).

5. The fielder collects the ball and runs to the pitching mound.

6. Everyone else on the fielding team runs to line up behind the player with the ball. The players on the fielding team pass the ball back over their heads so the ball moves down the line of players. The last player to receive the ball holds it above the head and shouts "Aerobic."

7. To score a point, all members of kicking group A must reach home plate before the ball reaches the last person on the fielding team.

8. Each kicking group (A, B, and C) has two turns—with groups switching after each kick—then the fielding and kicking teams switch places.

9. The kicking team has the right of way on the bases.

10. The fielding and kicking teams switch after six total kicks, two for each sub-group.

Wrap It Up!

Explain to students the rationale for playing this game. Emphasize how this game includes more activity for all students. Have students describe how this version of kickball is different from more traditional kickball games (they should focus on describing the differences in activity levels). Students can also compare the activity in baseball and softball to this version of kickball.

Teaching Notes

Each lesson has suggested modifications, whenever possible, to adapt the concepts to younger or older students.

Modifications for Younger Students

Younger students can kick a stationary ball or throw a ball out.

Modifications for Older Students

1. Vary the objects used by the kicking team. You can use a kickball, a rubber playground ball, a football, a Frisbee, or a tennis racket and tennis ball.

2. Vary the activities of the fielders. For example, students can form a circle around the pitcher's mound and pass the ball around the circle. Or the fielding team can remain in their original positions and pass the ball around the field until each team member touches the ball.

3. Make sure the distance between bases reflects the task required of the fielding team. This distance can be adjusted to create a larger running course. Runners on the kicking team can perform various movement skills, such as skipping, sliding, and galloping.

Modifications for Students With Autism

Students with autism typically experience motor clumsiness. When severe autism is present, a student may need a buddy to run with during this and other activities. A tether (a short towel or rope) may be used to connect the student with autism to a buddy. In this activity, the buddy can lead the student with autism around the bases. The length of the tether may be adjusted. Designated space is a useful management technique. Set up a place for the student to stand when waiting to run the bases. Do this by using a Poly spot to indicate a specific space for the student to stand and wait.

Concept Development

Tell students, *It is easier to kick a ball farther when the ball is rolled toward the kicker. The ball moves onto the top of the foot. The foot can move under the ball and lift it into the air. Therefore, greater height can be achieved.* Assist students with their kicking skills. If the ball is kicked on the right side, it will tend to go to the left. If the ball is kicked on the left side, it will tend to go to the right. A common kicking error is a lack of a follow-through. Therefore, encourage students to follow through with the kicking foot after contact is made.

Assessment Options

Each lesson includes assessment options for the lesson and may include additional assessment options for the skills performed within a lesson.

For the Lesson

Students will demonstrate a combination of cooperative and competitive skills to play the game successfully.

For Kicking

- The kicker has a rapid, continuous approach to the ball.
- The trunk is inclined backward during ball contact.
- The kicker uses a forward swing of the arm opposite the kicking leg.
- The kicker follows through by hopping on the nonkicking foot.
- The kicker uses the laces or instep to contact the ball.

Lesson 22: Cardio Hoops

Outcomes

At the end of this lesson, students will be able to do the following:

▶ Improve their cardiorespiratory endurance.

▶ Practice fitness activities using a hoop.

▶ Use fitness activities that reinforce shape recognition and mathematical language.

Connections to Health Education Standards

▶ Practice of health-enhancing behaviors

Connections to Other Standards

▶ Math standards: geometry

▶ Physical education standards: competency in motor skills and movement patterns; understanding of movement concepts, principles, strategies, and tactics

Connections to WOW! Lessons

▶ Blue level: lesson 6, "Crazy Hoops"

WOW! Vocabulary

▶ chord—A line segment that joins two points on a curve.

▶ circumference—The boundary of a circle.

▶ conflict resolution—The use of social and verbal skills that are developed to enable a person to resolve conflicts in a peaceful and responsible manner.

▶ diameter—A straight line passing through the center of a circle and meeting the circumference on each side.

▶ preferred (or dominant)—Selected most of the time.

▶ radius—A straight line extending from the center of a circle to the circumference.

▶ square—A shape with four equal sides.

▶ triangle—A shape with three sides (equilateral, scalene, or isosceles).

Get Ready to WOW! 'Em

You will need the following:

▶ Whistle, drum, or other signal device

▶ One hula hoop per student

▶ 40 cones or Poly spots

▶ CD player and music

Background Information

Physical activities can be used to reinforce classroom instruction in basic geometry concepts (such as **diameter, radius,** and **circumference**) and different geometric shapes (such as **triangle** and **square**).

Now WOW! 'Em

1. Review the background information presented for this lesson with the class.
2. Two separate workout plans are presented. Use one or the other or a combination of the two.

Hoop Workout

1. Hula hoops (one per student) are scattered throughout the playing area.
2. Students jog or run around the playing area. On your signals, students will each find a hoop and complete specified exercises.
3. Give students the following instructions:
   * *On my signal "one," find a hoop and complete one push-up.*
   * *On my signal "two," find a hoop and complete two cross-country skiers (see lesson 6 in section 1 on pag 60 for a description of this exercise).*
   * *On my signal "three," find a hoop and complete three mountain climbers.*

   Additional numbers can be added.
4. Using the previous sequence throughout the lesson, have students complete various locomotor activities. Here are some additional activity instructions you can give to the students:
   * *With your hoop on the ground, place your hands in the hoop and your feet outside the hoop. Walk your feet around the hoop in one direction, then in the other direction.*
   * *Use the hoop as a jump rope and see how many consecutive jumps you can make.*
   * *Jump as high as possible using a two-footed jump and land in the same place (see the "Assessment Options" section for more details).*
   * *Jump out of the hoop with two feet and land on two feet outside the hoop. Jump back in and land on two feet. Repeat using one foot, first the left foot then the right foot.*
   * *Hop all the way around the hoop in one direction, then hop around in the other direction. Use the left foot, then the right foot.*
   * *Hold the hoop around the waist and see if you can spin the hoop around the waist.*
   * *Roll the hoop forward, allowing it to fall to the ground. Jump into it and complete 10 jumping jacks.*
   * *Hold the hoop upright and make it spin around like a spinning top. Spin the hoop, run to a line or wall, and come back to the hoop before it stops spinning.*
5. Take away one hoop. Scatter the remaining hoops in the area and tell students to jog (or hop, gallop, skip, or slide). On a signal, each student finds a hoop. The student without a hoop can select an exercise (e.g., jumping jacks or cross-country skiers), and each student completes five repetitions of the exercise. Take away two hoops and each student without a hoop selects an exercise. This creates a competitive situation with students trying to find a hoop (some students may become upset if they cannot find a hoop).
6. Introduce music after students have learned some basic hoop activities.

7. If enough space is available, tell students to complete the following activities:

* *Hold the hoop in an upright position. Using your **preferred** or **dominant** hand, roll the hoop so it moves forward. Roll the hoop and move around the area with the hoop. Roll the hoop into the open spaces. Roll the hoop forward, then run ahead of it and catch it.*

Geometric Shapes Workout (Squares, Circles, Triangles)

1. Using cones or Poly spots, create large shapes (such as squares, circles, and triangles) in the playing area. These shapes can be as large as 10 to 15 yards (9 to 14 m) depending on the size of your class. Shapes can be color coded if you are using Poly spots.

2. Students skip, jog, or perform other locomotor activities until the music stops.

3. When the music stops, students find a large square, circle, or triangle with no more than five students to a shape.

4. Call out the exercise to be performed and the number of repetitions.

5. The next time the music stops, students must find a different shape than they were at previously.

Wrap It Up!

Check for students' understanding of basic geometrical terms.

Teaching Notes

Each lesson has suggested modifications, whenever possible, to adapt the concepts to younger or older students.

Modifications for Younger Students

Younger students can focus on basic shapes, such as triangles and squares.

Modifications for Older Students

Older students can discuss the mathematical properties of the shape (angle, sides, vertices, edges, names, types). More complex shapes, such as trapezoids and different types of triangles, can be presented.

Modifications for Students With Frustration or Anger

Use a "Resolution Corner" to teach students effective **conflict resolution.** This can help students learn to deal with frustration and anger when placed in competitive situations. They will also learn to develop social skills for effective peer group relations. The Resolution Corner can be used when two students get into a disagreement. The students go to a designated area, where they sit down and attempt to resolve their differences. Help students identify signs of anger in their own body, such as a quickly beating heart, a red face, aggressive facial expressions, loudness, and feeling overwhelmed or feeling there is no possibility of successfully completing the task. Make sure the Resolution Corner is reserved for those who are in conflict, rather than those who may want to sit out for a while.

Concept Development

1. After students have practiced some basic activities, add some music with a strong beat. Preview any music provided by students.

2. Demonstrate each specific activity.

3. Encourage students to bend at the knee to make a soft landing when jumping.

4. Hoops can be noisy indoors, so instruct students to place the hoops on the floor when listening to instructions.

5. Provide adequate space for activities.

6. Teach the concept of **circumference** by having students place the hoop on the ground and walk around the hoop.

7. Teach **diameter** by having students walk heel to toe across the middle of the hoop, which is lying on the ground.

8. Teach **radius** of a circle by having the students sit in the middle of the hoop and reach with one arm to touch the side.

9. Teach **chord** by having students grasp the hoop with their hands toward the top part of the hoop so that the line between their hands represents a chord (see figure 22.1).

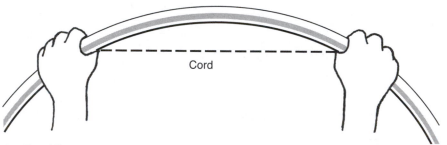

FIGURE 22.1   Chord line.

Assessment Options

Each lesson includes assessment options for the lesson and may include additional assessment options for the skills performed within a lesson.

For the Lesson

Students will demonstrate knowledge of geometric shapes and measurements of those shapes.

For the Vertical Jump

▶ The jumper starts in a crouched position with knees bent.

▶ The arms swing vigorously upward.

▶ The jumper reaches up with the arms and hands as high as possible.

▶ The jumper uses a two-footed jump and landing.

▶ The jumper lands lightly while bending at the hips, with the knees and ankles absorbing the force.

Explain to students that jumping higher depends on using all muscles and body parts in coordination. To demonstrate this, have students jump without using their arms and without starting from a crouched position.

Cardiorespiratory Fitness

In this part, students will learn about the three parts of an aerobic workout: the warm-up, the main activity, and the cool-down. By the end of these lessons, students will be able to create a sample aerobic workout that they can do at home.

Lesson 23: What's in a Workout?

Outcomes

At the end of this lesson, each student will be able to do the following:

▸ Understand the three parts of an aerobic workout.

▸ Create a sample workout to implement at home.

Connections to Health Education Standards

▸ Health promotion and disease prevention

Connections to Other Standards

▸ Science standards: science in personal and social perspectives; life science

▸ Physical education standards: responsible personal and social behavior; appreciation for the value of physical activity

Connections to WOW! Lessons

▸ Green level: lesson 8, "Physical Education"

▸ Blue level: lesson 6, "Crazy Hoops"

▸ Purple level: lesson 7, "Hockey and Yoga"

WOW! Vocabulary

▸ cool-down—A segment at the end of a workout where the person gradually reduces exercise intensity.

▸ warm-up—A period of moving slowly at the beginning of a workout to prepare the body for more vigorous activity.

Get Ready to WOW! 'Em

You will need the following:

▸ Worksheet 23.1, My Personal Workout (Sample; one copy per student)

▸ Worksheet 23.2, My Personal Workout (one copy per student)

▸ Transparencies of worksheets 23.1 and 23.2

▸ Overhead projector and transparency pens

▸ Sports-related magazines (e.g., *Runner's World, Sports Illustrated*)

▸ Scissors

Background Information

Successful and safe workouts involve three segments: the **warm-up,** the peak or main activity, and the **cool-down.** When designing a workout, people should make sure that all three segments are included.

Physical fitness has value in people's lives for the following reasons:

▶ Maintaining health (i.e., reducing the risk of heart disease and other diseases, such as cancer)

▶ Emergencies (e.g., running to get help when a friend has been hurt)

▶ Demands of everyday life (e.g., lifting and moving objects, changing a car tire)

▶ Playing sports and enjoying recreational activities

Now WOW! 'Em

1. Review the background information presented for this lesson with the class.

2. Tell students, *Developing and maintaining physical fitness is best achieved with exercise programs.* Explain that an exercise program has three phases:

   1. Warm-up (5 minutes): The warm-up involves a gradual increase in physical activity. The purpose of warming up is to prevent muscle strain and soreness and to increase the elasticity (stretchiness) of muscles in preparation for more vigorous exercise.

   2. Peak or main workout (15 to 20 minutes): This cardiorespiratory part of the workout is the most important because it strengthens the heart and increases the efficiency of the circulatory system. Many types of continuous or rhythmic exercises can be used in this phase of the workout. The key is that exercise is continuous and regular.

   3. Cool-down (5 minutes): The cool-down is similar to the warm-up. The cool-down is a gradual transition from strenuous to reduced activity. This helps prevent muscle soreness and tension.

3. Discuss ideas for a peak or main workout. Use examples from previous lessons and from student experiences from community sports programs. Students will develop a plan to share with a partner.

4. Have students review the sample workout on worksheet 23.1, My Personal Workout (Sample).

5. Next, the students each create their own workout plan using worksheet 23.2, My Personal Workout. Each student's plan should include all three components (warm-up, peak, and cool-down). Using sports-related magazines, students should cut out one picture that represents each of the three components.

6. Divide students into pairs. Students share their plans with their partner. After discussing each other's workout plan, the students complete their own plan, making any needed changes based on their partner's recommendations or feedback.

7. Ask for volunteers to share their workouts with the class.

Wrap It Up!

Have each student rank the reasons to value physical fitness (presented at the beginning of the lesson) in order of importance.

Teaching Notes

Each lesson has suggested modifications, whenever possible, to adapt the concepts to younger or older students.

Modifications for Younger Students

Younger students can rely more on pictures when creating their workout plans. They can then write key words to describe their pictures.

Modifications for Older Students

Older students can create different workouts based on different activity settings, such as a sports workout and a home or neighborhood workout. They can research workouts for specific sports or athletes.

Concept Development

1. Select three or four of the students' workouts to use as part of your physical education lessons. Students can act as "teachers" leading the class through their workout.

2. In a triathlon, athletes complete 3 fitness activities, such as running, swimming, and biking. A similar Olympic event is the decathlon (10 events). Create workouts in the form of "athlons" that include various amounts of activities: triathlon (3), pentathlon (5), hexathlon (6), octathlon (8), and decathlon (10). Workouts can be designed for the whole class to complete in a physical education lesson. They can also be designed for students to do with friends and family in their neighborhood. For example, the following is a neighborhood family pentathlon: Walk 1 mile to the park, run or jog 2 laps of the park, do 15 sit-ups, play catch for 5 minutes, and walk home. Create a name for each of the workouts.

Assessment Options

Each lesson includes assessment options for the lesson and may include additional assessment options for the skills performed within a lesson.

For the Lesson

Students will demonstrate the ability to plan workouts based on the model of a warm-up, main activity, and cool-down.

Worksheet 23.1:
My Personal Workout (Sample)

This is a sample workout designed to be used in a community setting, such as a park, school playground, or neighborhood.

1. Warm-up (5 minutes)

   - Stretch the legs and back.
   - Jog for a couple of minutes, starting slowly and gradually increasing speed.
   - Stretch the upper body.
   - Shoot a few hoops.

2. Peak or main activity (20 minutes). Select two of the following activities based on the facilities available:

   - Ride a bike for 10 minutes.
   - Jog for 10 minutes.
   - Play one-on-one basketball for 10 minutes.

3. Cool-down (5 minutes)

   - Jog and then gradually reduce speed to a walk.
   - Stretch the upper and lower body.

From C. Hopper, B. Fisher, and K.D. Munoz, 2008, *Physical Activity and Nutrition for Health* (Champaign, IL: Human Kinetics).

Worksheet 23.2:
My Personal Workout

Name: _____

Instructions: Develop a plan for a personal workout to be completed at home on weekends or at school during physical education. Label the amount of time needed to complete each phase and then fill in the activities to do during each section of the workout. Include cutouts of pictures to illustrate the workout (wait until you have discussed the workout with a partner before gluing the pictures).

1. Warm-up: minutes

-
-
-
-

2. Peak or main activity: minutes

-
-
-
-

3. Cool-down: minutes

-
-
-

From C. Hopper, B. Fisher, and K.D. Munoz, 2008, *Physical Activity and Nutrition for Health* (Champaign, IL: Human Kinetics).

Lesson 24: Challenge Course

Outcomes

At the end of this lesson, students will be able to do the following:

▶ Improve their cardiorespiratory endurance.

▶ Practice locomotor skills.

Connections to Health Education Standards

▶ Practice of health-enhancing behaviors

Connections to Other Standards

▶ Physical education standards: competency in motor skills and movement patterns; health-enhancing level of physical fitness

Connections to WOW! Lessons

▶ Blue level: lesson 7, "Four Parts"

▶ Purple level: lesson 6, "Skill-Related Fitness"

WOW! Vocabulary

▶ challenge—Testing a person's ability (and energy) to keep moving and attempting to improve performance.

Get Ready to WOW! 'Em

You will need the following:

▶ Cones (10)

▶ Mats (five or six)

▶ Benches (three or four)

▶ Hoops (four to six)

▶ Jump ropes (six)

▶ Yardstick (for bar) or meterstick

▶ Other equipment to include in the course design, such as chairs, scooter boards, and balance beams

Background Information

Challenge courses provide an opportunity to practice a variety of movement skills while performing continuous vigorous exercise. Students enjoy negotiating the obstacles on these courses. They also enjoy the challenge of completing the course as quickly and accurately as possible. This approach to exercise is often associated with adventure training.

Now WOW! 'Em

1. Review the background information presented for this lesson with the class.

2. Set up a challenge course in the gym or outdoors (see the example in figure 24.1). The course is a series of obstacles arranged in a circular rotation. The specific nature of the challenge course depends on available facilities and equipment. The course should be wide enough for several students to move safely around at the same time. Avoid using obstacles that create a line of students waiting to use a piece of equipment.

3. Demonstrate the specific movements. Tell students, *The objective is to keep moving as quickly as possible on the course.* The course can include all types of locomotor movements (running, jumping, galloping, and hopping); moving under, over, through, and around obstacles; and animal walks or movements (such as the bear walk, bunny hop, and crab walk).

4. Divide the class into pairs (or groups of four), with one student completing the course and the other jogging, walking, or dribbling a ball around the outside.

Wrap It Up!

Students should take their pulse rates before, during, and after the activity.

Teaching Notes

Each lesson has suggested modifications, whenever possible, to adapt the concepts to younger or older students.

Modifications for Younger Students

The partner who is not on the challenge course can jump rope. To ensure safety, make sure students complete movements under control. Also, make sure there is plenty of room for students to move around the course without bumping into each other.

Modifications for Older Students

▶ Discuss wheelchair accessibility issues.

▶ Design a course over a larger area that requires students to run longer distances between pieces of equipment. Time students on one lap of the course.

▶ Create a course that requires students to practice jumping and hurdling skills.

Modifications for Students With Spinal Cord Injuries

▶ Arrange the course so that any student in a wheelchair can participate and allow alternative movements. Students with spinal cord injuries have specific movement limitations depending on the location of the lesion. Students with quadriplegia have no trunk control or sitting balance. These students need a high-back chair, and they need to be strapped in for safety. Students with paraplegia have full use of the upper extremities; however, they have varying levels of trunk control and sitting abilities depending on the specific level of the injury. Lesson 44, "Back Yourself Up" on page 279 introduces the structure of the spinal column. Injuries disrupt the control of muscles at and below the injury

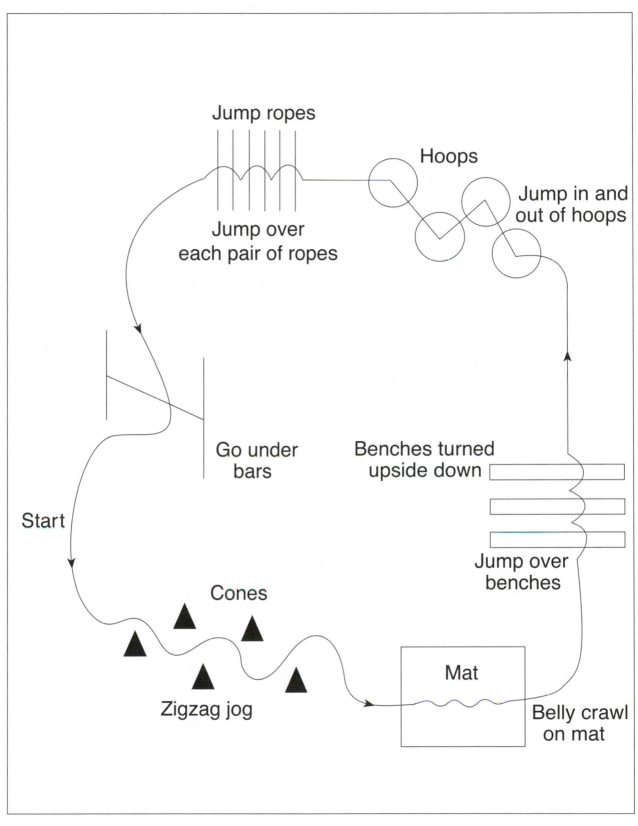

FIGURE 24.1   Challenge course.

Adapted, by permission, from C.A. Hopper, B.D. Fisher, and K.D. Munoz, 1997, *Health-Related Fitness for Grades 3 & 4* (Champaign, IL: Human Kinetics), 72.

level. The following body part movements are associated with the noted spinal nerves in the spinal column:

- Cervical 5: shoulder
- Cervical 7: elbow and wrist
- Cervical 8: hand
- Thoracic 1 to 8: chest
- Thoracic 9 to 12: abdomen
- Lumbar 1 to 5: legs

Concept Development

▶ Encourage partners to motivate each other with positive social interactions. Ask students to use different words of encouragement for each other, such as "good job" and "keep up the hustle." Students can then develop specific words to support and praise each other as they complete the activity.

▶ Challenge students to keep moving! An alternative format is for each partner to complete two circuits and then change to another partner. Use other equipment items, such as chairs, balance beams, inclined mats, climbing ropes, and scooter boards.

▶ Students can serve as station judges to keep equipment organized and ensure accuracy of movements.

▶ Vary the movement task on the outside of the course by using various pieces of equipment, such as balls, hoops, jump ropes, pull-up bars, and monkey bars.

▶ Teach the basic technique for hurdling and long jumping.

Assessment Options

Each lesson includes assessment options for the lesson and may include additional assessment options for the skills performed within a lesson.

For the Lesson

Students will demonstrate a variety of locomotor movements on the challenge course.

For Hurdling

▶ The lead foot is extended straight over the hurdle.
▶ The rear leg is bent, with the knee to the side.
▶ The lead foot reaches for the ground, followed by the trailing leg.
▶ Students should practice leading with the right and left legs.

For the Standing Long Jump

▶ Preparatory movement includes flexion of both knees, with the arms extended behind the body.
▶ The arms extend forcefully forward and upward, reaching full extension above the head.
▶ The jumper takes off and lands on both feet simultaneously.
▶ The arms are brought downward during landing.

Lesson 25: Station to Station

4. Teach students the basic dance steps for the single and double side steps (see the "Assessment Options" section).

5. Student A starts the challenge and can pick up one or two cards. If the student picks up two cards, both cards must be from the same row. As cards are picked up, the students must perform the activities listed on the back. If two cards are picked up and one of the activities for both students and the other is an activity for only one student, the activity for both students should be completed first.

6. As cards are picked up, students place them in one stack. The student who forces the other partner to pick up the last card is the winner of the challenge—and has solved the 7-5-3 puzzle.

Outcomes

At the end of this lesson, each student will be able to do the following:

► Improve physical fitness through cross-training.

► Complete a sequence of exercises following a station format.

Connections to Health Education Standards

► Practice of health-enhancing behaviors

Connections to Other Standards

► Physical education standards: competency in motor skills and movement patterns

Connections to WOW! Lessons

► Blue level: lesson 6, "Crazy Hoops"

► Purple level: lesson 7, "Skill-Related Fitness"

WOW! Vocabulary

► atlantoaxial—Vertebrae in the upper neck.

► cross-training—A training routine that involves several different forms of exercise.

► rotation—Moving from one station to another.

Get Ready to WOW! 'Em

You will need the following:

► Station cards (use the descriptions of the activities in this lesson to create station cards)

► Jump ropes (five)

► Cones (10)

► Two mats (if doing curl-ups)

► Basketballs (four or five)

► Whistle or other signal for rotation

► Family Activity 3 for section 2, Home Fitness Stations (one copy per student)

Concept Development

1. Emphasize working hard for 20 minutes to meet the FIT guideline.

2. Use the Intensity Guide in lesson 5 (page 53) to evaluate effort.

Background Information

Stations are an effective way of providing a variety of activities for a large group of students. Student motivation increases through the use of different exercise choices. Stations can include skill practice, exercises, and other activities, including jumping rope, running, and stretching. Stations provide opportunities for **cross-training** using a number of different physical activities that contribute to skill- and health-related fitness as well as physical conditioning. For example, although running is a great way to develop

---

Wrap It Up:

Ask students to share their successful strategies for solving the 7-5-3 puzzle.

Teaching Notes

Use lesson suggestions, whenever possible, to adapt the concepts to younger or older students.

Modifications for Younger Students

Students can take turns picking up a card and doing the activity without using the puzzle component. Teach the puzzle component to younger students in the classroom before using it in the activity.

Modifications for Older Students

Older students can take turns playing 7-5-3 with different students. Have students explain their **strategy** in writing and apply mathematics to their strategy.

Modifications for Students Who Get Easily Frustrated

For students who get easily frustrated, highly competitive activities will cause stress resulting from a fear of failure. Elimination activities should generally be avoided because the first student eliminated is usually a student with special needs. In the activity in this lesson, pair the easily frustrated student with a student who is trusted. Make sure the students understand the activities ahead of time so they are not surprised and worried by the demands of the activity.

Assessment Options

Each lesson includes assessment options for the lesson and may include additional assessment options for the skills performed within a lesson.

3. Allow students to pair up with a different partner.

4. Although not a primary goal, the activity can be completed by allowing winners to play each other.

5. Have students explain their strategies.

Cardiorespiratory endurance and leg strength, the upper body may not be included in a running workout. Using stations, additional activities such as push-ups and pull-ups can be added to the workout.

Now WOW! 'Em

1. Review the background information presented for this lesson with the class.

2. Set up an appropriate number of activity stations so that no more than three students are at each station. Assign one group per station to begin and designate a specific group to be responsible for the management of equipment. Large station cards (laminated) that contain the station numbers can help direct rotations between stations.

3. When first introducing the stations, demonstrate each activity and the order of **rotation.** Initially allow two minutes per station and gradually increase the duration as the endurance level of the students improves.

4. Start with familiar cardiorespiratory activities, such as the following:
   - Jump rope: Specify several basic jumps from lesson 48 (see page 297).
   - Strength and endurance: Select exercises from lesson 6 (starting on page 59), such as push-ups, curl-ups, mountain climbers, and cross-country skiers. If activity stations are located outdoors, mats should be provided for push-ups and curl-ups.
   - Ball skills (see figure 25.1):
     1. Soccer dribble: Use cones to set up a 10-by-10-yard (9 by 9 m) square. The first player dribbles around the cones. When the first player gets to the third cone, the next player can start dribbling around the square.
     2. Basketball rebound: Use a hoop and backboard. The first player dribbles to the free throw line and shoots. Player 2 rebounds the ball and passes to player 3, who then shoots. Player 1 rebounds, and the rotation continues.
     3. Basketball dribble and shoot: The first player dribbles the ball in and out, moving around five cones. This player then shoots, retrieves the ball, and goes directly to the end of the line without dribbling through the cones. After the first player shoots, the next player can begin.
     4. Frisbee in the middle: Set up a 12-by-15-yard (11 by 14 m) area with cones. Players 1 and 2 stand at the ends of the area in the center of the 12-yard line. Player 3 stands in the middle of the area. Player 1 throws the Frisbee to player 2. Player 3 tries to intercept. Players can move sideways, but not forward or backward. They play for a designated period of time and then switch positions.
     5. Volleyball passing: Three players pass and rotate in a 10-yard (9 m) space. Player 2 lines up behind player 1, with player 3 positioned across from them. Player 1 passes or serves the ball to player 3 and follows the pass to move behind player 3. Player 2 steps up in line after player 1 moves behind player 3. Player 3 passes to player 2 and follows the pass. Player 2 then passes to player 1 and follows the pass. Players should start with throws and then use serves and underhand or overhead passes.
     6. Handball rally: Use a wall and a playground ball. Players 1, 2, and 3 take turns striking the playground ball against the wall using their hands or fists. Allow any number of bounces.
   - Running activities:
     1. Agility run: Position 10 cones 3 feet (91 cm) apart in a straight line or pattern. Students take turns weaving through the cones. When all students reach one end, they take turns weaving in and out back to the start.
     2. Perimeter run: Students jog around the perimeter of the activity area, being careful not to interfere with other stations.

Lesson 28: Moving With Moo

Outcomes

At the end of this lesson, students will be able to do the following:

▸ Understand the differences in fat content in different types of milk.

▸ Improve their ability to complete cooperative tasks.

Connections to Health Education Standards

▸ Practice of health-enhancing behaviors

Connections to Other Standards

▸ Science standards: science in personal and social perspectives; life course

▸ Physical education standards: competency in motor skills and movement patterns; health-enhancing level of physical fitness

Connections to WOW! Lessons

▸ Purple level, Lesson 15, "Healthy Choices"

WOW! Vocabulary

▸ fluid ounce—A unit of volume; 8 ounces (240 ml) equals one cup.

▸ percent—A rate or proportion per hundred units.

▸ saturated fat—A type of fat that is most often of animal origin.

Get Ready to WOW! 'Em

You will need the following:

▸ Tall cones (6) to mark a start and end line

▸ Small cones or small cups (16 per pair of students)

▸ Soccer balls or other types of balls (one per pair of students)

Background Information

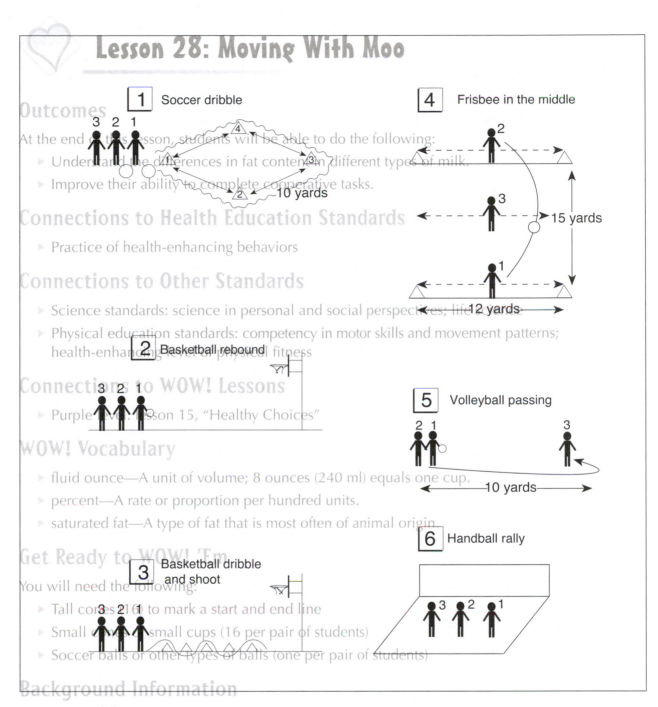

FIGURE 25.1   Skill stations.

Adapted, by permission, from C.A. Hopper, B.D. Fisher, and K.D. Munoz, 1997, *Health-Related Fitness for Grades 5 & 6* (Champaign, IL: Human Kinetics), 35.

A major source of **saturated fat** in the typical American diet is dairy products. Whole milk is a high-fat food. Different types of milk contain varying amounts of fat. Whole milk has 8 grams of fat per 8-**fluid-ounce** glass, 2 **percent** milk has 5 grams, 1 percent milk has 3 grams, and skim milk has less than half a gram. Soy milk varies from 2 to 5 grams per 8-ounce glass.

Refuel break: Students can get drinks when at this station. This helps ensure that the students replenish the water that their body loses during exercise.

5. When the entire activity is completed, the last group at each station is responsible for putting away the equipment for that station.

Now WOW! 'Em

1. Review the background information presented for this lesson with the class.

2. Explain the fat content of different types of milk.

3. Create a start line and an end line as shown in figure 28.1. The distance between the two lines can vary depending on the age of the students. Younger students can

Wrap It Up!

Use Family Activity 3, Home Fitness Stations, to encourage students to apply the concept of exercise stations with their family members.

Teaching Notes

Each lesson has suggested modifications, whenever possible, to adapt the concepts to younger or older students.

Modifications for Younger Students

Develop an easy-to-use format with jump rope and basic exercises for the activities at specific stations.

Modifications for Older Students

Students can design their own skill stations using different sports activities. Exercise machines, such as stationary bikes, designed for children can also be used at stations.

Modifications for Students With Down Syndrome (DS)

Students with DS are generally short with distinct facial features. They are often deficient in balance and cannot balance on one foot for more than a few seconds. In general, their movements appear awkward. A high percentage of students with DS are left-handed. In many cases, students with DS have visual, hearing, and heart and lung problems. Some have **atlantoaxial** instability in the first two cervical vertebrae. Students with atlantoaxial instability should not participate in activities that put pressure on the head and neck. Students with DS often enjoy and perform well in rhythmic activities, and they can excel in dance.

Concept Development

Establish a time period such as one minute at each station. Tell students to complete as many repetitions as possible within the one-minute period. Students can record their scores on a card. After a rest period, students can rotate around the same stations to try to improve their scores. The same stations can be used in a subsequent lesson, and students can again try to improve their scores.

Assessment Options

Each lesson includes assessment options for the lesson and may include additional assessment options for the skills performed within a lesson.

For the Lesson

Students demonstrate their ability to complete exercises and skills in a sequential manner following a station format.

For Frisbee Throwing (Forehand)

- The student grips the Frisbee between the thumb and forefinger, with the rim at the base of the thumb.
- The nonthrowing shoulder leads, facing toward the target.
- The student swings back the throwing arm as weight shifts to the rear foot.
- The arm swings low across the front of the body as weight shifts forward.
- The student releases the Frisbee in a flat, smooth, controlled motion; and the throwing arm follows through in the direction of flight.
- The student can use the left and right hands.

Pair   Pair   Pair   Pair   Pair   Pair

Each pair has 16 cones

30 yds

End

FIGURE 28.1   Moving with moo.

Section 2: Family Activity 3
Home Fitness Stations

Wrap It Up!

Ask students what type of milk they drink at home. Suggest replacing milk with a lower fat content.

Teaching Notes

Each lesson has suggested modifications, whenever possible, to adapt the concepts to younger or older students.

Name: _____

Select five exercises to use at stations in a family fitness course at home. Choose exercises ranging from easy to difficult, but be sure to select exercises that family members can successfully complete. Describe the stations on this sheet, and diagram the sequence of the exercises. Set up the five stations in the house, in the yard, or at a park. The objective is to complete three circuits of each station. Select the number of repetitions at each station, starting with a low number of repetitions (two to four) at each one.

Modifications for Younger Students

Younger students can take turns transporting the cones to the end line. Gradually introduce the concept of students developing another strategy rather than just taking turns. Students can identify the color of the milktops for each type of milk: red (whole milk), ...

1. List the names of family members.

Modifications for Older Students

Students can perform several movement patterns during this activity, such as running, skipping, hopping, or jumping while holding a soccer ball or basketball, dribbling the ball as they move to place the cones.

Modifications for Students With Seizures

A seizure occurs when an overload of electrical impulses to the brain causes the central nervous system to act to protect the person. In a convulsion, the body reacts by tensing or contracting involuntarily. Most students with epilepsy will be taking medication to prevent seizures. If a seizure occurs, you need to take steps to help prevent the student from sustaining an injury. Do not try to restrain the individual (a seizure cannot be stopped). Clear the area of hard and sharp objects. Do not put anything in the student's mouth.

2. Describe the exercises.

Exercise 1

Concept Development

1. Relay races are typically included in physical education. Competitive relay races such as the one in this lesson often reward those who are highly skilled and fit. Students whose skills and fitness levels are lower may feel less successful in relays. To help ensure that the skill levels of the teams are even, team up lower-skilled students with higher-skilled students. Include cooperative tasks so that teammates work together to achieve the goal.

Exercise 2

2. To enhance the relay format, make sure there are only two or three students per team. This will help prevent lines of students waiting for a turn. If creating larger teams, allow two or three students to be active in the task at the same time.

Exercise 3

3. Remember that the frequency of activity directly relates to the development of physical fitness. The more active the students are in these relays, the greater the potential for developing physical fitness.

Exercise 4

4. Students waiting in line for a turn can perform an activity or exercise.

Exercise 5

Assessment Options

Each lesson includes assessment options for the lesson and may include additional assessment options for the skills performed within a lesson.

(continued)

(continued)

3. Diagram the sequence of exercises.

For the Lesson

Students will demonstrate their knowledge of the fat content in milk by carrying the correct number of cones during the relay activity.

For the Soccer Dribble

▸ The student uses the inside, outside, and front of foot surfaces.

▸ The student keeps the ball within a yard (m) of the feet.

▸ The student uses both the left and right foot.

▸ The body is behind the ball in a controlled running action.

4. Record the dates and the number of repetitions for each family member for one week.

5. Ask family members to write a short comment about this activity. Family members can comment on their enjoyment level or exertion level. They can also comment on whether they want to continue to do the workout regularly.

From C. Hopper, B. Fisher, and K.D. Munoz, 2008, *Physical Activity and Nutrition for Health* (Champaign, IL: Human Kinetics).

(continued)

Frequency, Intensity, and Time

In the next lessons, students are introduced to the FIT principle – which stands for frequency (F), intensity (I), and time (T) – as it relates to aerobic fitness. Students will participate in a variety of activities designed to improve their muscular strength, flexibility, endurance, and cardiorespiratory fitness.

...rove a particular skill or fitness component (e.g., aerobic fitness), practice should be specific to that skill or fitness component. Students will also review the differences between aerobic and anaerobic activities.

Lesson 26: FITget Practice

Outcomes

At the end of this lesson, each student will be able to do the following:

▶ Understand how often (frequency), how hard (intensity), and how long (time) to exercise in order to improve aerobic fitness.

Connections to Health Education Standards

▶ Practice of health-enhancing behaviors

Connections to Other Standards

▶ Physical education standards: health-enhancing level of physical fitness; appreciation for the value of physical activity

▶ Science standards: science in personal and social perspectives; life science

Connections to WOW! Lessons

▶ Blue level: lesson 6, "Crazy Hoops"

▶ Blue level: lesson 7, "Four Parts"

WOW! Vocabulary

▶ frequency—The number of times a person performs fitness activities within a given time period.

▶ intensity—The level of effort in a task.

▶ stress—A feeling of increased anxiety and arousal.

▶ target heart rate—A range that an individual's heart rate needs to be within in order for cardiorespiratory training to occur.

▶ time—The number of minutes spent exercising.

Get Ready to WOW! 'Em

You will need the following:

▶ Worksheet 26.1, Weekly Exercise Planner (one copy per student)

▶ Family Activity 4 for section 2, Weekend Workout (one copy per student)

▶ Family Activity 5 for section 2, Family Triathlon (one copy per student)

Background Information

Improved machinery, technology, and power equipment have reduced the amount of physical work in daily life. In the past, many people worked in fields and factories, but today a large number of individuals hold sedentary jobs. With more technological conveniences, there is less manual work. Cars, elevators, escalators, garage door openers, food processors, drive-up windows, and remote controls have reduced physical activity for most people. In the past, people participated in games and sports for recreation. Today many people participate in virtual games without the benefits of exercise. To increase physical activity levels, students should understand how to plan their own physical fitness routines. FIT stands for **frequency, intensity,** and **time,** which provides a formula to gain maximum benefit from aerobic exercise programs.

Now WOW! 'Em

1. Review the background information presented for this lesson with the class.

2. Use the following instructional sequence throughout the lesson:
   * Have students discuss ideas with a partner.
   * Have students share with the class.
   * Encourage students to justify answers and responses.

3. Introduce the FIT principle for students to follow when planning aerobic exercise. Share the following information with students and ask students the following questions:
   * F = Frequency. *How many times a week should you exercise to be physically fit?* (People should exercise a minimum of three days per week.)
   * I = Intensity. *How hard should you exercise?* (People should exercise until they reach their **target heart rate** or approximately 150 to 170 beats per minute.)
   * T = Time. *How long should you exercise?* (People should exercise continuously for 20 minutes.)

4. In a class discussion, identify and record the health benefits of physical activity (and of using the FIT principle) by reviewing concepts from previous lessons:
   * Enables the body to use more oxygen
   * Causes the heart to become more efficient and beat fewer times when the person is resting
   * Improves blood circulation to muscles and all body parts
   * Strengthens muscles and bones
   * Enables sleep
   * Reduces **stress**
   * Increases level of energy and concentration
   * Increases self-confidence (people feel better about themselves)
   * Promotes bone development

5. Use worksheet 26.1, Weekly Exercise Planner, to help students determine how they will meet the FIT guidelines. Students use the planner to report amounts of exercise in a week and then to evaluate the plan.

Wrap It Up!

Plan time in class for students to report their FIT plans. Use Family Activity 4 and 5 (Weekend Workout and Family Triathlon) as options for planning an exercise program.

Teaching Notes

Each lesson has suggested modifications, whenever possible, to adapt the concepts to younger or older students.

Modifications for Younger Students

Encourage younger students to plan active recess periods (these students are more dependent on their parents for activities outside of school).

Modifications for Older Students

Older students can use participation in community sport and recreation activities as part of their plans. However, you should still encourage them to participate in some individual activities outside of organized sports and recreation.

Concept Development

1. Start with a weeklong plan to help students take charge of their own fitness. Expand the plan into a multiple-week routine. Students can self-evaluate their progress and make modifications.

2. Fitnessgram physical fitness assessment can be used to make specific plans that address each fitness area.

3. Explain that the FIT concept primarily focuses on aerobic fitness. Flexibility and muscular strength are also important fitness components.

Assessment Options

Each lesson includes assessment options for the lesson and may include additional assessment options for the skills performed within a lesson.

For the Lesson

Students will demonstrate the ability to develop an individualized training program. They will establish a baseline score and track progress over a 10-session workout schedule.

Worksheet 26.1: Weekly Exercise Planner
Performance Profile

Name: _____

Instructions: Write the name of your planned activity or exercise in the "Activity" column. Record how many times you plan to exercise, how hard you plan to exercise, and how long you plan to exercise. On completing each activity, have an adult initial the "Completion" column.

Day	Activity	Frequency: How many times per week?	Intensity: Vigorous, moderate, or light?	Time: Minutes of activity	Completion
Monday					
Tuesday					
Wednesday					
Thursday					
Friday					
Saturday					
Sunday					

(continued)

(continued)

Evaluating Your FIT Plan (complete this section after week 1):

1. Was your FIT plan too easy or too difficult? Explain.

Lesson 30: Aerobic Voyage

Outcomes

At the end of this lesson, students will be able to do the following:

- ▶ Improve their cardiorespiratory fitness.
- ▶ Distinguish between aerobic and anaerobic activities.

Connections to Health Education Standards

2. What changes do you need to make to your FIT plan?

- ▶ Practicing healthy behaviors to enhance
- ▶ Access to valid health information, products, and services

Connections to Other Standards

- ▶ Physical education standards: understanding of movement concepts, principles, strategies, and tactics

Connections to WOW! Lessons

- ▶ Blue level: lesson 6, "Crazy Hoops"

3. List or describe obstacles (e.g., weather, equipment) that prevented you from completing your plan.

WOW! Vocabulary

- ▶ energy—The capacity for work or vigorous activity.

Get Ready to WOW! 'Em

You will need the following:

- ▶ 40 sports and fitness cards (use the laminated cards created in lesson 20), with an equal mix of aerobic and anaerobic cards
- ▶ 30 cones to mark off a large playing area and create a center dividing line. The playing area can be as large as 50 by 50 yards (46 by 46 m). Mark a safe area and a "nonguarding" zone at the end of each team's area (as shown in figure 30.1).
- ▶ Pinnies (enough for half of the students in the class)
- ▶ Foam balls for tagging (one each for half of the class)

Background Information

Anaerobic activities are carried out without using oxygen for **energy.** The intensity of anaerobic activities is so high that oxygen is not used to produce energy. Since energy production is limited in the absence of oxygen, these activities (e.g., a 20-yd [18 m] sprint) can be done for only short periods. Anaerobic activities do not contribute to the development of the cardiorespiratory system. However, they are part of the total activity profile of an individual and are therefore a critical part of an active lifestyle.

Aerobic activities require continuous effort, and they involve using the large muscle groups of the body. Examples include running, bicycling, jumping rope, swimming, and

From C. Hopper, B. Fisher, and K.D. Munoz, 2008, *Physical Activity and Nutrition for Health* (Champaign, IL: Human Kinetics).

Section 2: Family Activity 4
Weekend Workout

Name: _____

Take the family to the school track, fitness course, or a similar area. These are perfect places to work out.

Instructions

1. Warm up by walking once around the track.

2. Complete some stretches.

3. Keep walking or break into an easy jog.

4. If there are bleachers, stride up and down the bleachers to give the legs and buttocks a workout.

5. Next, complete a series of exercises. Every 100 yards (91 m) around the track, complete 10 repetitions of an exercise (such as mountain climbers, jumping jacks, cross-country skiers, stride jumps, or jump twisters). Students can show family members how to perform the exercises. Include four different exercises in each lap.

6. Walk or jog another lap and complete 15 repetitions of the same exercises.

7. Cool down by walking a lap and doing some gentle stretching.

8. Begin easy and gradually build in intensity over time.

Section 2: Family Activity 5
Family Triathlon

Name: _____

A triathlon consists of running, swimming, and bicycling. Triathletes are recognized as being outstanding endurance athletes. Use the triathlon concept to have some fun with your family.

Instructions

1. Choose three activities that your family enjoys, such as walking, swimming, bicycling, jogging, jumping rope, or playing certain sports (e.g., soccer, basketball, or touch football).

2. Perform the three sports or activities one after the other for a total of 30 minutes. One activity may last longer than the others.

3. Be prepared to discuss the results of your triathlon in class.

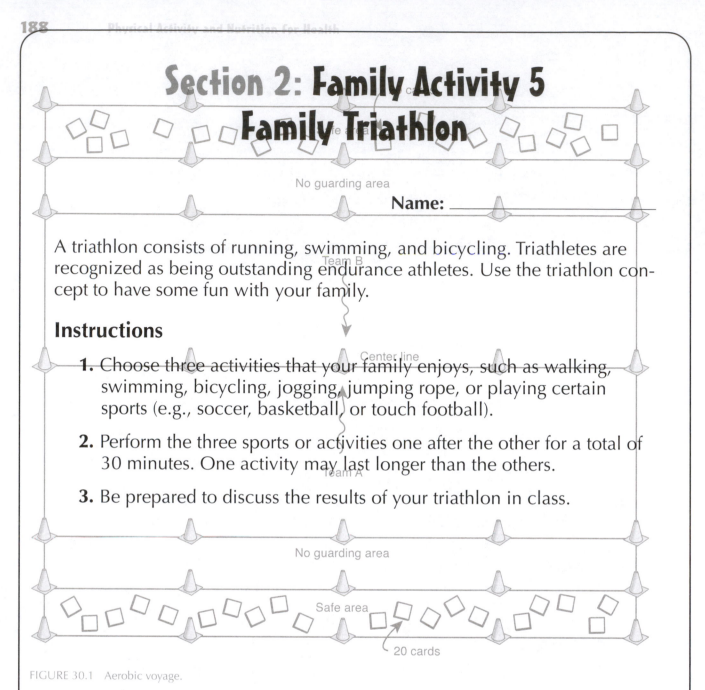

FIGURE 30.1   Aerobic voyage.

Wrap It Up!

Using some cards as examples, further reinforce the difference between aerobic and anaerobic activities. Stress that both types of activities are beneficial and that a combination of both types is a good way to achieve an active lifestyle.

Teaching Notes

Each lesson has suggested modifications, whenever possible, to adapt the concepts to younger or older students.

Modifications for Younger Students

Students can play an aerobic game with each student having a foam ball and throwing the ball into the other team's playing area. Divide the playing area into two halves with a center dividing line. The goal is to try to get all the balls in the other team's area.

Lesson 27: 7-5-3

Outcomes

At the end of this lesson, each student will be able to do the following:

▶ Use math skills to practice making estimations.

▶ Complete various activities to develop muscular strength and endurance as well as aerobic fitness.

Connections to Health Education Standards

▶ Practice of health-enhancing behaviors

Connections to Other Standards

▶ Math standards: number and operations

▶ Physical education standards: health-enhancing level of physical fitness

Connections to WOW! Lessons

▶ Green level: lesson 8, "Physical Education"

▶ Blue level: lesson 6, "Crazy Hoops"

WOW! Vocabulary

▶ estimation—Looking ahead to project a future amount or size.

▶ puzzle—A problem designed to challenge by presenting difficulties to be solved.

▶ strategy—A plan or method for obtaining a goal.

Get Ready to WOW! 'Em

You will need the following:

▶ Cones (four per pair of students)

▶ Jump ropes (one per student)

▶ Balls (one per pair of students)

▶ One set of 15 activity cards for each pair of students (see lesson 6 for a description of each exercise). Each card designates an activity for one (A or B) or both (A and B) students. See "Assessment Options" later in this lesson for the dance steps.

- Complete 10 skiers (students A and B).
- Complete 5 squat thrusts (student A).
- Complete 5 repetitions of the "single side step" dance step (students A and B).
- Run around 4 corners of the grid (student B).
- Jog around the outside of the grid and back to high-five each other (students A and B).
- Jump rope 30 times (students A and B).
- Complete 5 push-ups (student A).
- Complete 10 jumping jacks (student B).

- Jog in place for 15 seconds (students A and B).
- Dribble a basketball around cones (student A).
- Complete 10 bounce passes to each other from the side of the grid (students A and B).
- Complete 5 repetitions of the "double side step" dance step (students A and B).
- Complete 10 kick backs (dance step) (student A).
- Complete 10 chest passes to each other from the side of the grid (students A and B).
- Complete the back-saver sit-and-reach stretch for 15 seconds (students A and B).

▶ Each activity is designated for one or both students. These designations can be adjusted as needed.

Background Information

7-5-3 is a mathematical **puzzle.** Students are challenged to play with a partner and develop **strategies** to win the game. To be successful, students must use math skills to make accurate **estimations** of how to avoid picking up the final card in a set of 15. Throughout the challenge, students complete activities that help improve muscular strength and cardiorespiratory fitness. The emphasis is on continuous activity for 20 minutes.

Now WOW! 'Em

1. Review the background information presented for this lesson with the class.
2. A set of 15 activity cards is needed for each pair of students playing the challenge. Write the names of exercises, running activities, and various tasks (as noted in the "Get Ready to WOW! 'Em" section) on the back of each card. Students can write exercises on cards to assist you in preparing for this challenge. Organize the cards as shown in figure 27.1.
3. Divide students into pairs and designate student A and B in each pair. Provide a space for each pair to work together by creating a series of 10-by-10-yard (9 by 9 m) grids (squares). These grids may be smaller depending on space available. The goal of the game is for students to force their partner to pick up the last remaining card out of all 15 cards.

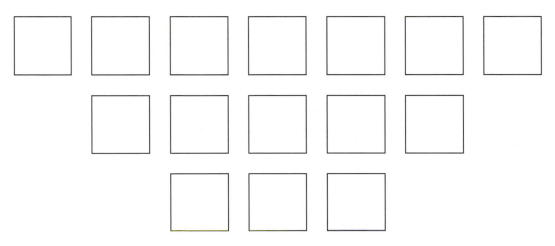

FIGURE 27.1   Card setup for 7-5-3.

4. Teach students the basic dance steps for the single and double side steps (see the "Assessment Options" section).

5. Student A starts the challenge and can pick up one or two cards. If the student picks up two cards, both cards must be from the same row. As cards are picked up, the students must perform the activities listed on the back. If two cards are picked up and one lists an activity for both students and the other lists an activity for only one student, the activity for both students should be completed first.

6. As cards are picked up, students place them in one stack. The student who forces the other partner to pick up the last card is the winner of the challenge—and has solved the 7-5-3 puzzle.

Wrap It Up!

Ask students to share their successful strategies for solving the 7-5-3 puzzle.

Teaching Notes

Each lesson has suggested modifications, whenever possible, to adapt the concepts to younger or older students.

Modifications for Younger Students

Students can take turns picking up a card and doing the activity without using the puzzle component. Teach the puzzle component to younger students in the classroom before using it in the activity.

Modifications for Older Students

Older students can take turns playing 7-5-3 with different students. Have students explain their **strategy** in writing and apply mathematics to their strategy.

Modifications for Students Who Get Easily Frustrated

For students who get easily frustrated, highly competitive activities will cause stress resulting from a fear of failure. Elimination activities should generally be avoided because the first student eliminated is usually a student with special needs. In the activity in this lesson, pair the easily frustrated student with a student who is trusted. Make sure the students understand the activities ahead of time so they are not surprised and worried by the demands of the activity.

Concept Development

1. Emphasize working hard for 20 minutes to meet the FIT guideline.
2. Use the Intensity Guide in lesson 5 (page 53) to evaluate effort.
3. Allow students to pair up with a different partner.
4. Although not a primary goal, the activity can be completed by allowing winners to play each other.
5. Have students explain their strategies.

Assessment Options

Each lesson includes assessment options for the lesson and may include additional assessment options for the skills performed within a lesson.

For the Lesson

Students will demonstrate an understanding of how to solve a mathematical puzzle as well as their ability to complete a variety of exercises.

For the Dance Steps

1. Single side step
   - The student steps to the left with the left foot and then steps together with the right foot.
   - The student steps to the right with the right foot and then steps together with the left foot.
   - The student repeats the movement to each side.

2. Double side step
   - This is the same movement as the single side step, except the step is completed twice in each direction.

3. Kick backs
   - The feet are shoulder-width apart, and the right foot is stationary.
   - The student lifts the left foot behind the right and touches the ground (then reverses the action).

Lesson 28: Moving With Moo

Outcomes

At the end of this lesson, students will be able to do the following:

▸ Understand the differences in fat content in different types of milk.

▸ Improve their ability to complete cooperative tasks.

Connections to Health Education Standards

▸ Practice of health-enhancing behaviors

Connections to Other Standards

▸ Science standards: science in personal and social perspectives; life science

▸ Physical education standards: competency in motor skills and movement patterns; health-enhancing level of physical fitness

Connections to WOW! Lessons

▸ Purple level: lesson 15, "Healthy Choices"

WOW! Vocabulary

▸ fluid ounce—A unit of volume; 8 ounces (240 ml) equals one cup.

▸ percent—A rate or proportion per hundred units.

▸ saturated fat—A type of fat that is most often of animal origin.

Get Ready to WOW! 'Em

You will need the following:

▸ Tall cones (16) to mark a start and end line

▸ Small cones or small cups (16 per pair of students)

▸ Soccer balls or other types of balls (one per pair of students)

Background Information

A major source of **saturated fat** in the typical American diet is dairy products. Whole milk is a high-fat food. Different types of milk contain varying amounts of fat. Whole milk has 8 grams of fat per 8-**fluid-ounce** glass, 2 **percent** milk has 5 grams, 1 percent milk has 3 grams, and skim milk has less than half a gram. Soy milk varies from 2 to 5 grams per 8-ounce glass.

Now WOW! 'Em

1. Review the background information presented for this lesson with the class.

2. Explain the fat content of different types of milk.

3. Create a start line and an end line as shown in figure 28.1. The distance between the two lines can vary depending on the age of the students. Younger students can

start with a distance of 30 yards (27 m), and older students can use a distance of 40 to 50 yards (37 to 46 m) depending on the facilities available.

4. Divide the class into pairs and give each pair 16 small cones or small cups. Each pair should also have one soccer ball (or other type of ball).

5. Each pair is positioned at the start line (see figure 28.1).

6. Call out a type of milk, such as whole milk. Students have to place the correct number of small cones on the end line to represent the fat content (number of grams of fat) for the specified type of milk. For whole milk, eight cones would be placed at the end line.

7. As different types of milk are called, each pair of students must place the correct number of cones, moving the cones one at a time. When 2 percent milk is called, five cones are carried (one at a time). When 1 percent milk is called, three cones are moved to the end line. When skim milk is called, the students place the ball on the end line. For skim milk, both students run together and stand side by side with one student holding the ball above the head.

8. Only one student can carry a cone at a time (this activity is similar to a relay race). Students can decide on a strategy regarding who goes each time to carry the cones to the end line. When returning to the start line, the student's foot must touch the start line before the next student can run. Start with each pair taking turns running to move the correct number of cones to the end line as soon as possible. However, allow each pair to develop a different strategy, such as one person making two consecutive trips (although overall participation should be equal).

9. After the correct number of cones have been transported, the pair stand one behind the other at the start line to indicate they have finished the task. Check that the correct number of cones have been delivered. As the lesson continues, add different movement activities, such as dribbling the soccer ball while carrying the cones.

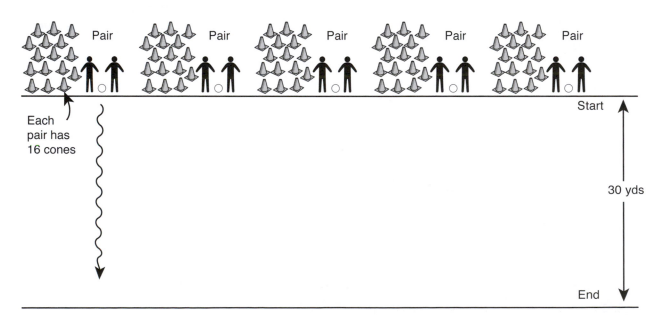

FIGURE 28.1   Moving with moo.

Wrap It Up!

Ask students what type of milk they drink. Challenge them to try drinking milk with a lower fat content.

Teaching Notes

Each lesson has suggested modifications, whenever possible, to adapt the concepts to younger or older students.

Modifications for Younger Students

Younger students can take turns transporting the cones to the end line. Gradually introduce the concept of students developing another strategy rather than just taking turns. Students can identify the color of the milk tops for each type of milk: red (whole milk), pink (2 percent), green (1 percent), white (skim).

Modifications for Older Students

Students can perform several movement patterns during this activity, such as running, skipping, hopping, and galloping. Groups can use a soccer ball or basketball, dribbling the ball as they move to place the cones.

Modifications for Students With Seizures

A seizure occurs when an overload of electrical impulses to the brain causes the central nervous system to act to protect the person. In a convulsion, the body reacts by tensing or contracting involuntarily. Most students with epilepsy will be taking medication to prevent seizures. If a seizure occurs, you need to take steps to help prevent the student from sustaining an injury. Do not try to restrain the individual (a seizure cannot be stopped). Clear the area of hard and sharp objects. Do not put anything in the student's mouth.

Concept Development

1. Relay races are typically included in physical education. Competitive relay races such as the one in this lesson often reward those who are highly skilled and fit. Students whose skills and fitness levels are lower may feel less successful in relays. To help ensure that the skill levels of the teams are even, team up lower-skilled students with higher-skilled students. Include cooperative tasks so that teammates work together to achieve the goal.

2. To enhance the relay format, make sure there are only two or three students per team. This will help prevent lines of students waiting for a turn. If creating larger teams, allow two or three students to be active in the task at the same time.

3. Remember that the frequency of activity directly relates to the development of physical fitness. The more active the students are in these relays, the greater the potential for developing physical fitness.

4. Students waiting in line for a turn can perform an activity or exercise.

Assessment Options

Each lesson includes assessment options for the lesson and may include additional assessment options for the skills performed within a lesson.

For the Lesson

Students will demonstrate their knowledge of the fat content in milk by carrying the correct number of cones during the relay activity.

For the Soccer Dribble

- ▸ The student uses the inside, outside, and front of foot surfaces.
- ▸ The student keeps the ball within a yard (m) of the feet.
- ▸ The student uses both the left and right foot.
- ▸ The body is behind the ball in a controlled running action.

Specificity

To improve aerobic fitness, people need to perform physical activity that is specific to this type of fitness. In the lessons in this part, students will practice various activities to improve their skills and aerobic fitness levels. These lessons will help students understand the principle of specificity—that is, to improve a particular skill or fitness component (e.g., aerobic fitness), practice should be specific to that skill or fitness component. Students will also review the differences between aerobic and anaerobic activities.

Lesson 29: Target Practice

Outcomes

At the end of this lesson, each student will be able to do the following:

- ▶ Understand that improvement in a particular skill or fitness component requires training that is specific to that skill or fitness component.
- ▶ Examine the effects of practice routines on the development of skills and fitness.

Connections to Health Education Standards

- ▶ Practice of health-enhancing behaviors

Connections to Other Standards

- ▶ Physical education standards: understanding of movement concepts, principles, strategies, and tactics; regular participation in physical activity

Connections to WOW! Lessons

- ▶ Blue level: lesson 8, "The Goliath Beetles"
- ▶ Purple level: lesson 6, "Skill-Related Fitness"

WOW! Vocabulary

- ▶ baseline—A score serving as a basis for measurement and comparisons.
- ▶ performance—A permanent change in behavior.
- ▶ profile—A comprehensive overview showing main features.

Get Ready to WOW! 'Em

You will need the following:

- ▶ Worksheet 29.1, Performance Profile (one copy per student)
- ▶ Sports equipment (depending on the selected sport skills)
- ▶ Stopwatch (for the running activity)

Background Information

Students' ability to learn and perform movement skills depends on many factors, such as innate abilities and body types. To improve a specific fitness component, such as aerobic fitness, practice should be specific to that activity. This principle applies to fitness activities as well as sport skills. With sustained practice, all students can improve in most activities.

Now WOW! 'Em

1. Review the background information presented for this lesson with the class.
2. This activity takes place over a two- to three-week period and can be integrated into physical education lessons.

3. After **baseline** scores have been established in each activity, 10 days are assigned to the practice program, but these should not be consecutive days. Several days off should be inserted into the schedule (e.g., two or three days of practice, followed by a day off).

4. Students use worksheet 29.1, Performance Profile, to track their progress. They should write the names of the selected activities. Additional spaces (1-10) are provided to record scores and establish a performance **profile.**

5. Divide the class into pairs and then create three groups of paired students. These groups will rotate around to each of the three activities every 10 minutes in each 30-minute lesson.

6. The purpose of this activity is for each student to compare his or her **performance** across three contrasting activities: a sport skill, a muscular endurance exercise, and a running activity. In each activity, students first develop a baseline score. In the sport skill and muscular endurance activities, students develop a baseline by completing as many repetitions as possible. They also complete the running activity to establish their baseline time.

7. Sport skill options: Select one of the following sport skills depending on available equipment and facilities. Performing the activity over the time period will help students see how practice routines can positively influence skill development. Establish a practice routine with a specific number of repetitions of each skill. Describe how to practice each activity. Allow time for some warm-up and practice. Allow 10 minutes of practice in the selected skill each day.

   - Basketball free throw: From the free throw line or another designated point, students shoot the basketball. The score is the number of successful shots in 10 trials.
   - Soccer juggling: Students attempt to keep the ball in the air. They should use all body surfaces, including the thigh, foot, chest, and head. Each touch of the ball counts as one juggle. The challenge is to gain the highest number of consecutive juggles. The highest number achieved is the student's score for the activity.
   - Striking a tennis ball at a target: Identify a target area on a wall for students to hit. Students use a paddleball racket and a tennis ball. Establish a specific distance for students to hit from, such as 10 yards (9 m) from the wall. They should start by hitting the ball after a bounce. The score is the number of target hits in 10 consecutive attempts.
   - Frisbee throw for distance: Create a line to throw from and mark throws with cones. Move the cone to mark the farthest throw. The score is the distance in yards (m). If a football field is available, use the markings on the field to measure the distance.

8. Muscular endurance options: Select one specific exercise for the class to perform, such as push-ups, curl-ups, pull-ups, or squat thrusts. The score is the number of consecutive repetitions.

9. Running activity options: Select a specific timed running activity, such as a quarter or half mile, two laps of the track, or another running activity based on local facilities. The running activity should last about 5 minutes. The score is the time the student took to complete the running event (in minutes and seconds). Students practice the selected run each workout session.

Wrap It Up!

Describe how people have different talents in physical activities. Challenge students to find a physical activity that they enjoy and that matches their personal strengths. After each session, ask students to describe improvements.

Teaching Notes

Each lesson has suggested modifications, whenever possible, to adapt the concepts to younger or older students.

Modifications for Younger Students

Younger students can select two activities instead of three. Jump rope skills (see lesson 48) can be used instead of a sport skill.

Modifications for Older Students

Older students can approach this lesson as a type of fitness club activity. The variety of activities is typical of a well-rounded workout schedule that includes a sport skill, muscular endurance activity, and running. Use the exercise progression schedule presented in lesson 43 ("Overload") to help guide the workout in the muscular endurance activity. Use the PACER practice activity (lesson 14) as another option for the running activity. Other types of sports skills can be selected based on favorites and equipment.

Concept Development

At a later time in the year, students can select another activity to practice in each category and follow the same format. The Performance Profile includes space for additional activity options. Students can graph their performance to track improvement.

Assessment Options

Each lesson includes assessment options for the lesson and may include additional assessment options for the skills performed within a lesson.

For the Lesson

Students will demonstrate the ability to develop an individualized training program. They will establish a baseline score and track progress over a 10-session workout schedule.

Worksheet 29.1:
Performance Profile

Name: _____

Instructions: Write down the selected sport skill, muscular endurance exercise, and running activity. The baseline score is recorded on the first day. Chart practice schedule scores for 10 days over a 2- to 3-week period. Under 1-10, write in the date and score in each of the three categories.

	Baseline score	Practice Schedule									
		1	2	3	4	5	6	7	8	9	10
Sport skill: _____	Number										
Muscular endurance exercise: _____	Number										
Running activity: _____	Time										

From C. Hopper, B. Fisher, and K.D. Munoz, 2008, *Physical Activity and Nutrition for Health* (Champaign, IL: Human Kinetics).

Lesson 30: Aerobic Voyage

Outcomes

At the end of this lesson, students will be able to do the following:

- ▶ Improve their cardiorespiratory fitness.
- ▶ Distinguish between aerobic and anaerobic activities.

Connections to Health Education Standards

- ▶ Practice of health-enhancing behaviors
- ▶ Access to valid health information, products, and services

Connections to Other Standards

- ▶ Physical education standards: understanding of movement concepts, principles, strategies, and tactics

Connections to WOW! Lessons

- ▶ Blue level: lesson 6, "Crazy Hoops"

WOW! Vocabulary

- ▶ energy—The capacity for work or vigorous activity.

Get Ready to WOW! 'Em

You will need the following:

- ▶ 40 sports and fitness cards (use the laminated cards created in lesson 20), with an equal mix of aerobic and anaerobic cards
- ▶ 30 cones to mark off a large playing area and create a center dividing line. The playing area can be as large as 50 by 50 yards (46 by 46 m). Mark a safe area and a "nonguarding" zone at the end of each team's area (as shown in figure 30.1).
- ▶ Pinnies (enough for half of the students in the class)
- ▶ Foam balls for tagging (one each for half of the class)

Background Information

Anaerobic activities are carried out without using oxygen for **energy.** The intensity of anaerobic activities is so high that oxygen is not used to produce energy. Since energy production is limited in the absence of oxygen, these activities (e.g., a 20-yd [18 m] sprint) can be done for only short periods. Anaerobic activities do not contribute to the development of the cardiorespiratory system. However, they are part of the total activity profile of an individual and are therefore a critical part of an active lifestyle.

Aerobic activities require continuous effort, and they involve using the large muscle groups of the body. Examples include running, bicycling, jumping rope, swimming, and playing sports such as soccer and basketball (sports that include activity and movement for an extended period of time).

Now WOW! 'Em

1. Review the background information presented for this lesson with the class.

2. Use the sports and fitness cards created in lesson 20. Because these cards are laminated, they can be carried in the hands by students. You need 40 cards, 20 with pictures of aerobic activities and 20 with pictures of anaerobic activities. For aerobic activities, use pictures of jogging, bicycling, jump rope, basketball, soccer, dancing, swimming, and ice skating. For anaerobic activities, use pictures of football, baseball, shot put, weightlifting, discus, javelin throw, bowling, golf, and kickball. The goal of the game is for students to learn the difference between aerobic and anaerobic activities. The students should only select aerobic activity cards to bring back to their safe area.

3. Discuss with the class the characteristics of aerobic activity. Go through some examples and designate activities as aerobic and anaerobic.

4. Using cones, divide the playing area into two halves. Split the class into two teams, with one team in each half of the playing area.

5. Place 10 aerobic and 10 anaerobic cards in each team's safe area (see figure 30.1). Place the cards on the floor facedown.

6. Have one team wear colored pinnies for identification.

7. The objective of the game is for each team to get as many aerobic activity cards in their safe area as possible.

8. Team A tries to run through the area where team B is standing and reach the safe area at team B's end of the playing area. Require students to hop and skip as movement variations.

9. Team B tries to tag members of team A using foam balls. If a member of team A is tagged, that person must return deep into team A's playing area (no guarding area).

10. Members of team A who reach the safe area then select an aerobic activity card, leaving all anaerobic cards in the zone defended by team B. The goal for team A is to get as many aerobic cards back to their own safe area as possible. The safe area marked by cones cannot be guarded and is surrounded by a no guarding area also marked with cones. Members of team A then try to return to their area with the activity card without getting tagged by team B. If members of team A are tagged while holding a card, they must give up the card to team B (who return the card to their safe area). If members of team A return safely to their area, the card is placed in their own safe area.

11. After two minutes of play, the roles are reversed. After several tries by each team, count how many aerobic activity cards each team has in their safe area. The goal of the game can also be reversed so that students are trying to gain anaerobic cards instead of aerobic cards.

12. Emphasize the importance of fair play and being honest. Playing fair and being a good sport make the game fun for everyone. Teach safe tagging techniques by requiring tagging on the back and arm to avoid collisions between students and any grabbing or pushing of other students.

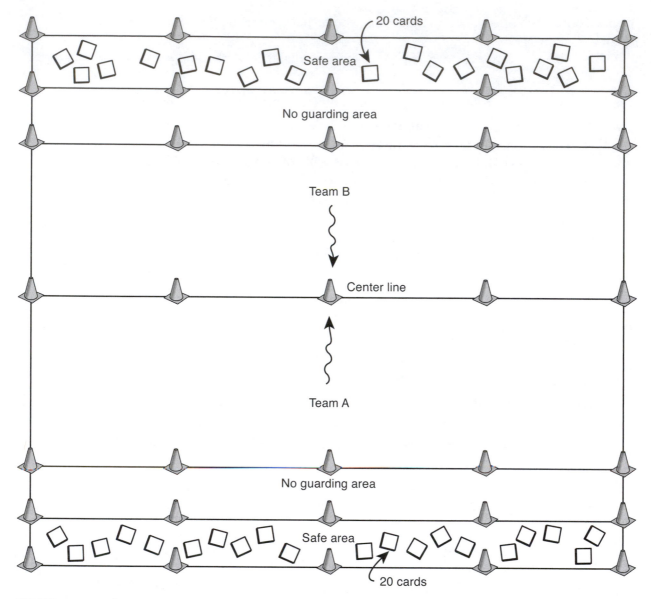

FIGURE 30.1   Aerobic voyage.

Wrap It Up!

Using some cards as examples, further reinforce the difference between aerobic and anaerobic activities. Stress that both types of activities are beneficial and that a combination of both types is a good way to achieve an active lifestyle.

Teaching Notes

Each lesson has suggested modifications, whenever possible, to adapt the concepts to younger or older students.

Modifications for Younger Students

Students can play an aerobic game with each student having a foam ball and throwing the ball into the other team's playing area. Divide the playing area into two halves with a center dividing line. The goal is to try to get all the balls in the other team's area.

As foam balls are thrown into the area, the other team throws them back as quickly as possible. Play for two to three minutes and then count the balls to see how many are in each area.

Modifications for Older Students

In the aerobic voyage game, add the rule that when a student is tagged, the student has to complete five jumping jacks or another designated exercise.

Modifications for Students to Improve Literacy and Number Skills

The game can be changed to include letters and numbers. Have students collect numbers with a specific theme, such as odd numbers. When using letters, ask students to collect consonants and vowels.

Concept Development

Vary the form of movement. Have students use hopping, skipping, or other ways of moving in addition to running.

Assessment Options

Each lesson includes assessment options for the lesson and may include additional assessment options for the skills performed within a lesson.

For the Lesson

Students will understand the basic differences between aerobic and anaerobic activities, while also learning that all physical activities have positive health benefits.

For Hopping

▶ The foot of the nonsupport leg is bent and carried in back of the body.

▶ The nonsupport leg swings in pendular fashion to produce force.

▶ The arms are bent at the elbows and swing forward on takeoff.

▶ The student is able to hop on the right and left foot.

SECTION 3

Power Fitness

To be strong and flexible and also have endurance, a person must eat a high-quality diet that includes sufficient proteins to build a better body. In addition to protein, water is also essential to prevent dehydration and improve endurance. In the upcoming nutrition lessons, students will learn to calculate their protein requirements and develop strategies to prevent dehydration.

In this section, students will also learn how exercise can improve flexibility and muscle strength while improving endurance. Students will participate in flexibility exercises and muscle-building activities aimed at building a physically fit body.

Protein

Protein is an essential nutrient used by the body to increase muscle mass. Muscles are necessary for performing activities that require strength, flexibility, and endurance. In the following lessons, students will learn that protein consists of long chains of both essential and nonessential amino acids. They will learn to calculate how much protein they need and how to eat high-quality protein by combining both animal and plant foods.

Lesson 31: Protein Power Chains

Outcomes

At the end of this lesson, each student will be able to do the following:

▸ Describe the importance of eating protein as part of a healthy diet.

▸ Construct model chains of amino acids to represent protein.

Connections to Health Education Standards

▸ Health promotion and disease prevention

Connections to Other Standards

▸ Science standards: science in personal and social perspectives; life science

▸ Math standards: geometry

Connections to WOW! Lessons

▸ Red level: lesson 16, "All Living Things"

▸ Purple level: lesson 9, "The Nutrient–Health Connection"

WOW! Vocabulary

▸ amino acids—Molecules that make up the protein found in food; sometimes called building blocks.

▸ DNA—The genetic instructions inside the body's cells. The body follows these instructions to make individuals who they are.

▸ enzymes—Catalysts for chemical reactions in the body.

▸ essential amino acids—The 9 amino acids that the body cannot make. These amino acids must be eaten every day for a person to be healthy.

▸ hormones—Proteins that control the processes in the body.

▸ nonessential amino acids—The 11 amino acids that the body can make each day.

Get Ready to WOW! 'Em

You will need the following:

▸ One transparency of figure 31.1 (mighty muscle)

▸ One transparency of figure 31.2 (protein chain)

▸ Overhead projector and transparency pens

▸ Two different paper chains, each at least 40 links long (with 20 different colors included in each)

▸ Strips of colored paper 1 inch (2.5 cm) wide and 4 inches (10.2 cm) long. You need strips in 20 different colors or shades of color to be used to make the protein chains (30 colored strips for each student).

▸ A bottle of paper glue for each student

Background Information

Protein is a nutrient found throughout the body. It makes up muscle, bone, skin, hair, and blood, as well as almost every tissue in the body. **Enzymes** (catalysts for chemical reactions in the body) and **hormones** (which control processes in the body) are also made up of protein.

As people grow, their body uses the protein they eat in the diet to manufacture new muscles and hair follicles, to lengthen the bones, and to produce the hormones that control these processes. If a person doesn't consume enough protein each day—or doesn't consume the right type of protein—the person won't have the parts to build a strong body.

So what type of protein should a person eat? The term *protein* refers to the form of the nutrient found in food. Each protein is made up of hundreds of molecules called **amino acids,** sometimes referred to as building blocks. Amino acids are arranged in chains in a pattern determined by the protein itself. For example, muscle is made up of a specific order of amino acids that might differ from other body proteins in only one amino acid in the sequence. A total of 20 different amino acids can be found in food. When a person eats protein, the body breaks down the protein chain into the individual amino acids for absorption. Once the amino acids are absorbed, the body reassembles them into individual proteins (such as muscle) following the genetic roadmap called **DNA.** After the chains of amino acids have been constructed, two of these chains combine in a coiled structure to form the protein. Of the 20 amino acids found in food, 9 of them are considered **essential amino acids,** which means they cannot be made by the body. The other 11 are called *nonessential amino acids* and can be made by the body.

Now WOW! 'Em

1. Before class, construct two different chains of amino acids by gluing at least 40 links (colored strips of paper—1 inch wide and 4 inches long). Each chain should be made up of 20 different colors. These chains of colored links will represent chains of amino acids. You should also prepare additional colored strips of paper (in 20 different colors or shades of color) for the students to use to make protein chains. You need enough strips for each student to have at least 30 colored strips.

2. Ask the students, *Do you remember what protein is?* They should respond that protein is one of the six nutrients along with carbohydrate, fat, vitamins, minerals, and water.

3. Begin a discussion about how the protein in food helps people build, maintain, and repair their muscles. For this discussion, use figure 31.1 (mighty muscle) and share the background information presented for this lesson.

4. Using figure 31.2 (protein chain), explain to the class that proteins are made up of long chains of individual molecules called amino acids. Write the term *amino acids* on the board. Tell the students, *Nine of those amino acids are called essential amino acids, which means the body can't make them. The body can make the other 11 amino acids, and they are called nonessential amino acids.*

5. Explain to the students, *When you eat protein, your body digests it by breaking apart the strands of amino acids and absorbing them. Your body then puts the strands back together inside your cells to make your muscles grow and increase in strength.*

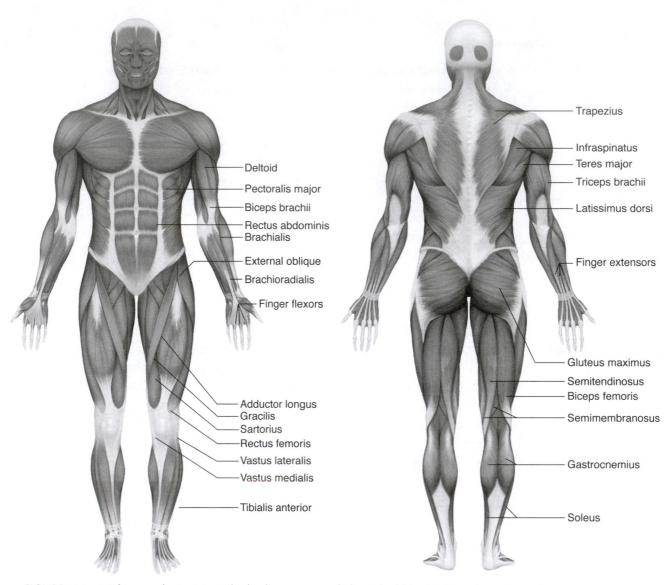

FIGURE 31.1 Mighty muscle. Protein in the food a person eats helps to build, maintain, and repair muscles.

Reprinted, by permission, from National Strength and Conditioning Association, 2008. *Essentials of Strength and Conditioning*, 3rd ed. (Champaign, IL: Human Kinetics), p. 68.

6. Show the students one of the sample chains of amino acids that you made. Explain the following to students: *The hundreds of proteins in your body have different configurations of amino acids in different sequences. For example, your hair is composed of different protein chains than your skin or fingernails.*

7. Take the two sample chains of amino acids and coil them together to make a double chain of protein. Explain to the students that the proteins in foods and in the body are made of two chains coiled together.

8. Hand out the strips of paper and a bottle of glue to each student. Students will be making their own unique protein chain of amino acids. Each student's chain must have at least 30 amino acids and must contain all 20 different amino acids (different colors of paper links) in whatever sequence the student wants.

9. Demonstrate how to make the protein chains. Choose one strip of paper and bend it to make a circle. Place a little glue on one end of the paper and then overlap the edges. Hold the edges together for a few seconds until the glue sticks. Next,

choose a strip of paper of a different color and slide it through the loop you just made. Bend that piece of paper, place a little glue on the end, overlap the edges, and hold them for a few seconds. Repeat this process until the protein chain is at least 30 links long.

Wrap It Up!

When all students have finished their chain, put the students into pairs. Each pair should put their chains together to make a double coiled protein. Hang the colorful proteins on the bulletin board.

Teaching Notes

Each lesson has suggested modifications, whenever possible, to adapt the concepts to younger or older students.

Modifications for Younger Students

With younger students, you can use the term *building blocks* instead of the term *amino acids*. Younger students should be able to construct the protein chains and understand that proteins are made up of many different types of amino acids.

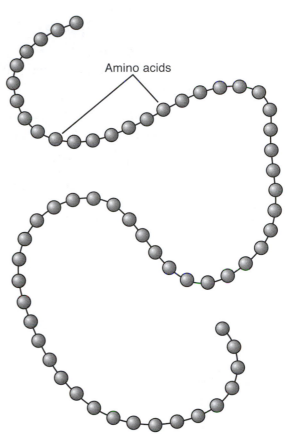

FIGURE 31.2   Protein chain. Proteins are long chains of amino acids (sometimes including hundreds of amino acids) in different combinations of essential and nonessential amino acids.

Modifications for Older Students

Older students can make a model of the hormone insulin, which is two protein chains, one with 21 amino acids and the other with 30 amino acids. The specific order or sequence of the different amino acids for each chain is listed below. Each number corresponds to a specific amino acid—that is, a specific color—in the chain. For example, 1 could be blue, 2 could be red, 3 could be green, and so on. You will need 17 different colors of paper and at least 6 strips of each color. Once the two chains are made, the students twist them together to make the protein insulin. Here is the correct sequence:

1-2-3-4-5-6-6-7-8-3-6-8-9-10-5-9-4-11-10-6-11

12-3-11-5-13-9-6-1-8-13-9-3-4-7-9-10-9-3-6-1-4-14-1-12-12-10-15-16-17-7

Concept Development

Assign the students to use math to determine how many total amino acids were used to construct their class protein chains. Explain that the body could only construct the protein represented by the model if the person ate the appropriate amino acids. If the person didn't eat an amino acid represented by one of the colors in the chain, then the chain would be incomplete, and the body would not be able to make the protein. As a result, if the protein was used to make hair, for example, the person would not be able to replace hair follicles that fall out in a brush. This will reinforce the importance of eating protein every day.

Assessment Options

Each lesson includes assessment options for the lesson and may include additional assessment options for the skills performed within a lesson.

For the Lesson

By completing their protein chains, students will demonstrate their ability to understand the concept of amino acids and protein.

Lesson 32: Pump It Up With Protein

Outcomes

At the end of this lesson, students will be able to do the following:

- Plan a meal that contains a variety of complete protein.
- Calculate their protein requirements for a day.
- Categorize foods as either complete protein or incomplete protein.

Connections to Health Education Standards

- Health promotion and disease prevention
- Interpersonal communication skills

Connections to Other Standards

- Science standards: science in personal and social perspectives; life science
- Math standards: number and operations

Connections to WOW! Lessons

- Red level: lesson 14, "Tacos by Cody"
- Purple level: lesson 9, "The Nutrient–Health Connection"

WOW! Vocabulary

None.

Get Ready to WOW! 'Em

You will need the following:

- Transparency 32.1, Training Table (one transparency)
- Transparency 32.2, Complete Protein (one transparency)
- Overhead projector and transparency pens
- Worksheet 32.1, Pump It Up With Protein (one copy per student)
- Worksheet 32.2, Protein Content of Various Foods Per Serving (one worksheet per student)
- Family Activity for Section 3, Mighty Mini-Pizzas

Background Information

The body doesn't store amino acids as it does excess body fat. Thus, to ensure that body proteins are built and repaired, people need to eat high-quality protein foods as well as the right quantity of protein.

Not all protein foods are alike. Some of them contain all the essential amino acids that a person needs each day, whereas other protein foods do not. Foods that contain all nine of the essential amino acids are referred to as complete protein. These are protein sources that come from animal foods such as egg white, meat, fish, and milk. If a food

Table 32.1 Protein Content Examples

Food	Grams of protein per serving
Tuna fish (3 ounces [84 g])	21
Hamburger (3 ounces)	21
Chicken (3 ounces)	21
Cow's milk (8 fluid ounces [240 ml])	8
Yogurt (1 cup [245 g])	11
Soy milk (1 cup [240 ml])	7
Peanut butter (2 tablespoons)	8
Cheddar cheese (1 ounce [28 g])	7
Boiled egg (1 whole egg)	7
Cottage cheese (1 cup [226 g])	28
Kidney beans, cooked (1/2 cup [89 g])	7
Whole wheat bread (1 slice)	3
Rice, cooked (1 cup [174 g])	4
Baked potato (1 medium)	3
Tofu (1/2 cup [124 g])	10
Cold cereal [28 g] (1 ounce)	3

lacks one or more of the essential amino acids, then that food is referred to as an incomplete protein. Plant sources of protein, such as nuts, seeds, grains, and legumes, are examples of incomplete protein.

To help ensure that they obtain all the essential amino acids needed each day, people should consume a wide range of protein foods. Animal foods, such as milk, cheese, eggs, or small amounts of meat, can be added to a meal to complement the vegetable protein. This will make the meal a source of complete protein.

Here are the recommendations for obtaining the required quality and quantity of protein each day:

1. Eat a wide variety of protein foods each day.
2. Choose low-fat or lean versions of animal protein and high-fiber plant protein, such as beans, legumes, and whole grains.
3. Eat a balance of carbohydrate and protein.

The amount of protein needed each day depends on body weight, age, and activity level. If someone is younger than 13, the amount of protein needed each day is calculated in the following way:

Weight in pounds × 0.43 grams of protein

If a person's body weight is 100 pounds, then 43 grams of protein is needed each day (0.43 grams of protein per pound, or 100 × 0.43).

Most foods contain some protein. The table on this page lists some examples.

Now WOW! 'Em

1. Review the background information presented for this lesson with the class.
2. Ask the students, *What foods are good sources of protein?* Using the Training Table transparency on page 201, begin to write the foods in the appropriate spaces as the students say them (e.g., if they say "apple," you would write apple on the fruit table). Ask students, *Which of the food groups come from animals and which ones come from plants?* Tell them, *Animal foods are complete protein, and plant foods are incomplete protein.*
3. Tell students, *When people eat animal foods, they get all nine essential amino acids in one food. If they combine plant foods, such as peanut butter and whole wheat bread, they also get all nine essential amino acids.* Use the Complete Protein transparency on page 203 to illustrate this concept. Ask the students, *Can you think of other foods that you can combine together to make complete protein?*

If the students struggle to come up with answers, provide examples to help them along:

- Grains + legumes (tortilla + beans = burrito)
- Grains + dairy (macaroni and cheese or cereal and milk)
- Grains + cheese + vegetables (pizza)

4. Tell students, *To be healthy, eating foods that are complete protein is important. However, in addition to the quality of protein, the quantity of protein you consume each day is also important.* Write the calculation for the grams of protein needed each day on the board: weight in pounds (100) $\times$ 0.43 grams of protein = 43 grams of protein needed per day.

5. Hand out worksheet 32.1, Pump It Up With Protein, to each student. Instruct students to calculate their own daily protein requirement. Ask the students to tell you what they calculated, and write each student's protein requirement up on the board to get an idea of the variation in protein needs for your class.

6. Provide students with worksheet 32.2, which lists the protein content of various foods per serving. Tell them to refer to this list as they complete the rest of worksheet 32.1. Students should determine how many grams of protein they usually eat in a day.

Wrap It Up!

After the students have finished adding up their protein intake for the day, discuss the results as a class.

Teaching Notes

Each lesson has suggested modifications, whenever possible, to adapt the concepts to younger or older students.

Modifications for Younger Students

With younger students, simply discuss the foods that contain protein and why the students need protein each day. Then, complete the Pump It Up With Protein worksheet as a class, asking the students to choose foods they would eat each day to meet their protein needs.

Modifications for Older Students

None.

Concept Development

Assign the students to write an essay about the foods they eat that are complete protein, including those that may be family traditions.

Assessment Options

Each lesson includes assessment options for the lesson and may include additional assessment options for the skills performed within a lesson.

For the Lesson

By completing the Pump It Up With Protein worksheet, students will demonstrate their ability to recognize which food groups contain protein as well as their ability to calculate their daily protein needs.

Transparency 32.1:
Food Groups

Dairy	Grains	Meat and Beans

Fruit	Vegetables

Transparency 32.2:
Complete Proteins

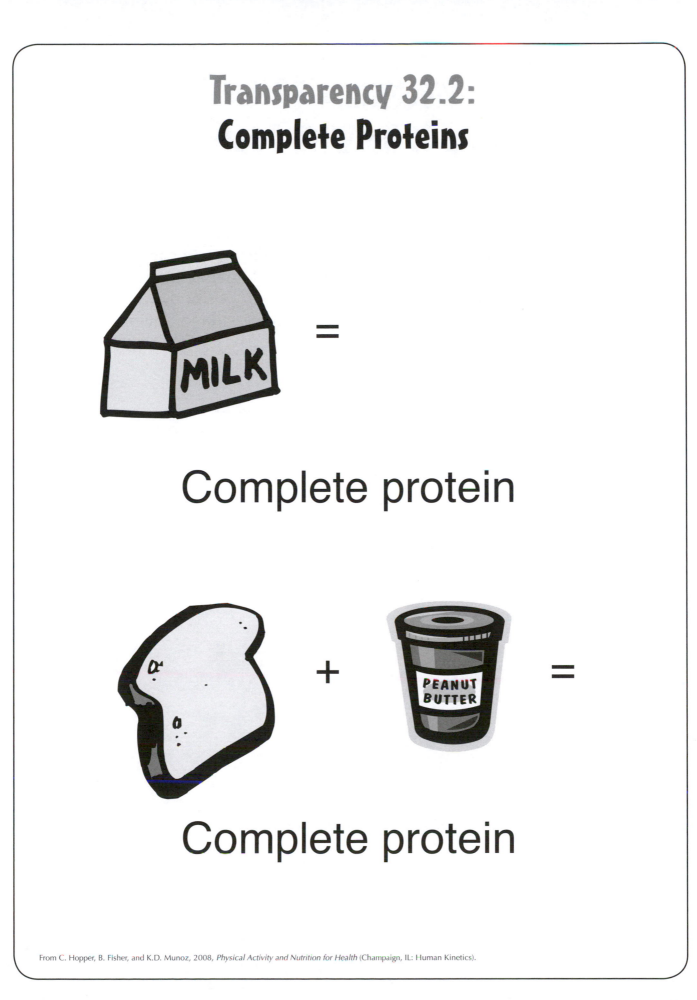

Complete protein

Complete protein

Worksheet 32.1:
Pump It Up With Protein

Name: _____

Instructions: To build stronger muscles, you need to eat enough protein each day. To "pump it up with protein," first calculate how many grams of protein you need each day. Use this calculation: Your body weight in pounds × 0.43 grams of protein. Write the answer in the following body shape.

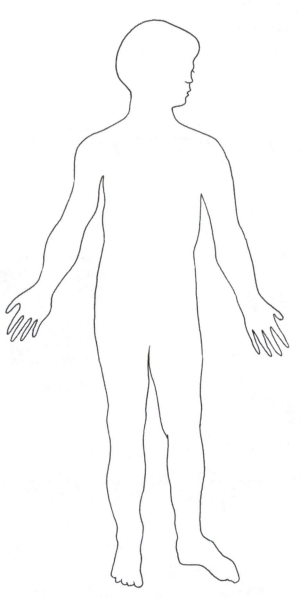

(continued)

From C. Hopper, B. Fisher, and K.D. Munoz, 2008, *Physical Activity and Nutrition for Health* (Champaign, IL: Human Kinetics). Illustration reprinted, by permission, from C.A. Hopper, B.D. Fisher, and K.D. Munoz, 1997, *Health-Related Fitness for Grades 5 & 6* (Champaign, IL: Human Kinetics), 5.

In the following spaces, write in the food you normally eat for breakfast, lunch, dinner, and snacks, along with the amount of protein in a serving of each food. Total up your grams of protein for the day. Are you "pumped up" with the correct amount of protein for your body weight?

▶ Breakfast foods   Protein (grams)

_____   _____

_____   _____

_____   _____

▶ Lunch foods   Protein (grams)

_____   _____

_____   _____

_____   _____

▶ Dinner foods   Protein (grams)

_____   _____

_____   _____

_____   _____

▶ Snack foods   Protein (grams)

_____   _____

_____   _____

_____   _____

Total protein (grams)   _____

Circle the answer that applies to you for the following questions.

Are you "pumped up" with protein?   Yes   No

Did you eat protein from both animal and plant sources?   Yes   No

Worksheet 32.2:
Protein Content of Various Foods per Serving

Food	Grams of protein per serving
Tuna fish (3 oz [84 g])	21
Hamburger (3 oz)	21
Chicken (3 oz)	21
Cow's milk (8 fluid oz [240 ml])	8
Yogurt (1 c [245 g])	11
Soy milk (1 c [240 ml])	7
Peanut butter (2 tbsp)	8
Cheddar cheese (1 oz [28 g])	7
Boiled egg (1 whole egg)	7
Cottage cheese (1 c [226 g])	28
Kidney beans, cooked (1/2 c [89 g])	7
Whole wheat bread (1 slice)	3
Rice, cooked (1 c [174 g])	4
Baked potato (1 medium)	3
Tofu (1/2 c [124 g])	10
Cold cereal (1 oz [28 g])	3

From C. Hopper, B. Fisher, and K.D. Munoz, 2008, *Physical Activity and Nutrition for Health* (Champaign, IL: Human Kinetics).

Section 3: Family Activity 1
Mighty Mini-Pizzas

Name: _____

Mighty mini-pizzas are a great after-school snack that provide a complete protein to meet your protein needs. They also provide carbohydrate for energy. Plus, mighty mini-pizzas are not difficult to make. Try the following recipe:

Ingredients

Sourdough or plain English muffins—1/2 for each pizza

Spaghetti sauce—1 tablespoon for each pizza

Mozzarella cheese—1 tablespoon for each pizza

Optional Ingredients

Unsweetened pineapple chunks, green pepper slices, sliced mushrooms, chopped onions, sliced tomatoes

Directions

1. Halve the muffins.
2. Spread 1 tablespoon of spaghetti sauce on each half.
3. Sprinkle on any or all of the optional ingredients you like.
4. Top each with 1 tablespoon of cheese.
5. Place on a cookie sheet and broil until the cheese is bubbly.

Write a paragraph comparing the mini-pizzas to the pizzas you usually eat.

From C. Hopper, B. Fisher, and K.D. Munoz, 2008, *Physical Activity and Nutrition for Health* (Champaign, IL: Human Kinetics).

Fluid

When people exercise, they produce energy in the form of heat. To keep the body cool so it doesn't overheat (similar to a car engine), people produce sweat from water within their cells. If a person loses too much water, the person becomes dehydrated, which can have some bad side effects. In the next two nutrition lessons, students will learn the importance of drinking plenty of water to prevent dehydration.

Lesson 33: Waterlogged

Outcomes

At the end of this lesson, each student will be able to do the following:

▸ Describe the role sweating plays in maintaining fluid balance.

▸ Understand the importance of replacing water lost during exercise.

Connections to Health Education Standards

▸ Health promotion and disease prevention

Connections to Other Standards

▸ Science standards: science in personal and social perspectives; life science

Connections to WOW! Lessons

▸ Red level: lesson 12, "Food for Thought"

▸ Red level: lesson 13, "A Crunch for Lunch"

▸ Orange level: lesson 12, "Food for Thought"

▸ Orange level: lesson 13, "A Crunch for Lunch"

▸ Orange level: lesson 15, "Go-Go-Go!"

▸ Yellow level: lesson 12, "Food for Thought"

▸ Green level: lesson 15, "Camels and Whales"

▸ Blue level: lesson 13, "Buyer Beware"

▸ Blue level: lesson 14, "Fuel for Thought"

WOW! Vocabulary

▸ dehydration—Excessive loss of water from the body.

▸ hypothalamus—The region of the brain that controls the pituitary gland.

▸ sweating—The body's method of cooling off during exercise by releasing water through the skin.

Get Ready to WOW! 'Em

You will need the following:

▸ Two-liter bottle of water

▸ Two sponges (one wet and one dry)

▸ Transparency 33.1, Sweating (one transparency)

▸ Worksheet 33.1, Waterlogged (one copy per student)

▸ Worksheet 33.2, My Water Log (one copy per student)

Background Information

The body functions best at a body temperature of about 98.6 degrees Fahrenheit (or 37 degrees Celsius). Exercise can produce large amounts of heat, but if the body doesn't have enough water (a condition called **dehydration**), the person's ability to exercise is impaired. Initially, the heart begins to work harder, and the pulse rate increases. Fatigue sets in, and some people can get headaches and become nauseated. These effects reduce the body's ability to exercise. Thus, **sweating** is an important mechanism to regulate body temperature. As the body sweats, the air dries the skin, and the body feels cooler. Sweat is mostly water—about 75 percent—with the remaining 25 percent being various salts and minerals. Therefore, a person needs to replace the water first and allow the salts and minerals to be replenished with food consumed after exercising. The best way to replace the water lost during exercise is to drink cool water in combination with a balanced diet on a day-to-day basis. A person loses about 2 to 3 quarts (1.9 to 2.8 liters) of water per day, sometimes more if the weather is really hot. People should weigh themselves before and after exercise. After exercising, if weight has been lost, that weight is partly water. For every pound of weight lost, a person should consume two cups of water. At least six to eight glasses of water (8-fluid-ounce [240 ml] glasses) should be consumed each day, plus additional water for sweat loss.

Now WOW! 'Em

1. Review the background information presented for this lesson with the class.

2. Describe to the class the following situation: *You're running up a hill as fast as you can. When you reach the top of the hill, your shirt, arms, and face are wet. Why does this happen?* They should answer that they are wet because of sweating.

3. Using transparency 33.1, Sweating, explain the following to students: *When your body gets hot, the **hypothalamus** in the brain sends a signal to your body telling it to sweat to cool off the cells in your body. The sweat comes through the skin with help from the sweat glands.*

4. Ask the students, *How often do you feel thirsty? Thirst is the brain's signal that the body is dehydrated and needs more water. People can get water by drinking it or drinking other fluids, such as juices. People also get water from foods such as fruits and vegetables and from metabolism.*

5. Show the class the two-liter bottle full of water. Tell students, *This is how much water is lost each day for most people. Trying to replace that water is important to prevent dehydration. You should try to drink a minimum of five to six glasses (8 ounces each) of water a day. You should drink more than this if you are exercising in the heat.*

6. Show the students a dried-out sponge and one that has water in it. Tell them, *This is what happens to our cells when we are dehydrated.*

7. Tell students the signs of dehydration: *Your lips and mouth feel dry, you feel light-headed or dizzy, and your heart rate is rapid. Other signs of dehydration include not having to urinate very frequently and having urine that is a dark yellow color.*

Wrap It Up!

Hand out worksheet 33.1, Waterlogged, and instruct the students to color the silhouette to show the amount of water the body contains (they should color 75 percent of the body). Next, tell them to color in the number of glasses of water they should drink each day (five to eight would be an appropriate range). When the students are done coloring, discuss the worksheet as a class.

Teaching Notes

Each lesson has suggested modifications, whenever possible, to adapt the concepts to younger or older students.

Modifications for Younger and Older Students

This lesson should be appropriate for students of all ages.

Concept Development

Assign the students to keep a log of the water they drink each day for two days using worksheet 33.2. Have them bring their log back to class for discussion.

Assessment Options

Each lesson includes assessment options for the lesson and may include additional assessment options for the skills performed within a lesson.

For the Lesson

When completing the class activity, students will demonstrate their understanding of a person's water requirements and the function of sweating.

Transparency 33.1: Sweating

Exercise = Sweat

Sweat = Thirst

Stop dehydration = Drink water

When people exercise, they produce energy in the form of heat. Their body produces sweat to cool them down so they don't overheat. If a person doesn't drink enough water, the person can become dehydrated. Drinking plenty of fluid before, during, and after exercise will help prevent dehydration.

From C. Hopper, B. Fisher, and K.D. Munoz, 2008, *Physical Activity and Nutrition for Health* (Champaign, IL: Human Kinetics).

Worksheet 33.1: Waterlogged

Name: _____

Instructions:

1. The body is approximately 75 percent water. Color in 75 percent of the body outline to represent the amount of water the body contains.

2. How many glasses of water do you drink each day? Color in the number of 8-ounce (240 ml) glasses you should drink each day to prevent dehydration.

From C. Hopper, B. Fisher, and K.D. Munoz, 2008, *Physical Activity and Nutrition for Health* (Champaign, IL: Human Kinetics). Body illustration reprinted, by permission, from C.A. Hopper, B.D. Fisher, and K.D. Munoz, 1997, *Health-Related Fitness for Grades 5 & 6* (Champaign, IL: Human Kinetics), 5. Glasses illustration reprinted, by permission, from C.A. Hopper, B.D. Fisher, and K.D. Munoz, 1997, *Health-Related Fitness for Grades 1 & 2* (Champaign, IL: Human Kinetics), 27.

Worksheet 33.2: My Water Log

Name: _____

Instructions: Keep a log of the fluids you drink during a two-day period. Write in the times and the approximate amount of fluid you drink. Be sure to identify the type of fluid you drink, such as water, soda, or milk.

Day	Time of day	Type of fluid	Amount of fluid
Example: Saturday	*7:00 a.m.*	*Milk*	*1 cup*

From C. Hopper, B. Fisher, and K.D. Munoz, 2008, *Physical Activity and Nutrition for Health* (Champaign, IL: Human Kinetics).

Lesson 34: Do Yourself a Flavor

Outcomes

At the end of this lesson, each student will be able to do the following:

▸ Understand the purpose of sport drinks to replace water and salt lost during exercise.

▸ Describe the role sweating plays in losing salts from the body.

Connections to Health Education Standards

▸ Health promotion and disease prevention

▸ Access to valid health information, products, and services

Connections to Other Standards

▸ Science standards: science in personal and social perspectives

Connections to WOW! Lessons

▸ Red level: lesson 12, "Food for Thought"

▸ Red level: lesson 13, "A Crunch for Lunch"

▸ Orange level: lesson 12, "Food for Thought"

▸ Orange level: lesson 13, "A Crunch for Lunch"

▸ Orange level: lesson 15, "Go-Go-Go!"

▸ Yellow level: lesson 12, "Food for Thought"

▸ Green level: lesson 15, "Camels and Whales"

▸ Blue level: lesson 12, "The Big Label Discovery"

▸ Blue level: lesson 13, "Buyer Beware"

▸ Blue level: lesson 14, "Fuel for Thought"

WOW! Vocabulary

None.

Get Ready to WOW! 'Em

You will need the following:

▸ Samples of sport drinks (about 1 quart [1 liter] of each), such as Gatorade, Erg, All Sport, and Propel. You also need a bottle of water. Label the drinks A, B, C, and so forth. Be sure the sport drinks are similar in color for the taste test.

▸ Worksheet 34.1, Do Yourself a Flavor (one copy per pair of students) 💿

▸ Small sample-size paper cups (enough for each student to taste each sample)

▸ Family Activity 2 for Section 3, Waterlogged 💿

Background Information

As discussed in lesson 33, exercise can result in dehydration if a person doesn't drink enough fluid and replace the salts. Therefore, people need to replace the water and salts lost during exercise. The best way to do this is to drink cool water (for more information, refer to lesson 33) and lightly salt your food. Many sport drinks have also been developed. Some of these drinks contain sugar in the form of glucose or fructose, as well as salts, such as potassium, sodium, and magnesium. Sport drinks are not necessary to replace fluids lost during exercise (water is the most important nutrient to replace), but these drinks can be helpful, especially in areas where the temperature gets extremely hot. When you sweat, you lose salts from the blood. Even though sweat is 75 percent water and 25 percent salts, the salts do need to be replaced. Sport drinks can do that easily.

Now WOW! 'Em

1. Before class, pour the sport drinks into containers marked A, B, C, and so forth. Also include a bottle of water along with the sport drinks. Use the empty drink bottles for the label-reading activity later in this lesson. Before the lesson, remove the labels from the sport drinks and make copies of them.

2. Begin a discussion about sweating. Ask students, *How many of you have felt your skin after exercise? Was it wet? Was it gritty feeling? If yes, why was it gritty?* Discuss the importance of water in sweat during exercise and how to replace fluid after exercise. Be sure to review the background information presented for this lesson with the class. You can also review the information from lesson 33.

3. Show the students the samples of sport drinks. Ask students, *Have you ever tried these drinks before? Did you like them? Why did you drink them?* Discuss briefly what the sport drinks contain.

4. Ask the students to work with a partner. Give each pair a copy of worksheet 34.1, Do Yourself a Flavor. Instruct them to read the labels of each of the drinks and record the ingredients on the comparison chart.

5. After they have completed the chart, ask the students to sample the drinks labeled A, B, C, and so forth. Ask them to rate the taste of each sample (they won't know which sample is which). Can they identify which drinks are which by the taste and by the list of ingredients?

Wrap It Up!

Ask the class the following questions:

▶ *Which drink had sugar added?*
▶ *What drink had salts added?*
▶ *Which drink did you like the best?*
▶ *How would you compare them to water?*
▶ *Which drink would be the most effective for preventing dehydration?*

Discuss the students' answers as a class.

Teaching Notes

Each lesson has suggested modifications, whenever possible, to adapt the concepts to younger or older students.

Modifications for Younger Students

For younger students, the label-reading part of this activity may be too difficult. Complete the taste test as a class activity.

Modifications for Older Students

None.

Concept Development

Assign the students to research the cost of each drinkand to evaluate these drinks compared to water.

Assessment Options

Each lesson includes assessment options for the lesson and may include additional assessment options for the skills performed within a lesson.

For the Lesson

By completing the group assignment and the class discussion, students will demonstrate their understanding of the contents of sport drinks compared to water for replacing fluids and salts.

Worksheet 34.1: Do Yourself a Flavor

Comparison Chart

Sport drink	Ingredients	Sugar? (Y/N)	Salt? (Y/N)
_____	_____	_____	_____
	_____		
	_____		
	_____		
_____	_____	_____	_____
	_____		
	_____		
	_____		
_____	_____	_____	_____
	_____		
	_____		
	_____		
	_____		

Taste Test

Drink	Salty (Y/N)	Sweet (Y/N)	Like it? (Y/N)
Drink A	_____	_____	_____
Drink B	_____	_____	_____
Drink C	_____	_____	_____

From C. Hopper, B. Fisher, and K.D. Munoz, 2008, *Physical Activity and Nutrition for Health* (Champaign, IL: Human Kinetics).

Section 3: Family Activity 2
Waterlogged

Name: _____

This is an activity for you and one additional family member. You need two large containers, one for you and one for the family member. On a weekend day, pour at least four large glasses of water into each container. Throughout the day, whenever thirsty, you and the family member should drink from your individual containers. On this log, record the times during the day when you drink. The goal is to drink all four glasses by the next morning. Place this log on the fridge door so it is handy for recording each drink.

Name: _____   **Name:** _____

Drinking times: Drinking times:

_____ _____   _____ _____

_____ _____   _____ _____

_____ _____   _____ _____

Exercise Progression

These lessons teach students about health and safety related to exercise. Students will participate in activities that improve flexibility, muscular strength, and endurance. Lessons focus on the importance of exercise progression and setting goals to reach a specific fitness target. Throughout the lessons, students will be challenged to reach a goal they have set.

Lesson 35: Better, Stronger, Quicker

Outcomes

At the end of this lesson, each student will be able to do the following:

▶ Practice progressive physical activity with increasing duration and intensity.
▶ Differentiate between light, moderate, and vigorous physical activity.

Connections to Health Education Standards

▶ Health promotion and disease prevention

Connections to Other Standards

▶ Science standards: life science
▶ Physical education standards: understanding of movement concepts, principles, strategies, and tactics

Connections to WOW! Lessons

▶ Red level: lesson 8, "Sturdy, Strong, and Stretchy"

WOW! Vocabulary

▶ light—An easy and gentle form of exercise.
▶ moderate—Describes exercise performed at a reasonable intensity, not extreme or excessive.
▶ progressive—Advancing in a logical and developmental manner.
▶ vigorous—Refers to strong, energetic, and active activities performed at a higher intensity.

Get Ready to WOW! 'Em

You will need the following:

▶ Jump ropes (one per student)
▶ Three foam balls
▶ Worksheet 35.1, Progressive Jump Rope (one copy per student)
▶ Stopwatch

Background Information

Exercise programs that involve **progressive** physical activity are an effective way to encourage students to stay active. Progressive physical activities gradually increase the intensity over time, such as increasing jump roping time by 30 seconds each day. Programs that include activities of **light** to **moderate** intensity, such as walking and bike riding, are more likely to be maintained than programs focused on **vigorous** physical activities. However, participating in some vigorous activity is important for overall health.

Now WOW! 'Em

1. Use the Intensity Guide in lesson 5 to distinguish between different levels of exertion.

2. Explain the procedures for calling 911 in an emergency situation. Tell students, *You should state your address, describe the situation, stay on the line, and follow directions from the 911 operator.* Briefly describe heart attack symptoms to the students, such as pain in the chest and arm and shortness of breath.

3. Be sure to review the background information presented for this lesson with the class. To help students identify vigorous activity, have them play 911 tag. Use a playing area the size of a basketball court.

4. Select two or three students to be taggers. Using foam balls, the taggers try to tag other students between the shoulder and waist. When players are tagged for the first time, they continue to play while holding their left arm above the elbow with their right hand. When tagged a second time, players grasp their chest with both hands. Explain to students how these actions relate to heart attack symptoms. When tagged a third time, players freeze, grab their throat, and shout "911."

5. "Frozen" players are freed by completing 10 jumping jacks with a player who has not been tagged. You should rotate taggers and occasionally change the exercise used to free the players with "heart attacks."

6. Describe how specific medications can help dissolve blood clots after a heart attack.

7. Tell students, *Many traditional games, such as softball, baseball, and kickball, include periods of inactivity.* Play one of these games so that students can make the comparison between a vigorous activity and a light or moderate activity.

8. Using worksheet 35.1, Progressive Jump Rope, introduce how to develop a progressive program of physical activity. Instruct students to jump rope and record their time for continuous jumping (in minutes and seconds) on each day. Select a two- to four-week period to record data. The objective is to increase the amount of time spent jumping rope. Students should record their times in 30-second intervals.

9. Use the stopwatch to call out 30-second intervals as the students are jumping. Set goals for each grade level:
   - Grades 1 and 2: 5 minutes of continuous jumping
   - Grades 3 and 4: 6 minutes of continuous jumping
   - Grades 5 and 6: 7 minutes of continuous jumping

Wrap It Up!

Use the Intensity Guide to help students identify their levels of effort. The 911 tag game requires intense effort. Explain that this intense effort produces health benefits for the cardiovascular system, such as a stronger and more efficient heart.

Teaching Notes

Each lesson has suggested modifications, whenever possible, to adapt the concepts to younger or older students.

Modifications for Younger Students

In the jump rope activity, have students start with 30 seconds of continuous jumping and slowly progress in increments of 30 seconds.

Modifications for Older Students

Encourage students to perform a series of progressive activities, such as 5 minutes of jumping rope followed by 5 minutes of jogging.

Concept Development

The concept of progressive physical activity can be applied to other activities, such as running and dribbling a soccer ball or basketball. Students may improve their performance in jump roping or any other selected physical activity at a variety of times throughout the day (e.g., during recess or at home). Students should see a pattern of improvement from the data on the worksheet. They should apply this concept to other daily physical skills and activities.

Assessment Options

Each lesson includes assessment options for the lesson and may include additional assessment options for the skills performed within a lesson.

For the Lesson

Students will complete a program of progressive physical activity (continuous jump roping) and track their progress.

Worksheet 35.1:
Progressive Jump Rope

Name: _____

Instructions: Your teacher will select a two- to four-week period to record data. The objective is to increase the amount of time spent jumping rope. Record your time for continuous jumping (in minutes and seconds) on each day. Record your times in 30-second intervals. Your teacher will use a stopwatch to call 30-second intervals as you are jumping.

Date	Time	Date	Time	Date	Time	Date	Time

From C. Hopper, B. Fisher, and K.D. Munoz, 2008, *Physical Activity and Nutrition for Health* (Champaign, IL: Human Kinetics).

Lesson 36: Fitness Challenge

Outcomes

At the end of this lesson, students will be able to do the following:

▶ Improve their muscular strength and endurance.

▶ Set personal goals for each exercise.

Connections to Health Education Standards

▶ Practice of health-enhancing behaviors

Connections to Other Standards

▶ Physical education standards: health-enhancing level of physical fitness

Connections to WOW! Lessons

▶ Red level: lesson 8, "Sturdy, Strong, and Stretchy"

▶ Green level: lesson 3, "Quadriceps"

WOW! Vocabulary

▶ improvement—An advance in performance and achievement.

▶ predict—Estimating future performance.

Get Ready to WOW! 'Em

You will need the following:

▶ Four mats (optional for floor exercises)

▶ 19 fitness exercise cards (use the cards from lesson 6)

▶ Worksheet 36.1, Fitness Challenge (one copy per student)

▶ Pencils (one per pair of students)

Background Information

Goal setting provides an opportunity to develop a plan for reaching a specific target. For physical fitness activities, students' goals should focus on individual **improvement** rather than comparison with other students. By practicing goal setting, students can become more aware of their exercise capabilities, and they can refine their ability to **predict** their future performances.

Now WOW! 'Em

1. Divide students into pairs. For each fitness exercise, one partner counts and records the other partner's score.

2. From the following list of exercises, select 10 exercises to use in one activity lesson. See activity descriptions on pages 59 to 68 in lesson 6.

Side leg raises	Squat thrusts	Curl-ups
Mountain climbers	Leg extensions	Obliques
Skier	Jump twisters	Chest raises
Clappers	Reverse sit-ups	Push-ups
Jumping jacks	Crunches	Reverse push-ups
Cross-country skier	Cross-body lift	Circles on one hand
Stride jumps		

3. Be sure to review the background information presented for this lesson with the class. For each of the selected exercises, ask students to estimate or predict the number of repetitions they can complete in 30 seconds. Students should record their estimates on worksheet 36.1, Fitness Challenge.

4. In pairs, students take turns completing each exercise. They record their scores on the worksheet.

5. Emphasize the correct technique for each exercise. Demonstrate one complete repetition of each exercise. Monitor the sequence of the exercises. To avoid fatigue, students should perform exercises that work different parts of the body in turn—for example, side leg raises (lower body), followed by crunches (abdomen), followed by push-ups (upper body). Keep each student's scorecard and repeat the challenge periodically throughout the year. This will allow students to observe their progress and improvement.

Wrap It Up!

Use these exercises in a "booster break" during the day to energize students. Spend 10 minutes on these exercises at some stage during the day.

Teaching Notes

Each lesson has suggested modifications, whenever possible, to adapt the concepts to younger or older students.

Modifications for Younger Students

Reduce the number of exercises. Students can perform four to six exercises, recording their scores on a modified worksheet. Add some other basic movements such as modified push-ups (from knees) and crab walk.

Modifications for Older Students

Additional exercises can be added (e.g., pull-ups). Discuss realistic goal setting with students. Ask them to set goals relative to their own level of performance.

Modifications for Students Who Are Hearing Impaired

Position yourself where students can see your lips when you talk. Students who are hearing impaired should be positioned close to you. Use only essential words or actions to transmit messages. Make use of demonstrations to explain movements. Pair a hearing student with a student who is hearing impaired. Teach the basic hand signals for "start" and "stop." Use these signals to begin and stop exercise periods (see figure 36.1). The student not exercising can look for these signals and then give the sign to his partner. Hand signals are useful substitutes for whistles and shouts.

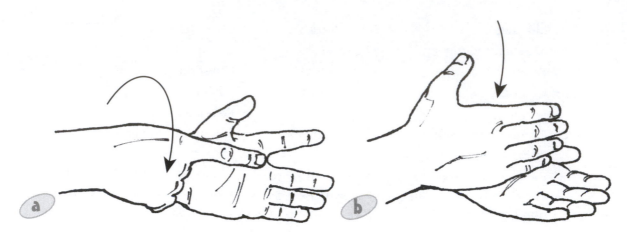

FIGURE 36.1 Hand signals for *(a)* start and *(b)* stop.

Concept Development

1. This format can be used for multiple lessons. Students should be challenged to improve, and they should chart their progress.

2. The length of the interval to complete each exercise can be varied according to age.

3. This lesson can be used in preparation for fitness testing. The activities selected can be matched to the items that will be used for fitness testing.

4. Students can graph their progress on the exercises.

5. Additional exercises can be selected for other workouts. The same procedure can be used for these additional exercises, with students making estimations and charting their progress over time.

Assessment Options

Each lesson includes assessment options for the lesson and may include additional assessment options for the skills performed within a lesson.

For the Lesson

Ensure that students perform the exercises using the correct form and make sure that the scores are recorded accurately. Each repetition is complete when the student returns to the original starting position.

Worksheet 36.1: Fitness Challenge

Name: _____

Key: E = estimate; A = actual

Exercise	Date: E	A	Date: E	A	Date: E	A	Date: E	A
Category 1: Lower body								
Side leg raises								
Mountain climbers								
Skiers								
Clappers								
Jumping jacks								
Cross-country skiers								
Stride jumps								
Squat thrusts								
Leg extensions								
Jump twisters								

From C. Hopper, B. Fisher, and K.D. Munoz, 2008, *Physical Activity and Nutrition for Health* (Champaign, IL: Human Kinetics).

(continued)

(continued)

	Date:		Date:		Date:		Date:	
Exercise	E	A	E	A	E	A	E	A
Category 2: Abdomen and body core								
Reverse sit-ups								
Crunches								
Cross-body lifts								
Curl-ups								
Obliques								
Category 3: Upper body								
Chest raises								
Push-ups								
Reverse push-ups								
Circles on one hand								

Lesson 37: Probability Fitness

Outcomes

At the end of this lesson, students will be able to do the following:

▸ Improve their cardiorespiratory fitness.

▸ Improve their strength and endurance.

▸ Understand new vocabulary related to mathematical probability.

▸ Practice mathematics skills.

Connections to Health Education Standards

▸ Practice of health-enhancing behaviors

Connections to Other Standards

▸ Math standards: data analysis and probability; representation

▸ Physical education standards: competency in motor skills and movement patterns

Connections to WOW! Lessons

▸ Blue level: lesson 6, "Crazy Hoops"

WOW! Vocabulary

▸ chance—An unknown or unpredictable element.

▸ data—Individual facts, statistics, or items of information.

▸ outcome—An end result or consequence.

▸ probability—A chance of something occurring.

Get Ready to WOW! 'Em

You will need the following:

▸ Six dice, two for each group (these can be made with 4-in [10 cm] foam cubes and permanent marking pens)

▸ 20 cones to form lines for the passing and running stations

▸ Balls (one per pair of students)

▸ Jump ropes (one per student)

▸ Large chart or portable white board (with dry erase pen) with a listing of the different jump rope moves and the different types of passes

▸ Three clipboards (one per group of students)

Background Information

Rolling dice provides an effective motivational strategy and an opportunity to practice basic addition skills while exercising. Dice games are found around the world, and they date back to ancient times. **Probability** is the science of **chance.** Probability is evident in aspects of our everyday lives, such as forecasting weather conditions or the results of sporting events. Probability can be calculated mathematically by determining all the possible **outcomes**. In this lesson, students learn that some events are more likely than others while some events are equally likely. Students will collect and analyze a **data** sampling.

Now WOW! 'Em

1. Review the background information presented for this lesson with the class.

2. Divide the class evenly into three groups at different stations: jumping rope, passing a ball, and running. Use the following list of activities for each station:

   • Jump rope: single bounce (1), skier (2), ringing the bell (3), double bounce (4), single side swing (5), side straddle (6). The numbers correspond to the numbers on a die (see step 3). See lesson 48, "Jump for Life," on page 297 for descriptions of these moves. Write the list on the white board or poster in numerical order.

   • Ball skills: chest pass, bounce pass, overhead pass. Students form pairs and complete the passes at a distance of 10 yards (9 m) or closer depending on skill level. Use two lines of cones 10 yards apart to organize the students at this station.

   • Running: Students run back and forth between two lines of cones 20 yards (18 m) apart.

   Review each activity to make sure everyone understands how to perform the activities.

3. At each station, one pair of students serve as the dice rollers and scorekeepers for the group (recording the dice combinations for that group). Students take turns as scorers and dice rollers. The two dice are rolled and scored as the left die and right die. For the jump rope station, use the left die to determine which jump rope activity the students should do (see the corresponding numbers in the list of jump rope activities in step 2). Multiply the number rolled on the right die by 3 to determine the number of jumps the students should complete. For the ball skills station, the left die determines the type of pass: chest (1 or 2), bounce (3 or 4), or overhead (5 or 6). Add the numbers rolled on the two dice together to determine the number of passes. For the running station, subtract the number on one die from the other to determine the number of 20-yard runs.

4. Each time the dice are rolled, the students record the sum of the number combination on their clipboard (see figure 37.1).

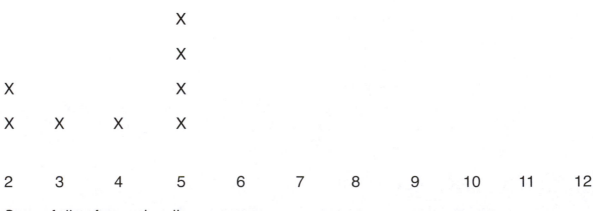

Sum of dice for each roll

FIGURE 37.1   Sample chart of dice scores. This chart indicates the number of times the roll of the dice resulted in each possible sum: The dice added up to 2 twice, added up to 3 one time, added up to 4 one time, and added up to 5 four times.

Wrap It Up!

On returning to class, students can determine the theoretical probability and actual probability of dice combinations. For older students, the number of rolls and outcomes can be represented as fractions.

Teaching Notes

Each lesson has suggested modifications, whenever possible, to adapt the concepts to younger or older students.

Modifications for Younger Students

Keep the class together as one group (instead of three groups) and use one activity, such as jumping rope. Roll the dice to determine the type of activity and the number of repetitions.

Modifications for Older Students

Each group collects and records a data sample at each station. Group samples can be compared or combined into one large class sample.

Modifications for Students With Amputations

Students with amputations may have balance difficulties. In some cases, students will be fitted with prostheses that need to be changed as the student grows. Single-leg amputees may have balance problems during throwing and kicking activities. Amputation reduces the surface area of the skin and affects heat dissipation and body cooling. Perspiration is increased in the rest of the body. Students may have muscle atrophy and contractures around the limb deficiency that require daily stretching. Generally, students with prostheses can participate in all types of activities if the prostheses are well-fitted. Students with upper-limb prostheses may have more success in passing using a softer and larger ball and in jumping rope may need to have a long rope turned for them.

Concept Development

1. Ask students to calculate how many ways each total can be made by the roll of the dice. For example, for the number 7, there are six possible combinations:

   1 6 + 1
   2. 5 + 2
   3. 4 + 3
   4. 3 + 4
   5. 2 + 5
   6. 1 + 6

2. The theoretical probability of rolling a "7" is one out of six (or 1/6). Theoretical probabilities will form a bell curve.

3. Dice combinations: Students can record dice combinations on a chart. Die 1 (left) faces are represented in the top row. Die 2 (right) faces are represented in the left column. The bolded numbers represent the sum of die 1 and die 2. Discuss the patterns that emerge, such as diagonal sums that repeat. Students can immediately see there is only one way for a sum of 12 to occur.

	1	*2*	*3*	*4*	*5*	*6*
1	**2**	**3**	**4**	**5**	**6**	**7**
2	**3**	4	5	6	**7**	**8**
3	4	5	6	7	8	**9**
4	5	6	**7**	8	**9**	**10**
5	6	7	8	**9**	**10**	**11**
6	**7**	8	**9**	**10**	**11**	**12**

Assessment Options

Each lesson includes assessment options for the lesson and may include additional assessment options for the skills performed within a lesson.

For the Lesson

Using the dice, students will demonstrate basic skills in addition and subtraction. They will also demonstrate their ability to complete the appropriate physical activity.

For the Overhead Pass

▶ The ball is held in both hands overhead, with arms slightly bent.

▶ The hands grip the sides of the ball.

▶ The student steps forcefully into stride position and transfers weight to the front foot.

▶ The arms follow through and the elbow extends.

▶ The wrists and fingers turn downward and snap forward.

For the Bounce Pass

▶ The ball is held chest high.

▶ The ball is pushed forward and downward.

▶ The student pushes the ball off the fingertips.

▶ The student steps forward in the stride stance.

▶ The ball contacts the floor about three quarters of the distance from the passer to the catcher.

Types of Flexibility

To be able to move effectively during exercise, a person's joints must be flexible, allowing the person to bend, stretch, and pivot. The following lessons introduce the concept of joint flexibility. Students will learn stretching activities that can improve flexibility.

Lesson 38: The Bends

Outcomes

At the end of this lesson, each student will be able to do the following:

▶ Understand that movements depend on joint flexibility.
▶ Know the difference between ball-and-socket and hinge body joints.
▶ Understand the importance of body joints in everyday life.

Connections to Health Education Standards

▶ Practice of health-enhancing behaviors

Connections to Other Standards

▶ Science standards: life science
▶ Physical education standards: health-enhancing level of physical fitness

Connections to WOW! Lessons

▶ Orange level: lesson 8, "Sturdy, Strong, and Stretchy"
▶ Yellow level: lesson 8, "Sturdy, Strong, and Stretchy"

WOW! Vocabulary

▶ ball-and-socket joint—A joint that allows a broad range of movement.
▶ cartilage—Tissue that provides a cushion between two bones.
▶ hinge joint—A joint that allows movement between two body parts.
▶ joint—A connection between body parts that permits movement.

Get Ready to WOW! 'Em

You will need the following:

▶ A door hinge or a box lid (attached to the box). Tape the lid to one side of the box to simulate hinge actions.
▶ A joystick from a video game, a TV antenna, a chair glide, or a showerhead
▶ Foam balls or playground balls (one per pair of students)
▶ Worksheet 38.1, Body Outline (one copy per pair)
▶ Tape and four brads or brass fasteners per student

Background Information

Joints enable the bones to move together so that the body can bend, stretch, and pivot. Students should learn to distinguish between **ball-and-socket joints** (e.g., a showerhead) and **hinge joints** (e.g., a door hinge), recognizing that the type of joint determines which type of movement is possible. Other types of body joints include gliding joints (forearm) and pivot joints (neck). Where bones meet, they are cushioned by **cartilage** that prevents the bones from crushing or grinding on each other.

Now WOW! 'Em

1. Review the background information presented for this lesson with the class.

2. Introduce the two types of joints by using the hinge and joystick. Help students identify the specific type of joints in the body.
   - Hinge joint examples—elbow, wrist, finger, knee, toe, and ankle
   - Ball-and-socket examples—shoulder and hip

3. Ask students, *Which parts of the arms and legs can move?* Point out parts of the body that have limited movement, such as the spine (back). Demonstrate that ball-and-socket joints (e.g., shoulder and hip) provide greater flexibility compared to hinge joints (e.g., wrist and knee). Show how throwing a ball overhand requires great flexibility, and point out that the ball-and-socket joint at the shoulder enables the throwing action to be completed.

4. Organize students into pairs. Have students try to throw a ball using their elbow but not rotating the arm at the shoulder. Point out how limited the movement and range would be if the shoulder were fused and acted only as a hinge.

5. Have students complete some stretches to demonstrate the amount of movement at the shoulder (see "Stretching Routines" in the introduction). Discuss how the arm can move. Also point out how the shoulder needs to be very mobile to catch a ball.

6. Using figure 38.1, students should cut out the various body parts. They should then reattach the body parts using tape for hinge joints (elbow, wrist, knee, and ankle) and brads or brass fasteners for ball-and-socket joints (shoulder and hip).

Wrap It Up!

To illustrate the importance of hinge joints, ask the students to demonstrate what their arm would be like if there was no joint at the elbow. Ask them to pick up and try to eat a food item without bending the elbow joint. Pose the following questions:

▶ *How would mealtime be different?*

▶ *How would this affect food choices?*

▶ *Would you be able to eat soup?*

▶ *How would you get dressed?*

Teaching Notes

Each lesson has suggested modifications, whenever possible, to adapt the concepts to younger or older students.

Modifications for Younger Students

Have students perform the shoulder stretch (see lesson 40). This is a relatively easy stretch for younger students, and it will allow them to see how the shoulder (ball-and-socket) and the elbow (hinge) can work together to provide flexible body movements.

Modifications for Older Students

Students can complete some of the stretches from the stretching routines presented earlier in the book (see the introduction). While stretching, students should identify which joints are ball-and-socket joints and which ones are hinge joints.

Concept Development

A skeleton (even a cardboard skeleton) is a useful teaching tool. Reinforce estimation skills by asking students to estimate the number of major joints in the arms and legs.

Assessment Options

Each lesson includes assessment options for the lesson and may include additional assessment options for the skills performed within a lesson.

For the Lesson

Students will demonstrate their ability to identify ball-and-socket and hinge joints in the body.

Worksheet 38.1:
Body Outline

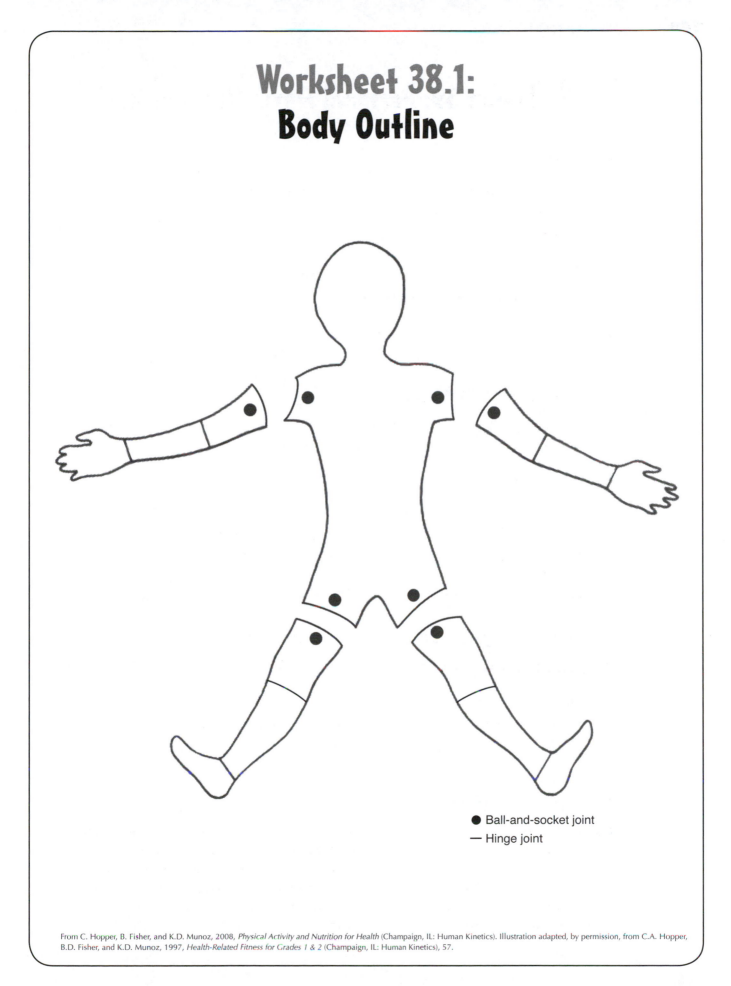

● Ball-and-socket joint
— Hinge joint

Lesson 39: Personal Flexibility Routine

Outcomes

At the end of this lesson, each student will be able to do the following:

▶ Devise an easy-to-use stretching routine.

▶ Understand how to stretch body joints.

Connections to Health Education Standards

▶ Practice of health-enhancing behaviors

Connections to Other Standards

▶ Physical education standards: health-enhancing level of physical fitness

Connections to WOW! Lessons

▶ Blue level: lesson 6, "Crazy Hoops"

▶ Yellow level: lesson 8, "Sturdy, Strong, and Stretchy"

WOW! Vocabulary

▶ contraction—The action of a muscle reducing in length to cause a movement.

▶ flexibility—The range of motion that joints have when bending and moving.

▶ muscles—Tissues composed of fibers capable of contracting to enable the body to move.

▶ range of motion—The area that a joint can be freely moved through without pain.

▶ tendons—Tough tissues that connect a muscle to bone.

Get Ready to WOW! 'Em

You will need the following:

▶ Mats (one per student) or a suitable surface for sitting and lying on the ground

▶ Worksheet 39.1, My Personal Flexibility Routine (one copy per student)

▶ Pencils or pens

Background Information

Range of motion around a joint is highly specific and varies from one joint to another. Individuals who have flexible joints are less likely to be injured in movement activities. Range of motion is dependent on the **muscles** surrounding the joints. Muscles tend to shorten and lose elasticity over time, and stretching can help retain **flexibility** of the joint. Muscles are connected to bones by **tendons.** Body parts are able to move when there is a **contraction** of a muscle or groups of muscles.

Now WOW! 'Em

1. Review the background information presented for this lesson with the class.

2. Tell students, *Flexibility exercises should be performed toward the end of a warm-up, such as a brisk walk, when muscle temperature is elevated. Warm tendons and muscles have more flexibility than cold ones.*

3. Demonstrate the different stretching exercises for the specific parts of the body (see figure 39.1). Give students the instructions italicized in the following list.
   - Focus of stretch: chest
     1. Chest stretche (see figure 39.1a): *In a prone (lying on belly) position, lift your upper body off the ground so your arms are straight.*
     2. Swimmer (see figure 39.1b): *While standing, tilt your trunk slightly forward. Imitate a freestyle swim stroke, alternating each arm.*
   - Focus of stretch: lower back
     1. Sit and reach (see figure 39.1c): *Sit with your knees slightly bent and your feet pointed upward. Reach toward your toes. Bend forward from the hips. Try to pull your chin toward your knees. Hold for 10 to 20 seconds.*
     2. Back stretcher (see figure 39.1d): *Pull your left leg toward the chest by holding onto your hamstrings. Keep your right leg slightly bent with your right foot on the ground. Hold for 20 to 30 seconds. Switch legs.*
     3. Both knees to chest (see figure 39.1e): *Pull both legs to your chest by holding onto the hamstrings. Curl your head up toward your knees. Hold for 5 to 15 seconds and then relax.*
   - Focus of stretch: upper legs
     1. Sitting stretcher (see figure 39.1f): *Sit with the soles of your feet together, legs flat on the floor. Place your hands on your knees and lean your forearms against your knees; resist while trying to raise your knees. Hold for 5 to 7 seconds, then relax.*
     2. Hip and thigh stretcher (see figure 39.1g): *Place your right knee directly above your right ankle, and stretch your left leg backward so the knee touches the floor. If necessary, place your hands on the floor for balance. Press your pelvis forward and downward and hold. Repeat on the other side.*
   - Focus of stretch: lower legs
     1. Calf stretch (see figure 39.1h): *Stand with your left leg forward and right leg back. Keep your right leg straight and bend your left leg. Lean forward, keeping the heel of your right foot on the ground. Hold for 3 seconds. Repeat for the left leg.*
     2. Shin stretcher (see figure 39.1i): *Kneel on both knees. Turn to your right and press down on your right ankle with your right hand. Hold this position, keeping your hips thrust forward to avoid hyperflexing the knees. Do not sit on your heels. Repeat on your left side.*
   - Focus of stretch: neck
     1. Neck stretch (see figure 39.1j): *Keeping your shoulders back and your spine straight, slowly roll your head to your right shoulder, straighten, then roll your head toward your left shoulder, and straighten. Do not roll your head in a fast, circular manner or roll your head backward.*
   - Focus of stretch: shoulders
     1. Shoulder shrug (helps to reduce muscle tension in the neck and shoulders; see figure 39.1k): *Shrug both shoulders up toward your ears. Hold and repeat. Shrug your shoulders backward as far as possible. Hold and repeat. Shrug your shoulders in opposite directions, up and down. Hold and repeat.*
     2. Reach for the stars (see figure 39.1l): *Reach above your head.*
     3. Shoulder squeeze (stretches the back of the arms and shoulder; see figure 39.1m): *Hold both hands behind your back (while in a standing position). Keeping your legs straight, bend forward at your waist. Raise your arms up over your head from behind.*

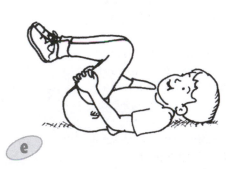

(continued)

FIGURE 39.1 Stretches for the chest, lower back, upper legs, lower legs, neck, and shoulder.

Reprinted, by permission, from C.A. Hopper, B.D. Fisher, and K.D. Munoz, 1997, *Health-Related Fitness for Grades 1 & 2* (Champaign, IL: Human Kinetics), 59, 61, 63.

g

h

i

j

l

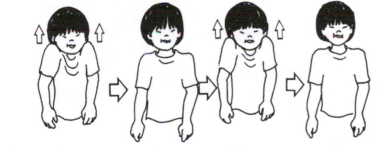

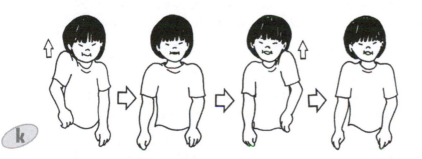

k

m

FIGURE 39.1   (continued)

4. Help students design their own flexibility routine (see worksheet 39.1). Students can select stretching exercises from the previous list. They can also use other stretches. Students should start with two repetitions of each stretch and then progress to additional repetitions.

Wrap It Up!

Students can identify the major muscles that are being stretched. One stretch that should be avoided is the standing toe touch. In this movement, too much pressure is placed on the lower back.

Teaching Notes

Each lesson has suggested modifications, whenever possible, to adapt the concepts to younger or older students.

Modifications for Younger Students

Younger students can select one stretch in each category and learn how to complete the stretch correctly.

Modifications for Older Students

Encourage students to create additional stretches. Some students may want to share with the class stretches they have learned in other settings (e.g., stretches learned in community sports and recreation activities). Advise students to always stretch with the knees slightly bent and not locked. Tell them to avoid any stretch that places excessive pressure on the spine.

Modifications for Students With Cerebral Palsy

Daily stretching activities are critical for those individuals with spastic cerebral palsy and other disabilities that result in muscle imbalances. In neuromuscular conditions that result in contractures, or shortening of soft tissues around the joint, muscles are reduced on one side of the joint and stretched on the other side. This results in a loss of range of motion.

Students with cerebral palsy are usually in a flexed posture. These students need to perform activities that strengthen their extensor muscles, such as straightening the elbow and knee. Throwing and kicking activities are good choices because they result in outward rotation and extension.

Concept Development

Students can pair up and show each other their flexibility routines. This can serve as a warm-up activity. Students may also want to prepare a separate flexibility plan for playing specific sports.

Assessment Options

Each lesson includes assessment options for the lesson and may include additional assessment options for the skills performed within a lesson.

For the Lesson

Students will be able to demonstrate stretching exercises that promote flexible joints for different parts of the body. Students will understand the term *range of motion*.

Worksheet 39.1:
My Personal Flexibility Routine

Name: _____

Instructions: Select one stretch for each area of the body and describe how to perform the stretch.

Chest

Lower back

Legs (upper)

Legs (lower)

Neck

Shoulders

Perform this routine on a daily basis, and teach the routine to family members.

From C. Hopper, B. Fisher, and K.D. Munoz, 2008, *Physical Activity and Nutrition for Health* (Champaign, IL: Human Kinetics).

Lesson 40: Flex Moves

Outcomes

At the end of this lesson, each student will be able to do the following:

- ▶ Understand that flexibility can be improved through stretching exercises.
- ▶ Develop a personal flexibility profile.
- ▶ Understand that some traditional stretching exercises can be harmful.

Connections to Health Education Standards

- ▶ Practice of health-enhancing behaviors

Connections to Other Standards

- ▶ Physical education standards: health-enhancing level of physical fitness

Connections to WOW! Lessons

- ▶ Red level: lesson 8, "Sturdy, Strong, and Stretchy"
- ▶ Yellow level: lesson 8, "Sturdy, Strong, and Stretchy"
- ▶ Orange level: lesson 8, "Sturdy, Strong, and Stretchy"

WOW! Vocabulary

- ▶ calisthenics—Exercises (without equipment) designed to develop and stretch muscles.
- ▶ dislocation—Displacement of a body part.
- ▶ elasticity—The ability of someone or something to stretch.

Get Ready to WOW! 'Em

You will need the following:

- ▶ Mats (one per student)
- ▶ Sit-and-reach box (see figure 40.1). The box should be 12 inches (31 cm) high, and a measuring scale should be placed on top of the box, with the 9-inch (23 cm) mark parallel to the face of the box. The zero end of the ruler is nearest the student.
- ▶ Worksheet 40.1, Flexibility Profile (one copy per student) 💿
- ▶ Family Activity 3 for section 3, Cable Calisthenics (one copy per student) 💿

Background Information

Flexibility is an important but often overlooked part of health-related physical fitness. Flexibility can be improved through stretching exercises. Adequate flexibility permits freedom of movement and may prevent some types of injuries. The term *flexibility* refers to the range of motion of a specific joint and its muscle groups. For example, at the shoulder, the arm can move up and down, move forward and back, and rotate in a circular motion. The flexibility of a joint depends on the **elasticity** of muscles around the joint. **Calisthenics** such as jumping jacks can assist in stretching muscles, but in most cases, additional specific stretching exercises are required for joint flexibility.

Now WOW! 'Em

1. Review the background information presented for this lesson with the class.

2. Tell students to form pairs and have them complete three flexibility activities from Fitnessgram: back-saver sit and reach, trunk lift, and shoulder stretch (see figures 40.1 through 40.3). The following descriptions are based on information from *Fitnessgram/Activitygram Test Administration Manual, Fourth Edition,* by M.D. Meredith and G.J. Welk (Champaign, IL: Human Kinetics, 2007).

   • Back-saver sit and reach: The objective is to reach forward on the right and left side of the body with the arms extended forward over the measuring scale and with the hands placed one on top of the other (see figure 40.1). Shoes are removed, and one leg is extended and placed flat against the sturdy box. The other leg is bent, with the foot flat on the floor. As the student reaches forward with the palms down along the measuring scale, the head is up and the back remains straight. Four reaches are completed on each side, and on the last reach, the position is held for at least one second. The score is recorded to the nearest half inch of the reach.

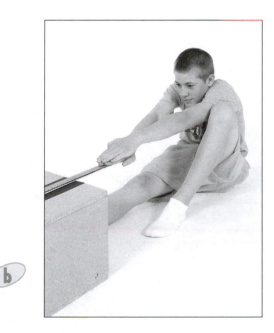

FIGURE 40.1   Back-saver sit and reach.

© Human Kinetics.

   • Trunk lift: The objective is to lift the upper body off the floor using the muscles of the back. The student lies facedown on a mat with the toes pointed and the hands secured under the thighs (see figure 40.2). A coin or other marker is placed on the mat beneath the eyes of the student. The student focuses on this coin during the upward movement of the upper body from the floor. In a slow fashion, the upper body is raised to a height of 12 inches (31 cm). A yardstick is used to measure the appropriate height of the chin. After the measurement is made, the student returns slowly to the mat. The highest chin raise is 12 inches; any scores beyond 12 inches are not counted.

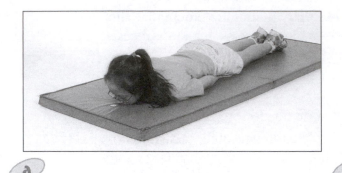

FIGURE 40.2   Trunk lift.

© Human Kinetics.

- Shoulder stretch: The objective is to touch the fingertips together behind the back by reaching over the shoulder with one hand and reaching behind the back with the other. This tests the flexibility of the upper arm and shoulder region. To test the right shoulder, the right hand reaches over the shoulder and down the back (see figure 40.3). At the same time, the left hand is placed behind the back and reaches up to join the right hand. If the fingers touch, the stretch is considered completed. The left shoulder is then tested in a similar manner.

3. Have students record their results on worksheet 40.1, Flexibility Profile. After testing, use the results to lead into a discussion of flexibility. The following basic information is important to share with students:

   - Tell students, *No ideal standards for flexibility exist. Some people are more flexible than others. A person who can reach one inch past her toes is not less fit than a person who can reach 5 inches past his toes. However, too little flexibility means that joints cannot move easily, and too much flexibility causes loose joints that may lead to* **dislocation.**

   - Tell students, *To keep joints flexible, regular exercises that improve range of motion (ROM) are essential. Flexible joints help prevent injuries.* Ask students to describe other stretching activities that improve flexibility of specific body joints.

   - Show students the preferred stretches and the nonpreferred stretches (see table 40.1). Explain why the preferred stretch prevents injury.

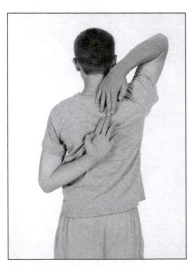
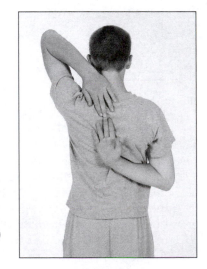

FIGURE 40.3   Shoulder stretch.

© Human Kinetics.

Table 40.1: Preferred Stretches Versus Nonpreferred Stretches

Preferred stretch	Nonpreferred stretch	Reason
Lateral straddle stretch	Hurdler stretch	In the preferred stretch, the knee is not placed in an unnatural position. The stretch does not stress the cartilage in the knee.
One-leg stretcher	The plow	The preferred stretch does not promote a forward head and hump back.
Sitting toe touch	Standing toe touch	The preferred stretch reduces stress on the muscles of the back.
Knee to chest	Double leg lifts	The preferred stretch reduces strain on the lower back.

- Describe the following techniques for successful stretching practice:
    1. *Exhale when moving into a stretch.*
    2. *Breathe normally while holding a stretch.*
    3. *Inhale when releasing a stretch.*
    4. *Always stretch slowly and never stretch by bobbing, bouncing, or jerking.*
- After telling students about these safe stretching techniques, have the students practice focusing on inhaling and exhaling at appropriate times without holding their breath.

Wrap It Up!

Hand out copies of Family Activity 3, Cable Calisthenic. Explain the activity for students to complete at home.

Teaching Notes

Each lesson has suggested modifications, whenever possible, to adapt the concepts to younger or older students.

Modifications for Younger Students

Younger students can easily perform these stretches without the measurement factor. The back-saver sit-and-reach stretch can be performed without the box and the trunk lift without the yardstick.

Modifications for Older Students

Older students may be involved in activities—such as martial arts, yoga, and ballet—that have specific flexibility routines as part of the training. Ask students to share with the class any additional stretching exercises that complement the ones from this lesson.

Modifications for Students With Balance Problems

Students with balance problems may need additional support when performing specific stretches. For stretches in a seated position, balance can be improved by sitting near a wall or stationary support. For standing exercises, a sturdy chair or wall is useful for support. Students may need to exercise on soft surfaces to protect them from falling. Use lighter equipment so that implements can be moved easily without causing load imbalances. When changing surfaces (e.g., from grass to blacktop to indoors), you should advise students regarding safety.

Concept Development

1. Tell students, *For safe and effective stretching, you should hold a sustained stretch for three to five seconds. Slow and gentle stretching helps reduce muscle tension. Bouncing movements produce a muscle contraction or tension in the muscle. Perform each stretch three times with relaxation between each stretch.*

2. Teach students that flexibility exercises should not be competitive.

3. Invite a speaker to talk to the class about stretching (e.g., an athletic trainer, physical therapist, aerobics instructor, dance instructor, or gymnastics coach).

4. Play a Native American game called Hacky Sack. Use a regular Hacky Sack or a leather glove turned inside out. In groups of two or three, students kick the object into the air and pass it around using only their feet. The objective of the game is to see how long the object can stay in motion without touching the ground. This is an excellent activity for hip flexibility.

Assessment Options

Each lesson includes assessment options for the lesson and may include additional assessment options for the skills performed within a lesson.

For the Lesson

Students will demonstrate three stretches that can be scored to develop an objective assessment of their personal flexibility.

For the Stretches

Back-Saver Sit and Reach:

- ▶ One leg is extended with the foot flat against the face of the box.
- ▶ The other knee is bent with the sole of the foot on the floor.
- ▶ The arms extend forward with one hand on top of the other and the palms down.
- ▶ The student reaches forward with the back straight and the head up.

Trunk Lift:

- ▶ The student lies on the mat facedown with the hands under the thighs.
- ▶ The student lifts the upper body off the floor in a slow manner.
- ▶ The head remains in a straight alignment with the spine.
- ▶ The student returns to the starting position in a controlled manner.

Shoulder Stretch:

- ▶ The right hand reaches over the right shoulder and down the back.
- ▶ The left hand moves behind the back and reaches up to touch the fingers of the right hand.
- ▶ The student reverses the positions to test the left shoulder.

Worksheet 40.1: Flexibility Profile

Name: _____

Instructions: The following three flexibility exercises are used in Fitnessgram. Record your score for each exercise and the date that you completed the exercise.

Back-saver sit and reach (left and right)	Date	Trunk lift	Date	Shoulder stretch (yes or no)	Date

Section 3: Family Activity 3
Cable Calisthenics

Name: _____

A Note to Parents

All students will spend some time watching TV, some a lot more than others. Two opportunities exist to exercise while watching TV. During programs, warm-up and cool-down stretches can be performed. Before the program begins, students can teach family members how to perform the stretches. Family members can then complete the stretches while watching TV.

In addition, during commercial breaks, there is time to complete a more vigorous exercise, such as push-ups, sit-ups, or jumping jacks.

Use this worksheet to help your child prepare a plan for family members to exercise while watching TV.

Instructions for Students

Write the names of the three stretches and three exercises you would like your family to learn.

Stretches	*Exercises*
1.	1.
2.	2.
3.	3.

(continued)

From C. Hopper, B. Fisher, and K.D. Munoz, 2008, *Physical Activity and Nutrition for Health* (Champaign, IL: Human Kinetics).

(continued)

Pick three TV programs you usually watch each week. Identify the family members who will be completing the stretches and exercises with you during the programs.

Programs	*Family members*
1.	1.
2.	2.
3.	3.

Get together a few minutes before the program begins to let the family members know what is going to happen. Demonstrate the stretches and exercises that you are going to complete. Ask the family members to carry out a stretch in each segment of the show. Ask them to complete five repetitions of the selected exercise during each commercial break.

Answer the following questions:

1. How did the family members like the approach?

2. Did family members provide excuses about why they did not want to participate? If so, what were they?

From C. Hopper, B. Fisher, and K.D. Munoz, 2008, *Physical Activity and Nutrition for Health* (Champaign, IL: Human Kinetics).

Muscles and Bones

The body contains over 600 muscles that provide structure to the body and allow it to move. In the upcoming lessons, students will learn the names of the major muscle groups and bones in the body. Students will also participate in physical activities that improve muscular strength and endurance as well as bone strength.

Lesson 41: Extreme Muscle Measures

Outcomes

At the end of this lesson, each student will be able to do the following:

▸ Identify the names and actions of major muscle groups.

▸ Locate the major muscle groups.

Connections to Health Education Standards

▸ Health promotion and disease prevention

Connections to Other Standards

▸ Science standards: life science

Connections to WOW! Lessons

▸ Red level: lesson 8, "Sturdy, Strong, and Stretchy"

▸ Red level: lesson 17, "Big and Strong"

▸ Orange level: lesson 18, "Busy Body"

▸ Yellow level: lesson 8, "Sturdy, Strong, and Stretchy"

▸ Green level: lesson 3, "Quadriceps"

WOW! Vocabulary

▸ cardiac muscle—The heart muscle.

▸ girth—The circumference of a muscle.

▸ muscle fiber—The parts that make up a muscle.

▸ muscular endurance—The length of time a muscle or muscle group can continue to exert force before fatiguing.

▸ muscular strength—The maximal amount of force that a muscle or muscle group can exert.

▸ muscular system—The body system that is made up of muscles and works with the skeletal system to enable movement.

Get Ready to WOW! 'Em

You will need the following:

▸ One piece of string (2 yd [183 cm] long) for each student

▸ Scissors (one per pair of students)

▸ Masking tape and markers to label strings

▸ Worksheet 41.1, Body Muscle Chart (one copy per student) ⊙

Background Information

Muscles are all made of the same material, a type of elastic tissue called **muscle fibers** (these tissues are sort of like the material in a rubber band). Tens of thousands of small fibers make up each muscle. The body contains three different types of muscles: smooth muscle, **cardiac** (kar-dee-ak) **muscle,** and skeletal (skeh-luh-tul) muscle. More than 600 muscles are in the body. They help in almost every movement—from pumping blood throughout the body to lifting objects and playing sports. Some muscles, such as the heart, do their jobs without any thought required by the person. **Muscular strength** and **muscular endurance** are fitness components that relate to cardiovascular health. An effective **muscular system** allows the body to participate in vigorous activities. Learning the names and actions of muscles provides an essential knowledge base for people developing exercise routines.

Now WOW! 'Em

1. Review the background information presented for this lesson with the class.

2. Divide students into pairs of the same sex. Students take turns measuring their partner's major muscles using string.

3. Students cut a length of string equal to the **girth** of the following major muscles. As they cut each piece of string, students should label the string (with masking tape) using the following key:
   - Upper arm (UA)
   - Lower arm (LA)
   - Waist (W)
   - Chest (C)
   - Upper leg (UL)
   - Lower leg (LL)

4. Have students sort and arrange the pieces of string from shortest to longest.

5. Next, students should tape or tie their strings in loops.

6. Select one pair of students to tape their strings to the chalkboard for a discussion of the measurement results. Ask the following questions:
   - *Why is the upper leg measurement greater than that of the upper arm?*
   - *Why do the waist and chest have greater girth than the arms and legs?*

7. Use figure 41.1 to help students locate the major muscle groups. With students in the original pairs (same sex), have the students write the names of the major muscles on pieces of masking tape. Partners then tape the names of the major muscle groups on each other in the correct locations on the body (placing the tape on exterior clothing).

8. Use the chart in table 41.1 to help students determine the action of each major muscle.

Wrap It Up!

Review how to pronounce the names of the muscles and describe some of the movements they allow.

▶ *A deltoid (del-toyd) muscle is located in each shoulder. The deltoid muscles help move the shoulders in all directions—allowing movements that range from swinging a baseball bat to lifting objects.*

▶ *The pectoralis (pek-tuh-rah-lus) muscles are found on each side of the upper chest. These are usually called pectorals (pek-tuh-rulz), or pecs for short. As boys*

Table 41.1 Muscle Action Table*

Muscle	Abbreviation	Action
Biceps	Bis	Bends elbow
Triceps	Tris	Straightens elbow
Deltoids	Delts	Lifts arm and shoulder
Quadriceps	Quads	Straightens knee
Hamstrings	Hams	Bends knee
Abdominal muscles	Abs	Bends hip and waist
Latissimus dorsi	Lats	Pulls up body
Trapezius	Traps	Lifts shoulders
Pectorals	Pecs	Pushes arms forward
Gastrocnemius	Calves	Bends ankle
Gluteus	Glutes	Moves legs and hips

*Represents the most basic muscle movement.

grow up, their pectoral muscles become larger. Many athletes and bodybuilders have large pecs.

▶ *Below the pectorals, down under the rib cage, are the rectus abdominis (rek-tus ab-dahm-uh-nus) muscles, or abdominal (ab-dahm-un-ul) muscles. They are also sometimes called abs for short.*

▶ *The biceps (bye-seps) muscle can be seen when flexing at the elbow. Contracting the biceps muscle results in a bulge under the skin.*

▶ *The quadriceps (kwad-ruh-seps), or quads, are the muscles on the front of the thighs. People who run, bike, or play sports develop large, strong quads.*

▶ *The gluteus maximus (gloot-e-us mak-suh-mus) is the muscle that you sit on.*

Teaching Notes

Each lesson has suggested modifications, whenever possible, to adapt the concepts to younger or older students.

Modifications for Younger Students

Younger students can create a body outline using butcher paper. With students in pairs of the same sex, one student lies on top of the butcher paper on the floor, and the other student traces the outline with a pencil. The outline is cut out and named. The students use the outline to attach the strings and name the major muscles.

Modifications for Older Students

Additional muscles can be identified. Bones can also be identified in relation to muscles (see lesson 42). Teach basic anatomical terms, such as *flexion* and *extension.*

Concept Development

Muscles are responsible for the body's every move. But muscles are more than just movers. Muscles keep the internal organs safe and protected. Muscles make the heat that keeps a person warm. All movements such as leaping, bending, or reaching result in muscle action. A muscle makes itself smaller when it contracts and larger when it relaxes. Students' bodies include varying amounts of muscle and body fat.

Assessment Options

Each lesson includes assessment options for the lesson and may include additional assessment options for the skills performed within a lesson.

For the Lesson

Students will demonstrate knowledge of the location and action of the major muscle groups.

Worksheet 41.1:
Body Muscle Chart

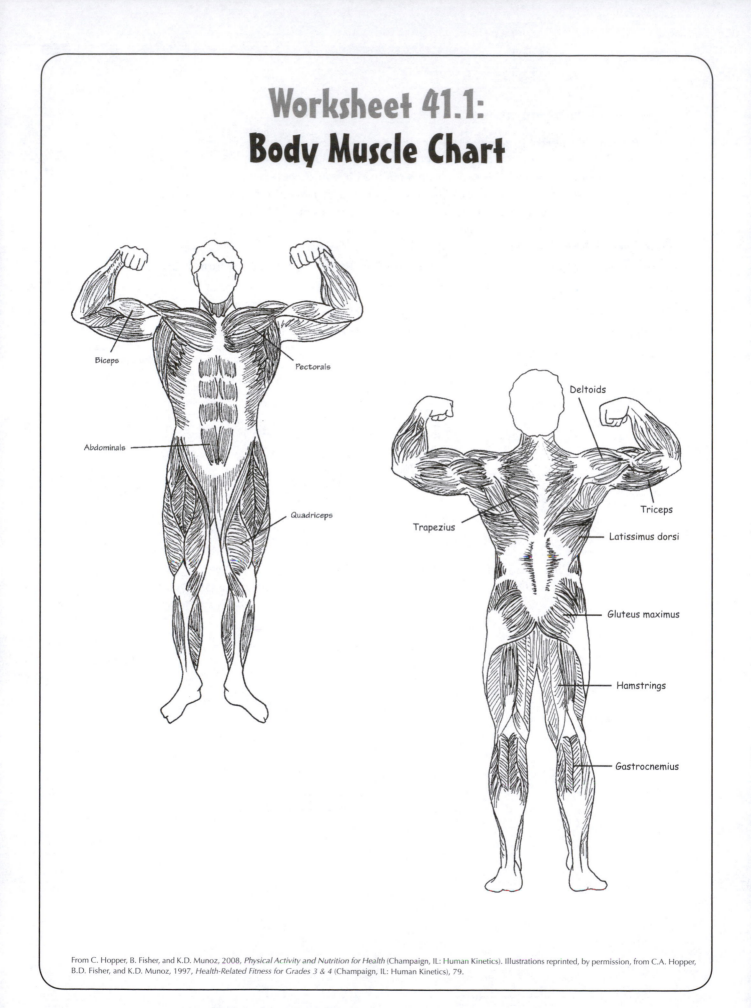

Biceps

Pectorals

Abdominals

Quadriceps

Deltoids

Trapezius

Triceps

Latissimus dorsi

Gluteus maximus

Hamstrings

Gastrocnemius

From C. Hopper, B. Fisher, and K.D. Munoz, 2008, *Physical Activity and Nutrition for Health* (Champaign, IL: Human Kinetics). Illustrations reprinted, by permission, from C.A. Hopper, B.D. Fisher, and K.D. Munoz, 1997, *Health-Related Fitness for Grades 3 & 4* (Champaign, IL: Human Kinetics), 79.

Lesson 42: Build a Better Body

Outcomes

At the end of this lesson, each student will be able to do the following:

- ▸ Understand the structure of the skeletal system.
- ▸ Identify the locations and names of individual bones.
- ▸ Practice basic techniques for dribbling a basketball.

Connections to Health Education Standards

- ▸ Health promotion and disease prevention

Connections to Other Standards

- ▸ Science standards: life science

Connections to WOW! Lessons

- ▸ Red level: lesson 8, "Sturdy, Strong, and Stretchy"
- ▸ Red level: lesson 17, "Big and Strong"
- ▸ Orange level: lesson 8, "Sturdy, Strong, and Stretchy"
- ▸ Orange level: lesson 17, "Big and Strong"
- ▸ Green level: lesson 3, "Quadriceps"

WOW! Vocabulary

- ▸ bone—Hard, dense, calcified tissue that forms the skeleton.
- ▸ femur—The long bone of the thigh.
- ▸ humerus—The long bone of the upper arm.
- ▸ skeletal system—The body system that is made up of bones and provides structure and shape to the body.

Get Ready to WOW! 'Em

You will need the following:

- ▸ Photocopies of Worksheet 42.1, Skeleton, on different colors of paper, including red, blue, green, yellow, and orange (one copy per pair of students) ⊙
- ▸ Jump ropes (one copy per pair)
- ▸ Playground balls (one copy per pair)
- ▸ Whistle or other signal

Background Information

The skeleton consists of a variety of different types of **bones.** The **skeletal system** is designed to support the structure of the body, protect internal organs, and provide attachments for muscles. Explain to students how they become taller. Growth occurs in

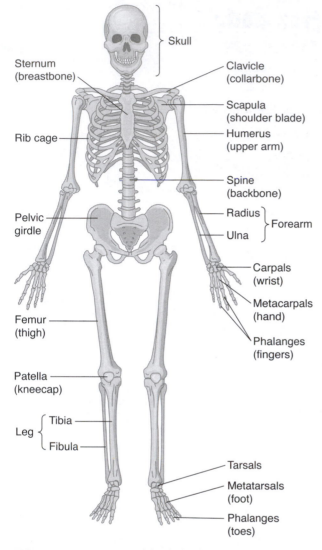

FIGURE 42.2 Structure of the skeletal system.

Reprinted, by permission, from M. Flegel, 2004, *Sport First Aid,* 3rd ed. (Champaign, IL: Human Kinetics), 5.

bones, and this growth results in an increase in height. Growth plates in bones enable the bones to increase in size. Reinforce the concept that calcium from milk helps to form strong bones. Explain that exercise aids in bone development. Muscles pulling on bone builds bone. Weight-bearing exercise builds denser and stronger bones. Like muscle, bone is a living tissue that responds to exercise by becoming stronger.

Now WOW! 'Em

1. Review the background information presented for this lesson with the class.

2. On the back of each copy of Worksheet 42.1 (which you photocopied onto the different colors of paper), write the name of an exercise on each separate skeleton part. These exercises may include push-ups, skiers, jumping jacks, and so on. For each exercise, also write down the number of repetitions the partners will complete.

3. Laminate the color copies and cut them into parts (skeleton pieces) designated by the lines on the photocopies. Use the appropriate number of copies so that there is one complete color set of skeleton pieces for each pair of students.

4. Divide students into pairs and assign each pair a color (red, blue, green, yellow, orange). Make sure there is an even distribution of pairs with each color. Designate partner A and partner B within each pair.

5. Spread skeleton parts around the floor. Arrange the pairs of students around the perimeter of the playing area. Provide a ball (playground ball or basketball) and jump rope to each pair.

6. On a signal, partner A dribbles out to find a part of the skeleton (designated by the pair's color) and then returns to the other partner. The partners both do the exercise specified on the back of the skeleton part.

7. Partners exchange the ball, and partner B now dribbles to find an additional skeleton part. When partner B returns, the partners do the exercise specified on the new skeleton part.

8. This pattern continues until all parts of the skeleton have been collected.

9. The stationary partner should jump rope while waiting for the dribbling partner to return with the next body part.

10. Use a whistle to signal the start of the activity and a changeover of pairs.

Wrap It Up!

Using figure 42.2, review the names of the main bones of the body (**humerus, femur,** and so forth).

Teaching Notes

Each lesson has suggested modifications, whenever possible, to adapt the concepts to younger or older students.

Modifications for Younger Students

For younger students, start the activity without using balls. Students run or jog to collect the skeleton parts.

Modifications for Older Students

- ▶ Have the students perform more advanced jump rope activities.
- ▶ Use the soccer dribble in addition to the basketball dribble.
- ▶ Call out the name of a specific body part or bone. Students find that piece of the skeleton to identify which exercise to complete.
- ▶ Describe the names and functions of the bones in each body category.
- ▶ Vary the movement categories, such as skipping, galloping, or sliding.

Modifications for Students With Disabilities

To encourage maximum participation, consider any of the following adaptations:

- ▶ Substitute different skills when appropriate, such as allowing a student in a wheelchair to dribble a ball with the hands or just carry the ball in the wheelchair.
- ▶ Let some air out of the ball to slow down the speed of the rebound, allowing students to keep better control of the ball.
- ▶ Organize a parallel area for those students with mobility problems who cannot move well in a crowded activity area.
- ▶ Use lighter equipment that is easy to hold and handle.
- ▶ Use small groups to enable students to participate.
- ▶ Change the rules to accommodate all students.

Concept Development

The best exercise for bones is weight-bearing exercise that works against the force of gravity, such as climbing stairs, jogging, and dancing. Ask students to identify exercises that do not work against gravity, such as swimming and bicycling.

Assessment Options

Each lesson includes assessment options for the lesson and may include additional assessment options for the skills performed within a lesson.

For the Lesson

By participating in the activity, students will learn the names of the various parts of the skeleton.

For Basketball Dribbling

▶ The body is held low with a bend at the knees and a slight forward lean.

▶ The ball is pushed slightly forward with each downward thrust.

▶ The ball is kept to the side of the body.

▶ The ball is pushed downward off the fingertips with a follow-through from the arm.

▶ The ball returns to about waist level.

▶ The student uses both the left and right hands to dribble.

For Soccer Dribbling

▶ Use laces, inside of foot, or outside of foot.

▶ Keep ball close to feet.

▶ Knees are slightly bent.

▶ Look up as frequently as possible for a sense of direction.

▶ Use inside and outside of foot to turn the ball in different directions.

Worksheet 42.1:
Skeleton

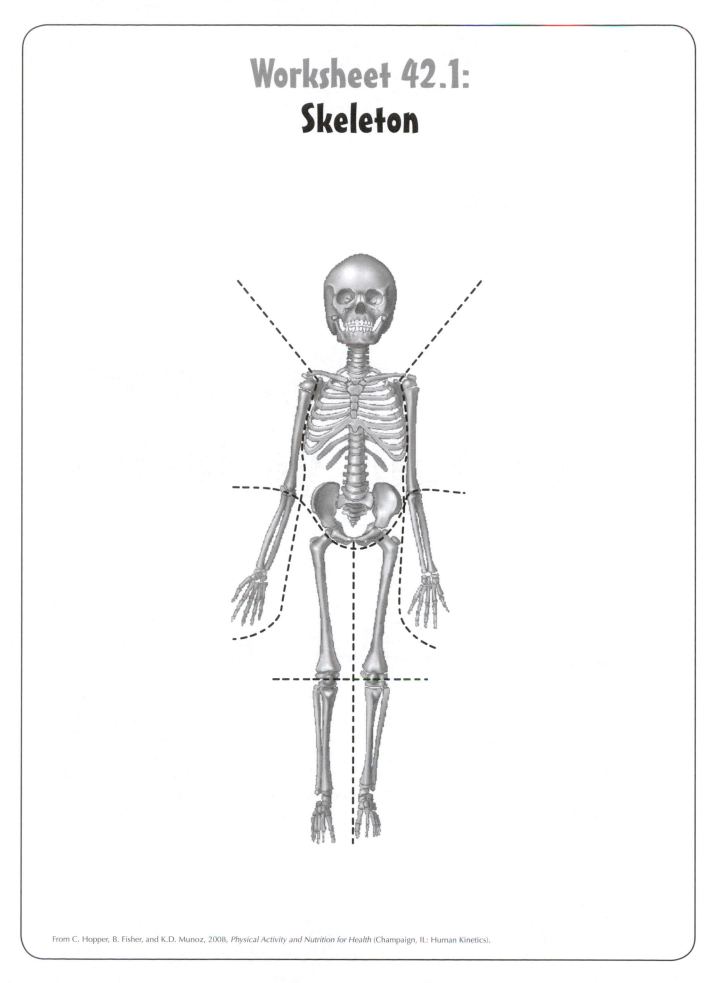

From C. Hopper, B. Fisher, and K.D. Munoz, 2008, *Physical Activity and Nutrition for Health* (Champaign, IL: Human Kinetics).

Overload

Each muscle requires a specific exercise to increase that muscle's strength and endurance. In these lessons, students will participate in a classroom experiment based on improving muscle strength through specific exercises. They will also learn exercises that improve the strength and flexibility of the back.

Lesson 43: Overload

Outcomes

At the end of this lesson, each student will be able to do the following:

▶ Understand the concept of performing an experiment.

▶ Improve the strength and endurance of specific muscles.

Connections to Health Education Standards

▶ Health promotion and disease prevention

Connections to Other Standards

▶ Science standards: life science

▶ Physical education standards: health-enhancing level of physical fitness

Connections to WOW! Lessons

▶ Red level: lesson 8, "Sturdy, Strong, and Stretchy"

▶ Red level: lesson 17, "Big and Strong"

WOW! Vocabulary

▶ posttest—A test of performance given after a period of training to measure improvement.

▶ pretest—A preliminary test of performance given before a period of training.

▶ repetition—One complete performance of an exercise.

▶ set—A series of repetitions of an exercise.

Get Ready to WOW! 'Em

You will need the following:

▶ Access to pull-up bars or modified pull-up bars (if those exercises are selected for the activity)

▶ Measuring strip for curl-ups (30 to 35 in [76 to 89 cm] long; 3 in [8 cm] wide for five- to nine-year-olds, 4 1/2 in [12 cm] wide for older students). For more information, refer to *Fitnessgram/Activitygram Test Administration Manual, Fourth Edition,* by M.D. Meredith and G.J. Welk (Champaign, IL: Human Kinetics, 2007).

▶ Worksheet 43.1, Pre- and Posttest Scores for Exercises (one copy per student)

Background Information

For muscles to increase in strength and endurance, a person's training must be specific to those muscles. The physical activities performed must exercise the specific muscles to be developed.

Now WOW! 'Em

1. This activity uses the exercise protocols in the *Fitnessgram* manual by Meredith and Welk (2007).

2. Be sure to review the background information presented for this lesson with the class. This activity is completed over a five-week period and is conducted in the form of an experiment.

3. Assign students to two groups, A and B. Explain how the program will consist of progressive **repetitions** and **sets.** Select two exercises from the following list:
   - Push-ups
   - Curl-ups
   - Modified pull-ups
   - Pull-ups

   Designate exercises 1 and 2. For example, exercise 1 is push-ups and exercise 2 is curl-ups (see figure 43.1). Randomly assign one of these exercises to each group. Ensure that each member of the group knows and can demonstrate how to perform the exercise correctly. Have students record results on Worksheet 43.1, Pre- and Posttest Scores for Exercise.

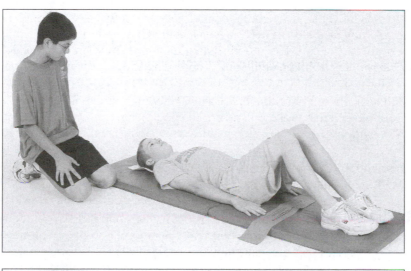

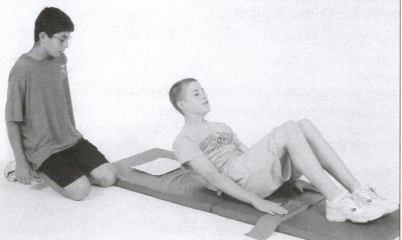

FIGURE 43.1   Curl-ups.

4. For each group, test the students on both exercises to see how many repetitions they can perform. This is the **pretest.**

5. Over the next five weeks, have students practice their designated exercise for five minutes per day, three times a week.

6. Progressive overload plan: Help students develop a personal training plan that gradually increases the number of repetitions and sets (how many times the repetitions are performed in an exercise period). The following is an example of a progressive overload plan for push-ups with a pretest score of 5:
   • Week 1: day 1—two sets of 4; day 2—two sets of 5; day 3—two sets of 5
   • Week 2: day 1—two sets of 5; day 2—two sets of 6; day 3—two sets of 6
   • Week 3: day 1—three sets of 4; day 2—three sets of 5; day 3—three sets of 6
   • Week 4: day 1—two sets of 7; day 2—two sets of 8; day 3—two sets of 9
   • Week 5: day 1—two sets of 8; day 2—two sets of 9; day 3—two sets of 10

7. Provide a short rest in between sets on each day. Allow for a day of rest in between each workout day. This plan should be modified if it is too easy or too difficult.

8. At the end of the five-week training period, test each student on both exercises to determine the maximum number of repetitions. This is the **posttest.**

Wrap It Up!

Make sure students are performing each exercise correctly. Help students develop a workout schedule that is challenging but will not cause excessive muscle soreness. Compare the scores of the two groups. Individual students should see an improvement in the score of their designated exercise but not in their posttest performance of the other group's exercise.

Teaching Notes

Each lesson has suggested modifications, whenever possible, to adapt the concepts to younger or older students.

Modifications for Younger Students

Other exercises such as jumping jacks can be used. Jump rope is also an option. With younger students, the emphasis should be on fun and enjoyable movements.

Modifications for Older Students

Older students should use pull-ups as one of their exercises to improve upper body strength. If students are unable to complete one pull-up, they can use "jump-up" pull-ups in the training program. In this form of pull-ups, students use their legs to jump up into the pull-up position, and then they slowly come down. The palms should face the body when gripping the bar.

Concept Development

Muscular strength and endurance are highly specific. A person can have a high level of strength and endurance in the arms and shoulders while having very low strength and endurance in the leg muscles. For the training plan in this lesson, students can graph data and engage in goal setting and additional planning.

Assessment Options

Each lesson includes assessment options for the lesson and may include additional assessment options for the skills performed within a lesson.

For the Lesson

Students will follow a five-week training program and track their performance to evaluate their progress.

Worksheet 43.1:
Pre- and Posttest Scores for Exercises

Name: _____

Instructions: Record pre- and posttest scores and chart the total number of repetitions performed each day.

Exercise: _____

My pretest score: _____

Week	Day	1	2	3
1				
2				
3				
4				
5				

My posttest score: _____

From C. Hopper, B. Fisher, and K.D. Munoz, 2008, *Physical Activity and Nutrition for Health* (Champaign, IL: Human Kinetics).

Lesson 44: Back Yourself Up

Outcomes

At the end of this lesson, students will be able to do the following:

▶ Perform specific exercises to maintain flexibility and strength of the back.

▶ Increase their awareness of back pain and problems.

▶ Understand survey techniques.

Connections to Health Education Standards

▶ Practice of health-enhancing behaviors

Connections to Other Standards

▶ Science standards: life science

▶ Physical education standards: health-enhancing level of physical fitness

Connections to WOW! Lessons

▶ Red level: lesson 8, "Sturdy, Strong, and Stretchy"

▶ Red level: lesson 17, "Big and Strong"

▶ Orange level: lesson 8, "Sturdy, Strong, and Stretchy"

▶ Yellow level: lesson 8, "Sturdy, Strong, and Stretchy"

▶ Purple level: lesson 15, "Healthy Choices"

WOW! Vocabulary

▶ summary—A comprehensive yet brief overview of facts.

▶ survey—To collect and examine information about a topic.

▶ trunk—The part of the body not including the head and limbs.

Get Ready to WOW! 'Em

You will need the following:

▶ Exercise mats (one per student)

▶ Worksheet 44.1, Structure of the Back (one per student)

▶ Worksheet 44.2, Back Survey (one copy per student)

▶ Family Activity 4 for section 3, Backpack Check (one copy per student)

Background Information

Although elementary students rarely have back problems, learning flexibility exercises will provide them with the knowledge to maintain a regular stretching program. For a person's back to stay healthy and less prone to injury, the person needs strong, flexible muscles to support the back's natural balanced position. Sitting is more stressful to the back than standing or walking, yet many jobs require people to sit all day long. In many cases, people sit incorrectly. Here are the guidelines for sitting correctly:

- ▶ Sit with the back straight and the shoulders back.
- ▶ Sit with the buttocks touching the back of the chair and with weight distributed evenly on both hips.
- ▶ Bend the knees at a right angle and keep the feet flat on the floor.
- ▶ Keep the knees even with or slightly higher than the hips.

Now WOW! 'Em

1. Be sure to review the background information presented for this lesson with the class. Tell students, *The back has three natural curves: the cervical (neck) curve, the thoracic (middle back) curve, and the lumbar (lower back) curve. When all three curves are balanced, the ears, shoulders, and hips line up straight.*

2. Complete these flexibility exercises with your class by giving them the following instructions:
   - Single knee to chest (see figure 44.1a): This exercise stretches the muscles of the lower back and hamstring, as well as the ligaments of the lumbar spine.
     1. *Lie down flat on the floor.*
     2. *Bend one leg at approximately 100 degrees and place that same foot on the floor.*
     3. *Gradually pull the opposite leg toward your chest.*
     4. *Hold the final stretch for a few seconds.*
     5. *Switch legs and repeat the exercise.*
   - Double knee to chest (see figure 44.1b): This exercise stretches the muscles of the upper and lower back. It also stretches the hamstring muscles and spinal ligaments.
     1. *Lie flat on the floor and then slowly curl up into a fetal position.*
     2. *Hold for a few seconds.*
   - Gluteal stretch (see figure 44.1c): This exercise stretches the buttock area (gluteal muscles).
     1. *Sit on the floor with your knees bent and both feet on the floor.*
     2. *Bend the left leg and place your left ankle on your right thigh slightly above the knee.*
     3. *Grasp under your right thigh with both hands and gently pull the leg toward your chest.*
     4. *Repeat the exercise with the opposite leg.*
   - Trunk rotation and lower back stretch (see figure 44.1d): This exercise stretches the lateral side of the hip and thigh, as well as the trunk and lower back.
     1. *Sit on the floor and bend the left leg, placing the left foot on the outside of the right knee with the right leg straight.*
     2. *Place the right elbow on the left knee and push against it. At the same time, try to rotate the trunk to the left (counterclockwise).*
     3. *Hold the final position for a few seconds.*
     4. *Repeat the exercise with the other side.*
   - Pelvic tilt (see figure 44.1e): This is an important exercise for the care of the lower back.
     1. *Lie flat on the floor with the knees bent at about a 60-degree angle.*
     2. *Tilt the pelvis by tightening the abdominal muscles, flattening your back against the floor, and raising the lower gluteal area slightly off the floor.*
     3. *Hold the final position for several seconds.*
     4. *The exercise can also be performed against a wall.*

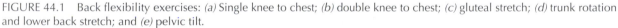

FIGURE 44.1   Back flexibility exercises: *(a)* Single knee to chest; *(b)* double knee to chest; *(c)* gluteal stretch; *(d)* trunk rotation and lower back stretch; and *(e)* pelvic tilt.

(a-b) Reprinted, by permission, from C.A. Hopper, B.D. Fisher, and K.D. Munoz, 1997, *Health-Related Fitness for Grades 5 & 6* (Champaign, IL: Human Kinetics), 83. *(d)* Reprinted, by permission, from C.A. Hopper, B.D. Fisher, and K.D. Munoz, 1997, *Health-Related Fitness for Grades 5 & 6* (Champaign, IL: Human Kinetics), 116.

3. Have students select five adults to collect **survey** data from regarding back health. Tell students, *Select family members, neighbors, or relatives who you know well.*

4. Tell students to record the results of the survey on the **summary** sheet portion of worksheet 44.2.

5. Tell students to analyze the data by writing a short statement of the results. Give students this example: *The majority of individuals who scored 3 or 4 on question 1 were over 50 and did not stretch once a day.*

Wrap It Up!

1. Ask students to help their parents and other adults who may have back problems by demonstrating exercises that will assist in strengthening and stretching back muscles. Select one or two exercises for them to use.

2. Ask students to complete Family Activity 4, Backpack Check.

Modifications for Safety: Exercises Not to Perform

▶ Straight leg lifts: These are often performed with the students lying on their back and raising both legs about six inches (15 cm) off the ground. This places extreme pressure on the lower back, and this exercise should not be performed.

FIGURE 44.2   Half knee bends.

Reprinted, by permission, from K. Thomas, A. Lee, and J. Thomas, 2000, *Physical Education for Children: Daily Lesson Plans for Elementary School*, 2nd ed. (Champaign, IL: Human Kinetics), 37.

▶ Yoga plow: In this exercise, students lie on their back and bring the legs up and over the head, with the toes touching the ground beyond the head. This places excess pressure on the back and neck, and this exercise should not be performed.

▶ Deep knee bends: Knee bends will stretch the calves and thighs. Deep knee bends can tear cartilage in the knees, and this exercise should not be performed. Instead, students may perform half knee bends, keeping the heels on the ground and not bending the knee beyond 90 degrees (see figure 44.2).

Teaching Notes

Each lesson has suggested modifications, whenever possible, to adapt the concepts to younger or older students.

Modifications for Younger Students

Teach one or two of the exercises to be used as part of a warm-up.

Modifications for Older Students

Students can work in pairs to help each other perform the exercises correctly. They should identify the important teaching cues for each stretch. Older students can complete the survey and analyze the data.

Concept Development

1. Use the topic of back health to teach survey skills to students. The Back Survey introduced in the "Now WOW! 'Em" section is designed to gather information from five adults about their incidence of back problems. Since many adults have back problems, this survey will reveal information.

2. Use the Back Survey to teach students about surveying techniques. Indicate how the questions collect different types of information:

   • Question 1 uses a scale that includes words but can also be connected to a numerical score.
   • Question 2 provides data regarding a specific category and frequency.
   • Question 3 provides limited information about a specific event. It does not provide any information about frequency or severity.
   • Question 4 is open ended and therefore the information cannot be tallied into categories (this question could also not provide a response).

Assessment Options

Each lesson includes assessment options for the lesson and may include additional assessment options for the skills performed within a lesson.

For the Lesson

Students will learn about the basic structure of the back. They will demonstrate the ability to complete stretching exercises that help develop flexibility.

Worksheet 44.1:
Structure of the Back

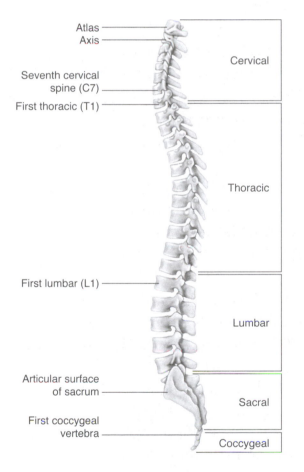

Atlas

Axis

Cervical

Seventh cervical spine (C7)

First thoracic (T1)

Thoracic

First lumbar (L1)

Lumbar

Articular surface of sacrum

Sacral

First coccygeal vertebra

Coccygeal

From C. Hopper, B. Fisher, and K.D. Munoz, 2008, *Physical Activity and Nutrition for Health* (Champaign, IL: Human Kinetics). Illustration © Human Kinetics.

Worksheet 44.2:
Back Survey

Name: _____

Instructions: On the summary section of this worksheet, record the first name of five adults, along with your relationship to each of them. Specify the age and sex of each adult. Ask the adults the following questions and record their responses on the summary sheet.

1. Have you ever experienced any back pain (use the following scale to answer this question)?

> 1—Never
>
> 2—Rarely (one or two times per year)
>
> 3—Sometimes (once a month)
>
> 4—Regularly (once or more per week)

2. How often do you complete stretching exercises for your back?

> Once a day
>
> Every other day
>
> Once or twice a week
>
> Only when having back pain
>
> Never

3. Have you ever had back surgery?

> Yes
>
> No

If yes, did the surgery improve the back problem?

4. Do you perform any other activities to maintain or strengthen the back muscles?

From C. Hopper, B. Fisher, and K.D. Munoz, 2008, *Physical Activity and Nutrition for Health* (Champaign, IL: Human Kinetics).

(continued)

(continued)

Summary Sheet

	Question 1	Question 2	Question 3	Question 4
1. Name and relationship: Age: Sex:				
2. Name and relationship: Age: Sex:				
3. Name and relationship: Age: Sex:				
4. Name and relationship: Age: Sex:				
5. Name and relationship: Age: Sex:				

Section 3: Family Activity 4
Backpack Check

Name: _____

Backpacks are an effective way to carry books and supplies to and from school. However, unless it is packed and carried correctly, a backpack may cause back and neck problems. Symptoms that a backpack is too heavy or improperly balanced may include aching shoulders, neck and back pain, and red marks and creases on the shoulders.

Students with backpacks that are too heavy will tend to bend forward to try to support the weight on their back rather than on their shoulders. Too much weight at the top of the backpack will cause an off-center shift of weight. Similarly, if the backpack is positioned over only one shoulder, the weight is shifted to one side, possibly causing back and neck pain.

Complete the following check:

▶ The backpack should weigh no more than 5 to 10 percent of the student's body weight. If the backpack is heavier, the student should carry some books in the arms instead of in the backpack.

▶ The contents of the backpack should be positioned so that the heaviest items are on the bottom.

▶ The backpack should not hang more than 3 or 4 inches (8 or 10 cm) below the waist.

▶ The backpack should have padded straps to help protect the shoulders.

▶ The student should use both shoulder straps to even out the load rather than carrying the backpack on just one shoulder.

▶ Shoulder straps should be adjustable and fitted to the body to prevent the backpack from shifting from side to side.

▶ When used correctly, backpacks provide an exercise opportunity and add resistance to walking.

From C. Hopper, B. Fisher, and K.D. Munoz, 2008, *Physical Activity and Nutrition for Health* (Champaign, IL: Human Kinetics).

SECTION 4

Promoting a Healthy Lifestyle

Physical activity and nutrition are two major factors that influence health. In section 4, key elements in maintaining a healthy lifestyle are introduced. These lessons focus on the value of participating regularly in physical activity, especially those activities that improve heart health (e.g., cardiorespiratory activities). The concept of physical activity for everyone regardless of physical ability is also emphasized. Students are encouraged to participate in a wide variety of activities and to engage in activities that meet personal needs. These strategies are designed to promote physical activity for a lifetime.

These lessons also teach students the importance of eating a balanced diet based on the MyPyramid food guide. Students will learn how much to eat and how the body systems assimilate food and provide the body with energy. Finally, students will participate in goal-setting activities to help them continue active living throughout their lifespan.

Active Living

In the past, people were much more active in their daily lives than they are today. Technology has changed the way in which we accomplish daily chores. In part 1, students will discuss the risk factors associated with today's lack of physical activity and participate in fun exercises they can continue later in life.

Lesson 45: My Physical Activity Pyramid

Outcomes

At the end of this lesson, each student will be able to do the following:

▶ Develop a personal physical activity plan.

▶ Engage in regular physical activity after school, on weekends, during holidays, and over the summer.

Connections to Health Education Standards

▶ Health promotion and disease prevention

▶ Practice of health-enhancing behaviors

▶ Goal-setting skills

Connections to Other Standards

▶ Physical education standards: appreciation for the value of physical activity

Connections to WOW! Lessons

▶ Red level: lesson 9, "Family Fitness Fun"

▶ Orange level: lesson 9, "Family Fitness Fun"

▶ Yellow level: lesson 9, "Family Fitness Fun"

▶ Green level: lesson 3, "Quadriceps"

▶ Blue level: lesson 8, "The Goliath Beetles"

▶ Purple level: lesson 15, "The Goliath Beetles"

WOW! Vocabulary

▶ lifestyle—A way of life that reflects the values of a person or a group.

▶ physical activity pyramid—A pyramid-shaped model for planning physical activity in a person's life, with a broad base of everyday activities at the bottom and more specialized activities at the top.

Get Ready to WOW! 'Em

You will need the following:

▶ Worksheet 45.1, Pyramid Planner (one copy for each student)

▶ Worksheet 45.2, Pyramid Building Blocks (one copy for each student)

▶ Scissors (one per student)

▶ Glue stick (one per student)

▶ Pen or pencil (one per student)

▶ Plastic bags for storage of students' pyramids (one per student)

Background Information

Promoting regular participation in enjoyable physical activity is a major goal of physical education programs. Students are more likely to participate in physical activity if they have developed movement skills that are meaningful to them on a daily basis. These skills should be part of the routines of life, including easy-to-complete individual and community activities. Encouraging students to take responsibility for including physical activity in their daily life is a key factor in helping them develop an active **lifestyle.** Physical activity provides opportunities for enjoyment, challenge, and self-esteem. It also reduces health problems.

Now WOW! 'Em

1. Review the background information presented for this lesson with the class.
2. Use Worksheet 45.1 to help students evaluate their current interests.
3. Each student should create a personal **physical activity pyramid** using the templates found in Worksheet 45.2.
4. Before cutting out each level of the pyramid, students write activities on each section to reflect their desired profile of physical activities. Each activity should be included in one activity level only.
   - Level I: individual everyday physical activity. Students should write at least three of their current everyday physical activities. Level I activities are those that can be completed throughout the day. Some examples include household chores, walking to school, riding a bicycle, walking in the neighborhood, and climbing the stairs (instead of taking the elevator).
   - Level II: home and community activities with family and friends. Level II activities are completed with groups of family members and friends and may include some activities that are similar to level I activities. An example would be a family walk through the neighborhood.
   - Level III: school activities. These activities include recess, physical education, before- and after-school recreation (at school), and schoolwide events (e.g., jump rope club). Organized team sports are not included in this level.
   - Level IV: team sports and specialized activities. Students should indicate what activities they would like to do to complete their personal pyramid of physical activity. Discuss with students possible activity areas, including dance, aquatics, martial arts, gymnastics, games, sports, and outdoor activities. Team and individual sports (school and community) are in this category. All students will have favorite activities, and their selection of activities should include a personal analysis of interests and skills.

Wrap It Up!

Conduct a class discussion focusing on how students can increase their everyday lifestyle activities. Ask students to explain their ideas and plans in this area. Suggest small adjustments to increase their levels of physical activity.

Teaching Notes

Each lesson has suggested modifications, whenever possible, to adapt the concepts to younger or older students.

Modifications for Younger Students

Younger students can glue pictures from magazines on the pyramid (using old sports magazines). They can focus on writing key words. For level IV activities (team sports and specialized activities), allow students to include the activities that they enjoy the most. The focus should not be on competitive team sports. Using a one-dimensional model of the pyramid may be easier than cutting out the three-dimensional plans.

Modifications for Older Students

For each activity listed on the pyramid, students can analyze the best ways to support their participation. A support chart can be developed. The following factors can be discussed: cost, availability of equipment, skill level required, safety, enjoyment, parental support, convenience, and success. Select an activity to use as an example:

Factor	*Activity: Soccer*
Cost	Registration fee (team fee)
Equipment	Cleats, shin guards, and uniform
Skill level required	Most areas have programs for recreational and competitive players.
Safety	Some risk of injury
Enjoyment	Is this an activity I would enjoy?
Parental support	Would my parents transport me to practice and games?
Convenience	How close are the playing fields?
Success	Would I be good at this activity?

Concept Development

1. The physical activity pyramid can include a description of activities for different times of the year. One side of the pyramid could be for fall and winter, while the other side is for spring and summer. Activities for each season can be written in different colors.

2. This lesson can include creating awareness of available community activities. Set up a schoolwide bulletin board to publicize a broad range of community and recreational activities.

3. Periodically, students should revisit and update their personal pyramid to reflect changes in their interests.

Assessment Options

Each lesson includes assessment options for the lesson and may include additional assessment options for the skills performed within a lesson.

For the Lesson

Using the Pyramid Planner, students will demonstrate the ability to develop a personal plan for engaging in a variety of individual, school, and community activities.

Worksheet 45.1: Pyramid Planner

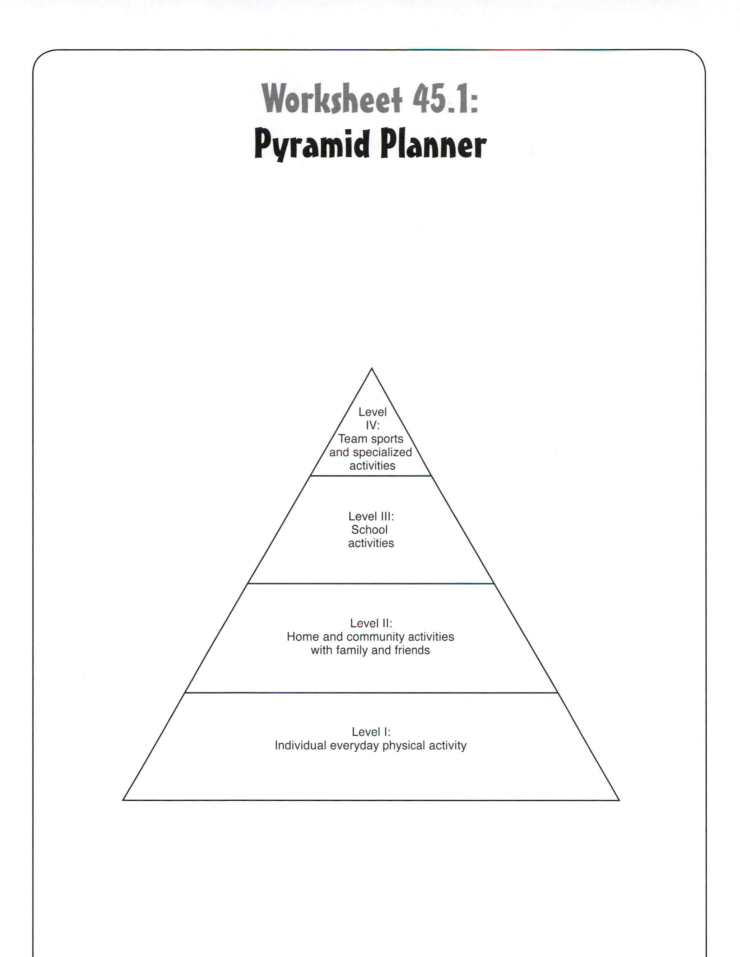

Level IV:
Team sports
and specialized
activities

Level III:
School
activities

Level II:
Home and community activities
with family and friends

Level I:
Individual everyday physical activity

Worksheet 45.2:
Pyramid Building Blocks

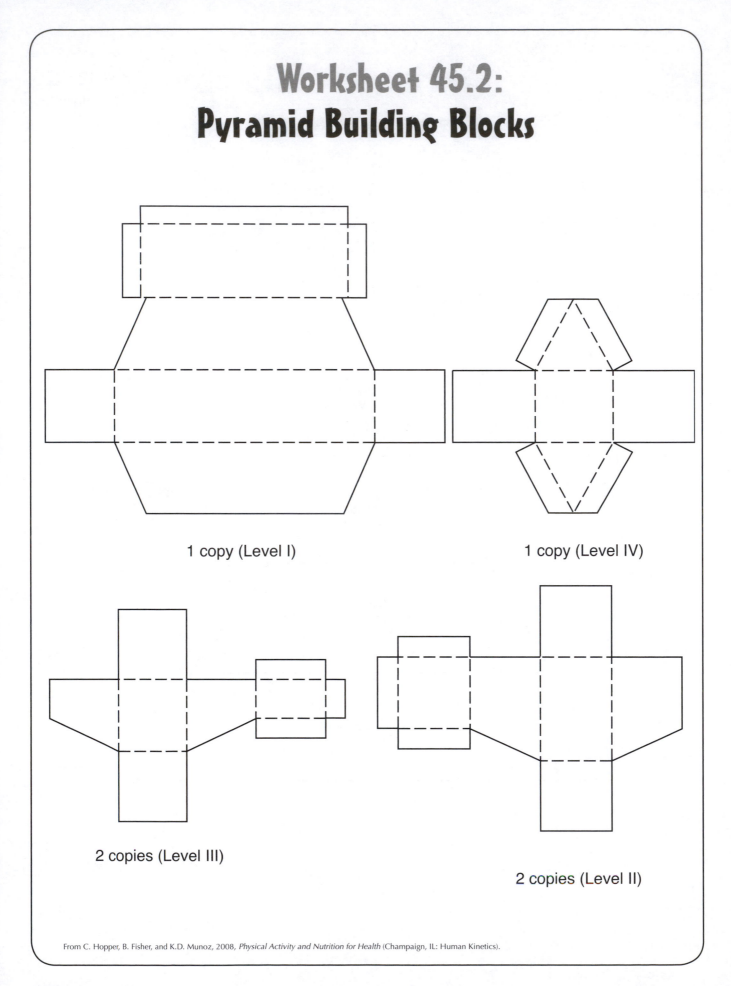

1 copy (Level I)

1 copy (Level IV)

2 copies (Level III)

2 copies (Level II)

From C. Hopper, B. Fisher, and K.D. Munoz, 2008, *Physical Activity and Nutrition for Health* (Champaign, IL: Human Kinetics).

Lesson 46: Healthy Living

Outcomes

At the end of this lesson, each student will be able to do the following:

▶ Understand the risk factors for disease, specifically cardiovascular disease.

▶ Understand how lifestyle changes over the years have affected physical activity levels.

Connections to Health Education Standards

▶ Decision-making skills

▶ Health promotion and disease prevention

Connections to Other Standards

▶ Physical education standards: responsible personal and social behavior

▶ Science standards: science in personal and social perspectives

Connections to WOW! Lessons

▶ Red level: lesson 7, "Heart Healthy"

▶ Orange level: lesson 9, "Heart Healthy"

▶ Yellow level: lesson 9, "Heart Healthy"

▶ Purple level: lesson 15, "Healthy Choices"

WOW! Vocabulary

▶ blood pressure—A measure of the force exerted against the walls of the blood vessels.

▶ diabetes—A condition involving high sugar content in blood and urine.

▶ heredity—Passing of biological traits from parents to children.

▶ obesity—Increased body weight caused by excessive fat.

▶ risk factors—Lifestyle habits that put individuals at risk for diseases.

Get Ready to WOW! 'Em

You will need the following:

▶ Worksheet 46.1, Lifestyles Long Ago (one copy per student)

▶ Worksheet 46.2, Healthy Changes (one copy per student)

Background Information

Inactivity is one of the major **risk factors** for heart disease and other health problems. Teaching students how to stay active helps reduce their likelihood of developing health problems later in life. Risk factors can be **hereditary** elements or lifestyle habits that increase the possibility of diseases. Lifestyles have become more sedentary because of the creation of new technologies, and those changes put people at risk for severe health problems (heart disease, **obesity,** and **diabetes**). The challenge is to find opportunities for physical activity in daily life.

Now WOW! 'Em

1. Have students complete worksheet 46.1, Lifestyles Long Ago. Students can do this individually or in pairs. This worksheet enables students to compare the lifestyles of people in the 1800s to those of people today. Students will see how the changes in lifestyle have reduced physical activity. For example, people in the 1800s would chop wood in order to heat their homes, whereas people today can just turn on the furnace. After students complete the worksheet, discuss the results as a class. Students can also trade papers or form small groups to discuss the results.

2. Review the background information presented for this lesson with the class.

3. Explain risk factors and how the following factors can influence health: *Some risk factors can be controlled, while others, such as age, sex, and* **heredity***, are beyond an individual's control. The following are considered factors that contribute to cardiovascular disease and health problems.*

   - Age: *Age is a risk factor for heart disease because other factors—such as a poor diet, lack of exercise, and obesity—are more likely to exist in older persons.*
   - Sex: *Men are much more likely to develop cardiovascular disease than women.*
   - Heredity: *Children inherit both physical and health-related characteristics from their parents. If parents have heart disease, there is a chance that heart disease will be passed on to their children.*
   - Inactivity: *Children and adults need to participate in activities that are vigorous enough to improve cardiorespiratory endurance. Lack of exercise and sitting in front of the television will lead to increased weight and poor physical fitness. Exercise includes daily household chores and gardening as well as sports and exercise. Stress to the students that they need to include moderate to vigorous physical activity for at least one hour per day.*
   - Obesity: *Children and adults with high amounts of body fat are at a greater risk for heart disease. The heart has to work harder to pump blood through a body with many fat cells. Children who carry extra weight do not feel comfortable or confident in physical activities and are often easily fatigued.*
   - High blood pressure: *Blood vessels run throughout the body. As the heart forces the blood through these vessels, the blood is under pressure.* **Blood pressure** *is a measure of the force exerted against the walls of the blood vessels. Normal blood pressure is 120/80 or below. The higher number reflects the pressure exerted during the forceful contraction of the heart, and the lower number reflects the pressure during the heart's relaxation phase. The American Heart Association considers all blood pressures over 140/90 to be high. This level of pressure damages the blood vessels.*
   - Smoking: *Cigarettes contain nicotine that damages the insides of the blood vessels and increases blood pressure. Smoking cigarettes has been strongly linked to lung cancer. It also causes shortness of breath and fatigue.*
   - Stress and tension: *Fear, anxiety, frustration, fatigue, and hostility increase heart rate and blood pressure. In turn, the heart and blood vessels are adversely affected by the chemicals and hormones the body produces under stress.*
   - Cholesterol and fatty foods: *Everyone needs to have some cholesterol. In fact, the body depends on cholesterol to form cells and hormones. But, when people eat too many foods rich in saturated and trans fat, plus consume more than there commended 300 milligram of dietary cholesterol per day, the cholesterol builds up in the bloodstream. It can form a thick, hard coating on the inner walls of blood vessels, reducing blood flow to the heart and brain and increasing the risk of heart attack.*

4. Students then complete worksheet 46.2, Healthy Changes. This worksheet requires students to evaluate their personal food choices and activity habits. It also provides students with healthy guidelines and recommendations. Students describe their current habits and provide a plan.

Wrap It Up!

Focus on those lifestyle factors that are within the students' control, such as reducing the number of soda drinks consumed each week, not purchasing large portions of food (supersizing) at restaurants, and limiting the amount of time spent watching television. Ask students, *How can you increase your levels of physical activity and improve your eating habits for greater health benefits?*

Teaching Notes

Each lesson has suggested modifications, whenever possible, to adapt the concepts to younger or older students.

Modifications for Younger Students

Younger students can write one- or two-word answers on the Lifestyles Long Ago worksheet. They can also draw pictures for their answer. When discussing risk factors, focus on diet and physical activity.

Modifications for Older Students

Link this lesson with other schoolwide initiatives to promote health, such as a tobacco education program or a school health fair. For example, ask a school nurse to describe the health consequences of smoking.

Concept Development

1. During a class discussion, create a chart titled "Ways to Increase Physical Activity." Post the chart in the classroom for ongoing reference.

2. Before the lesson, students may want to interview their grandparents to gain a better perspective on how life has changed during this century.

3. To extend the discussion, use this additional activity:

- Divide the class into groups and ask them to list possible explanations for the following fact: People living in the United States are the world's most overweight people.
- After the groups share their lists of possible explanations, split the class into two-person teams. Have each team select an item from the list. Working in pairs, the students illustrate a positive behavior change that children or adults could implement in their daily lives to increase fitness and combat obesity. For example, instead of going to the car wash, people could wash the family car by hand. Challenge the teams to illustrate how life today has become less physically demanding and to make recommendations for increasing physical activity in daily life.

Assessment Options

Each lesson includes assessment options for the lesson and may include additional assessment options for the skills performed within a lesson.

For the Lesson

Students will have a basic understanding of the various risk factors for disease. By completing the Healthy Changes worksheet, students will be able to present plans for changes in their lifestyles to reduce risk of disease.

Worksheet 46.1: Lifestyles Long Ago

Name: _____

Instructions: In the "Lifestyles now" column, write in the modern-day equivalent to compare with the "Lifestyles long ago" column. Describe the differences between lifestyles long ago and lifestyles now.

Lifestyle components	Lifestyles long ago (1800s)	Lifestyles now (2000s)
Heating homes	Cutting trees; chopping wood; gathering limbs	
Travel to school	Walk; horse or mule	
Family transportation	Walk; horse or mule; carriage or wagon	
Cleaning clothes and houses	Hand scrubbing; line drying	
Tools	Hand tools (saws); tools powered by animals	
Food	Grow, hunt, trap, or trade	

From C. Hopper, B. Fisher, and K.D. Munoz, 2008, *Physical Activity and Nutrition for Health* (Champaign, IL: Human Kinetics).

Worksheet 46.2: Healthy Changes

Name: _____

Instructions: Fold your paper in half so that the right side is under the left side. On the left side of the paper, write what you consume daily (or the amount of time you spend daily) under each category.

Your daily routine	*Health recommendations*
1. Drinking soda:	**1.** Drinking soda: Drink plenty of water or moderate amounts of fruit juice; limit soda to a minimum. Soda is high in sugar and has little nutritional value.
2. Playing computer or video games and watching TV or movies:	**2.** Playing computer or video games and watching TV or movies: Limit these activities to one to two hours per day. Remove TV from bedrooms.
3. Eating breakfast foods:	**3.** Eating breakfast foods: Eat fortified, whole grain cereals or oatmeal with raisins every day for a good start to your day. These breakfast foods are high in fiber and nutrients, and they are low in fat.
4. Eating fast food:	**4.** Eating fast food: Limit fast-food intake to only occasionally. When you do eat fast food, make low-fat choices such as salads and fresh fruit.
5. Snacking on foods:	**5.** Snacking on foods: Snack on fruit (such as blueberries, oranges, kiwi, cantaloupe, or strawberries) and vegetables (including carrots and tomatoes).

Describe two behaviors that you can change and practice by tomorrow:

1.

2.

From C. Hopper, B. Fisher, and K.D. Munoz, 2008, *Physical Activity and Nutrition for Health* (Champaign, IL: Human Kinetics).

Lesson 47: Aerobic Bowling

Outcomes

At the end of this lesson, each student will be able to do the following:

▶ Perform the underhand roll.

▶ Understand number concepts and multiples of numbers.

Connections to Health Education Standards

▶ Practice of health-enhancing behaviors

Connections to Other Standards

▶ Math standards: number and operations

▶ Physical education standards: competency in motor skills and movement patterns

Connections to WOW! Lessons

▶ Red level: lesson 9, "Family Fitness Fun"

▶ Yellow level: lesson 9, "Family Fitness Fun"

▶ Orange level: lesson 9, "Family Fitness Fun"

WOW! Vocabulary

▶ multiples—Multiplying a number by itself (e.g., 2 × 2)

▶ technique—The correct execution of the performance.

Get Ready to WOW! 'Em

You will need the following:

▶ Playground balls (one for every four students)

▶ Bowling pins or cones (one for every four students). You could also use empty one-liter bottles filled with a small amount of sand.

Background Information

Learning the **technique** of the underhand roll provides students with a movement skill used in many activities and sports. The underhand roll is the technique used for bowling.

Now WOW! 'Em

1. Review the background information presented for this lesson with the class.

2. Organize your class into groups of four students. One student stands behind the bowling pin, and the other three students form a line 10 to 15 yards (9 to 14 m) away, depending on age and skill.

3. The first student in line rolls the ball underhand to try to **strike** or knock over the bowling pin. After rolling the ball, the student runs to take the place of the student standing behind the pin.

4. The student behind the pin collects the ball and runs back to give it to the next student in line. If the pin was knocked over, the bowler places the pin in an upright position.

5. Each time the pin is knocked over, the team shouts out a predetermined multiple number, such as **multiples** of 2, 4, 7, or any number.

6. Teams play until a designated number has been reached—for example, multiples of 7 are selected to play to 63. Students should perform underhand rolls with both the left and right hands.

Wrap It Up!

Ask students to identify strategies that worked well in their group. Strongly reinforce suggestions that focus on teamwork.

Teaching Notes

Each lesson has suggested modifications, whenever possible, to adapt the concepts to younger or older students.

Modifications for Younger Students

Use mathematics appropriate for the grade level—for example, first graders can use basic addition.

Modifications for Older Students

Increase the distance between the ball roller and the bowling pin to make the task more difficult. Increase the difficulty of the math. Reduce the size of the groups to three students to increase the speed of the activity.

Modifications for Students With Diabetes

Students with diabetes should have an individual plan for emergency protocols, medication, diet, and snacks. Diabetes is a chronic disease. Individuals with diabetes have high blood sugar, which can affect many organs and body systems. Regular exercise is usually part of the diabetes management plan, and aerobic exercise will lower blood glucose. Insulin is not produced by the pancreas in people with diabetes. Insulin gives the signal to move glucose from the blood to body cells. Students with diabetes should be protected from sunburn, falls, blows, and other skin-damaging situations. Encourage students to wear clean, dry socks and proper shoes. When planning class parties and special events, you should include alternative foods for students with diabetes.

Concept Development

1. With students in groups of three, one student stands in the middle of the other two students, who are positioned 20 yards (18 m) apart.

2. The outside students roll the ball to each other, and the student in the middle must jump over the ball as it is rolled.

3. After jumping over the ball, the middle student then turns and faces the other outside student, who will roll the ball back to the other student.

4. The middle student can also jump and turn in one motion.

5. Students roll the ball slowly and then increase the speed of the roll. The student in the middle can decide when to increase speed.

6. Have students change places after two minutes.

Assessment Options

Each lesson includes assessment options for the lesson and may include additional assessment options for the skills performed within a lesson.

For the Lesson

Students will demonstrate their knowledge of basic math by calling out the correct score in aerobic bowling.

For the Underhand Roll

▶ The student stands with one foot positioned farther forward than the other.

▶ The student holds the ball in the hand corresponding to the trailing leg.

▶ The arm swings forward as weight transfers from the rear to the front foot.

▶ The ball is released in front of the leading foot.

▶ The arm follows through with a swing in the direction of the target.

Lesson 48: Jump for Life

Outcomes

At the end of this lesson, each student will be able to do the following:

▶ Learn a variety of jump rope activities for self-testing.

▶ Practice a physical fitness activity.

Connections to Health Education Standards

▶ Health promotion and disease prevention

Connections to Other Standards

▶ Physical education standards: competency in motor skills and movement forms; appreciation for the value of physical activity

Connections to WOW! Lessons

▶ Red level: lesson 9, "Family Fitness Fun"

▶ Yellow level: lesson 9, "Family Fitness Fun"

▶ Purple level: lesson 7, "Hockey and Yoga"

WOW! Vocabulary

▶ circular—Moving the jump rope in the shape of a circle.

▶ straddle—To move the legs apart over the jump rope.

Get Ready to WOW! 'Em

You will need the following:

▶ Jump ropes (one per student)

▶ A bell with a clapper (for demonstrating the type of movement in the "ringing the bell" jump rope activity)

Background Information

Rope jumping is an ideal recreational activity for all ages. It is an indoor or outdoor activity that requires one piece of inexpensive equipment. Jumping rope provides opportunities for many movement combinations. After some basic moves are learned, students can add creativity and individuality to the activity. Jumping rope is a lifelong skill that is easy to integrate as a warm-up or station activity.

Now WOW! 'Em

1. Review the background information presented for this lesson with the class.

2. Select the proper rope length for each student. The student's height determines the correct length of the jump rope. When the student stands on the rope with feet together, the handles should reach to the underarms. Ropes may be shortened by

tying knots about four inches (10 cm) below the handles. General guidelines for rope length are as follows:

- Grades K through 3: 7 to 8 feet (2.1 to 2.4 m)
- Grades 4 through 6: 8 to 9 feet (2.4 to 2.7 m)

3. Students form pairs and take turns jumping. One partner performs the activity while the other one rests. Allow space between jumpers so ropes do not touch. Initially, use one-minute activity periods and gradually increase the duration. Figures 48.1 through 48.10 illustrate the specific moves for each type of jump. Start with the basic jump and build new jumps as skill levels improve. Give students the following instructions for each activity:

4. Basic jump (single bounce)

  1. *Start with the rope behind your feet and with your hands together in front.*

  2. *Swing your hands down to your sides, then back, up, and over. The rope will hit in front of your toes. Step over the rope and repeat until your arm motion is correct.*

  3. *Swing the rope over and jump with both feet as the rope comes down in front. Land on the balls of the feet. Keep jumping and turning the rope with a* **circular** *wrist motion.*

5. Basic jump (double bounce)

  1. *Start with the rope behind your feet and with your hands together in front.*

  2. *Swing the rope over and jump with both feet as the rope comes down in front. Land on the balls of the feet. As the rope goes overhead, jump again. Keep jumping and using a circular wrist motion to turn the rope.*

 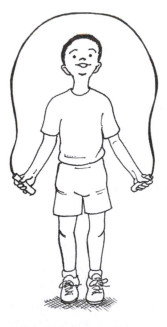

FIGURE 48.1   Basic jump (single bounce).

FIGURE 48.2   Basic jump (double bounce).

6. Side swing

  1. *Start with the rope behind your feet.*

  2. *Swing the rope up overhead, and as it comes down toward the feet, bring both hands to the right side so the rope hits the floor to the right of your feet.*

3. *Lift up with your hands, making a circular motion, and bring your hands across the front of your body to the left side so the rope hits the floor to the left of your feet.*

4. *Bring your hands back to the center and take the rope under your feet and back overhead to continue the sequence.*

FIGURE 48.3   Side swing.

7. Double side swing and jump

1. *Swing the rope to the right side.*

2. *Swing the rope to the left side.*

3. *As the rope comes down on the third turn, spread your hands apart and jump over the rope.*

FIGURE 48.4   Double side swing and jump.

8. Single side swing and jump

1. *Swing the rope to the left side.*
2. *On the next rope turn, spread your hands apart and jump.*
3. *As the rope comes over, swing it to the right side.*
4. *On the next turn, spread your hands apart again and jump.*

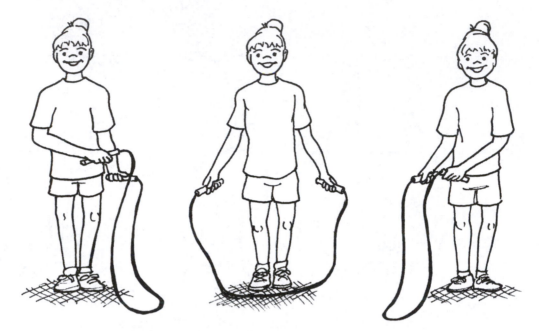

FIGURE 48.5   Single side swing and jump.

9. Skier

1. *Jump over the rope sideways 6 to 12 inches (15 to 31 cm) to the left and land on both feet together.*
2. *Jump over the rope sideways 6 to 12 inches to the right and land on both feet together.*

FIGURE 48.6   Skier.

10. Ringing the bell
    1. *Jump forward 6 to 12 inches over the swinging rope. Land on both feet together.*
    2. *Jump backward 6 to 12 inches over the swinging rope. Land on both feet together.*

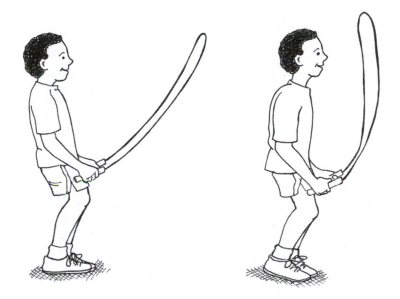

FIGURE 48.7   Ringing the bell.

11. Side **straddle**
    1. *Jump over the rope and land with your feet spread shoulder-width apart.*
    2. *Jump over the rope again and land with your feet together.*

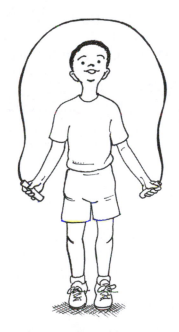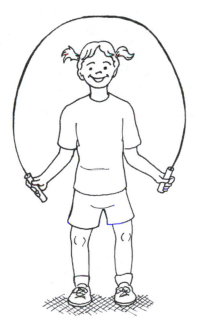

FIGURE 48.8   Side straddle.

12. Forward straddle

   1. *Jump over the rope and land with your left foot forward and your right foot back. The feet should be about 8 to 10 inches (20 to 25 cm) apart.*

   2. *Jump over the rope again and reverse your feet before landing.*

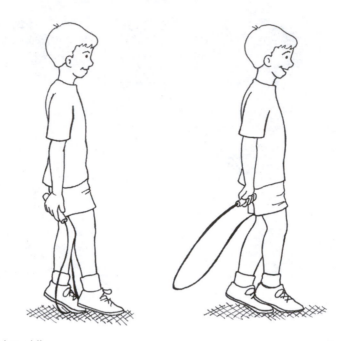

FIGURE 48.9   Forward straddle.

13. Moving on

   1. *Start by stepping over the rope while jogging in place.*

   2. *Step over the rope while slowly jogging forward.*

   3. *Complete three or four turns and return to the same place, then continue to increase the length of the jog.*

FIGURE 48.10   Moving on.

Wrap It Up!

Use the Intensity Guide in lesson 5 (page 53) to help students evaluate their effort. After the students have learned the jumps, encourage them to increase the sustained effort.

Teaching Notes

Each lesson has suggested modifications, whenever possible, to adapt the concepts to younger or older students.

Modifications for Younger Students

As an introduction to jump rope movements, teach students to jump in place without turning the rope and to swing the rope from side to side without jumping. Students can start by stepping over a rope on the ground. Ensure safety by providing young students with some personal space to jump rope. To provide a safe jumping area, use Poly spots to mark out designated locations for students.

Modifications for Older Students

Students who can jump well may assist others. Create pairs of students so that a more-skilled jumper can assist a lesser skilled jumper. Have partners create a two-person routine where they perform the same movements in time with each other.

Modifications for Students With Disabilities

Introduce each activity and have students practice without a rope. Students in wheelchairs can place the rope on the ground and move their wheelchairs over and back. Students who cannot swing and jump at the same time may be able to jump over a slow-moving long rope held by other students. Students with balance problems can step over a rope on the ground.

Concept Development

1. Introduce music with a beat.
2. The activities are designed progressively. Teach the activities in sequence. Teach one or two activities per session, and as the students' skill level progresses, introduce a new activity to challenge them.
3. Students can develop jump rope routines by combining activities.

Assessment Options

Each lesson includes assessment options for the lesson and may include additional assessment options for the skills performed within a lesson.

For the Basic Jump (Single Bounce)

▶ The head is erect, not leaning forward or backward.
▶ The feet are close together with weight on the balls of the feet.
▶ The hands are kept at waist level and just in front of the body.
▶ The student jumps once for each rope revolution.
▶ The feet and knees are kept close together.
▶ The student makes small circles with the wrists.
▶ The student bends the knees slightly.

▸ The student jumps only 1 or 2 inches off the ground.

▸ Students should also practice the backward basic jump by starting with the rope in front of the feet, lifting it up over the head, and jumping as it comes down behind.

For the Basic Jump (Double Bounce)

▸ The student jumps twice for each rope revolution and turns the rope slowly.

▸ Students should start with the single bounce because it transfers to other skills.

For the Side Swing

▸ The student swings the rope slowly.

▸ The student keeps one handle in each hand.

▸ The student keeps the hands and feet close together.

▸ The student keeps the feet together but doesn't jump.

▸ The student keeps the hands close to the side (the rope should hit the floor near the feet).

For the Double Side Swing and Jump

▸ See tips for the side swing.

▸ The student stands during the side swings.

▸ Students should practice swinging to the left side first.

For the Single Side Swing and Jump

▸ See tips for the side swing and the double side swing and jump.

▸ On the side swing, the hand crossing in front of the body should extend past the other hand.

For the Skier

▸ The student keeps the feet together.

▸ The student jumps in small steps.

▸ The student stays on the balls of the feet.

For Ringing the Bell

▸ The student keeps the feet together.

▸ The student uses small steps forward or back.

▸ The student stays on the balls of the feet.

▸ The motion is similar to a bell clapper swinging back and forth.

For the Side Straddle

▸ The student waits until the rope passes under the feet before spreading the feet apart.

For the Forward Straddle

▸ The student leans slightly forward.

▸ Students can add a basic jump between straddles.

For Moving On

▸ The student keeps the hands at waist level.

▸ Students should start slowly and gradually increase speed.

MyPyramid Food Guide

Using a food guide makes planning healthy meals much easier. In this part, students will learn about the MyPyramid developed by the U.S. Department of Agriculture. Students will use the MyPyramid to design power meals and snacks, and they will learn how to determine the number and size of the servings they should eat.

Lesson 49: Pyramid Power

Outcomes

At the end of this lesson, each student will be able to do the following:

▶ Name the six food groups in the MyPyramid.

▶ Name at least one key nutrient found in each food group.

▶ Plan a snack and a meal that contains at least one food from each of the six food groups in the MyPyramid.

Connections to Health Education Standards

▶ Health promotion and disease prevention

▶ Access to valid health information, products, and services

Connections to Other Standards

▶ Science standards: science in personal and social perspectives

Connections to WOW! Lessons

▶ Red level: lesson 12, "Food for Thought"

▶ Red level: lesson 14, "Tacos by Cody"

▶ Red level: lesson 16, "All Living Things"

▶ Yellow level: lesson 12, "Food for Thought"

▶ Green level: lesson 12, "Tacos by Cody"

▶ Green level: lesson 13, "Oodles of Noodles"

▶ Green level: lesson 14, "The Balancing Act"

▶ Blue level: lesson 11, "Moderation"

▶ Purple level: lesson 11, "V Is for Variety"

WOW! Vocabulary

▶ food groups—A classification of foods into groupings that contain similar nutrient content.

▶ MyPyramid—A guide developed by the U.S. Department of Agriculture that provides information on how many servings a person should eat from the six food groups.

▶ nutrient-dense foods—Foods that supply generous amounts of vitamins and minerals with few calories.

Get Ready to WOW! 'Em

You will need the following:

▶ Large strips of colored construction paper, approximately 3 feet (91 cm) in length (the colors that make up the MyPyramid)

▶ Food cards (use the cards from lesson 3)

▶ Worksheet 49.1, MyPyramid (one copy per student, plus one transparency)

▶ Worksheet 49.2, Pyramid Power (one copy per pair of students)

▶ Overhead projector and transparency pens

Background Information

MyPyramid was designed to help consumers plan healthy diets. MyPyramid is composed of vertical strips of different colors and widths. Each color represents a **food group,** while the width of the strip represents how much or how little of the food people should eat. The first strip on the left is orange and represents the grains group, followed by green for vegetables, red for fruits, yellow for oils, blue for milk, and purple for meat and beans. Notice the thin yellow line between the red and blue groups. This thin line represents fats, oils, and discretionary sweets, which people need very little of each day. For more detailed information regarding each group, go to the MyPyramid Web site at www.MyPyramid.gov.

Each group contains important nutrients that people need for energy and health. Some foods within each food group are more **nutrient-dense** than others. For example, oranges have more vitamin C than apples. Choosing a wide variety of foods within each group will improve the overall quality of the diet.

▶ Grains: This group contains foods made from rice, oats, wheat, cornmeal, barley, or any grain. Products such as bread, cereals, pasta, and rice are examples of foods found in this group. Students should be encouraged to choose whole grain foods (such as whole wheat bread, brown rice, whole rolled oats, and bulgur) rather than refined grains (such as white bread, white rice, and quick cooking oats). The grain group provides carbohydrate, protein, vitamins, and minerals as important nutrients required for health.

▶ Vegetables: Any vegetable or vegetable juice is considered part of this group. Encourage students to eat many different colors of vegetables (e.g., dark green, orange, and red) each day because the colors reflect the vitamin content of the food. This group contains carbohydrate, protein, vitamins, and minerals as important nutrients required for health.

▶ Fruits: Any fruit or 100 percent fruit juice counts as a serving from this group. Encourage students to eat at least two servings per day of a variety of different fruits (fresh, frozen, canned, or dried). This group contains carbohydrate, vitamins, and minerals required for health.

▶ Dairy: Dairy products—including milk, cheese, and yogurt—are part of this group. Encourage students to consume low- or nonfat dairy choices. This group provides carbohydrate, protein, fat, vitamins, and minerals required for health.

▶ Meat and beans: This food group includes meat, poultry, fish, and eggs, as well as plants such as dried beans or peas, nuts, and seeds. Dried beans and peas are also part of the vegetables group. Encourage students to choose lean or low-fat meats. This group contains protein, fat, vitamins, and minerals as well as carbohydrate from the plant protein.

▶ Oils: Foods in this classification include all oils, as well as fats from fish and nuts. Most plant and seed oils are high in healthy fats and do not contain cholesterol.

The only exceptions are the oils called tropical oils which include coconut and palm kernel oil and are high in saturated fats.

Now WOW! 'Em

1. Begin the class by showing students the transparency of the MyPyramid diagram. Ask the students if they recognize the pyramid. Describe what it is and the purpose of using the pyramid as a guide for planning food intake each day. Be sure to share the background information presented for this lesson.

2. Hand out worksheet 49.1, MyPyramid, to each student. Ask students to fill in the worksheet as you discuss each food group. Begin to describe the six different food groups that make up the pyramid.

3. Start by putting the orange strip of paper on the board and telling students that this represents the grains group. Ask the students if they know which foods belong in this group. As they mention the right foods, put the pictures of grain foods (the food cards) on the orange strip.

4. Following the same procedure, continue through the strips of colored food groups (moving from left to right) until you complete the purple group. Do not put the yellow (oils) group on the board until last.

5. When all but the yellow group is finished, take the yellow strip of paper and put it in the correct place between the red and blue strips. Explain to the class, *This group contains the healthy plant oils, nuts, and fish oils. Your diet should be low in this group, which is why the yellow strip is small.* Follow the same procedure as you did for the other food groups.

Wrap It Up!

Once students understand the food groups, nutrients, and typical foods found in the MyPyramid, the students should form pairs to complete worksheet 49.2, Pyramid Power. Instruct the students to choose foods from the MyPyramid groups to complete each section of the worksheet.

Teaching Notes

Each lesson has suggested modifications, whenever possible, to adapt the concepts to younger or older students.

Modifications for Younger Students

To modify the lesson for younger students, have them draw foods on the Pyramid Power worksheet rather than write the words. Complete the lesson as a class activity rather than in student groups.

Modifications for Older Students

None.

Concept Development

1. Assign the students to each develop a riddle that can be used to test their knowledge about foods in each of the food groups. Here are some examples:

- "What is round and purple, grows in a bunch, and is found in the fruits group?"
- "What is white, pours, and is found in the dairy group?"

2. Ask the students to each choose a food from the different food groups and explore the following questions:
   - *Where is the food grown (if it's a plant)?*
   - *What are some recipes that use the food as a main ingredient?*
   - *Name some different cultures that use the food as a staple.*
   - *How is the food processed?*

3. Use other activities found at www.MyPyramid.gov to enhance student learning.

Assessment Options

Each lesson includes assessment options for the lesson and may include additional assessment options for the skills performed within a lesson.

For the Lesson

Students will demonstrate their knowledge of the MyPyramid by completing the Pyramid Power worksheet and through their participation in the class discussions.

Worksheet 49.1: My Pyramid

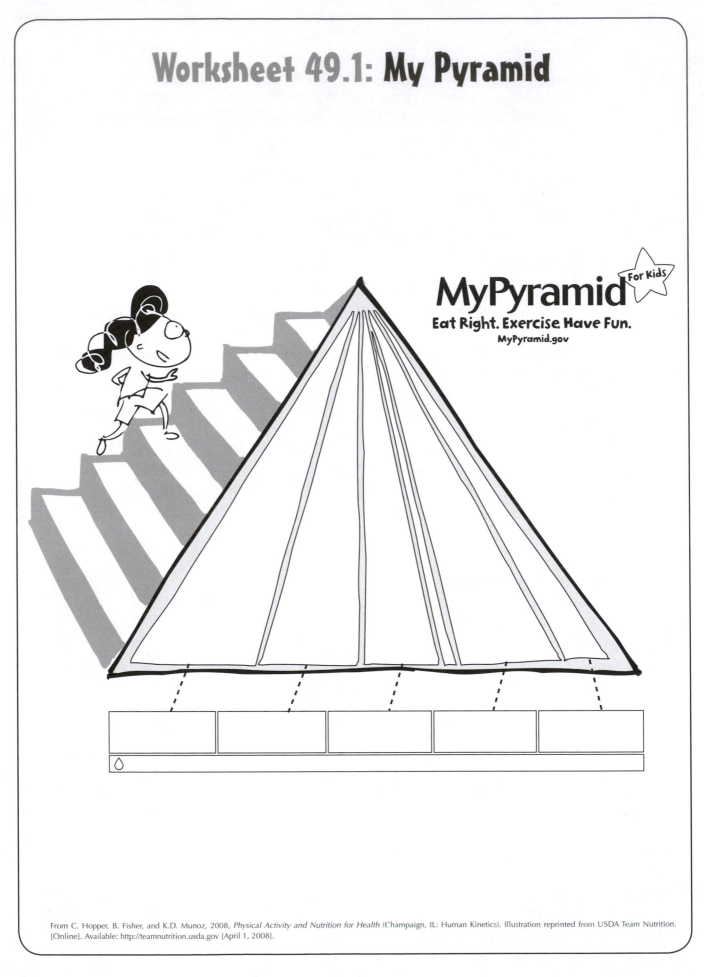

MyPyramid For Kids
Eat Right. Exercise. Have Fun.
MyPyramid.gov

Worksheet 49.2: Pyramid Power

Instructions: Your team will be competing in the Pyramid Power competition to see which team can construct the strongest power snacks and power meals.

Power Snack

Identify power snacks based on the MyPyramid:
- ▶ List two snacks that contain a food from at least one food group.
- ▶ List two snacks that contain a powerful carbohydrate source.

1. _____   1. _____

2. _____   2. _____

Identify snacks that will weaken your power:
- ▶ List two snacks containing added fats or oils.
- ▶ List two snacks containing discretionary sugars.

1. _____   1. _____

2. _____   2. _____

Power Meal

Create a meal from the MyPyramid that
- ▶ contains at least five foods from the MyPyramid,
- ▶ contains at least one food from each food group, and
- ▶ contains nutritious sources of carbohydrate and protein.

1. _____

2. _____

3. _____

4. _____

5. _____

6. _____

(continued)

From C. Hopper, B. Fisher, and K.D. Munoz, 2008, *Physical Activity and Nutrition for Health* (Champaign, IL: Human Kinetics).

(continued)

Identify meals that will weaken your power:

▶ Create a meal containing too much fat or sugar.

▶ Create a meal that does not contain a variety of foods from all six food groups.

1. _____   **1.** _____

2. _____   **2.** _____

3. _____   **3.** _____

4. _____   **4.** _____

5. _____   **5.** _____

From C. Hopper, B. Fisher, and K.D. Munoz, 2008, *Physical Activity and Nutrition for Health* (Champaign, IL: Human Kinetics).

(continued)

Lesson 50: Stack 'Em Up

Outcomes

At the end of this lesson, students will be able to do the following:

- ▶ Describe the number of recommended daily servings from each of the food groups in the MyPyramid.
- ▶ Analyze their food intake compared to the guidelines provided by the MyPyramid.

Connections to Health Education Standards

- ▶ Health promotion and disease prevention

Connections to Other Standards

- ▶ Science standards: science in personal and social perspectives

Connections to WOW! Lessons

- ▶ Green level: lesson 10, "Tasty Tillies"
- ▶ Green level: lesson 11, "Soup and Salad?"
- ▶ Green level: lesson 13, "Oodles of Noodles"
- ▶ Green level: lesson 14, "The Balancing Act"

WOW! Vocabulary

- ▶ portion—The amount of a specific food an individual eats at a meal. It could be one or more serving sizes of a specific food depending on an individual's body size, age, and activity level. Larger portions usually contain more than one serving; smaller portions usually contain less than one serving.
- ▶ serving—A unit of measure used to describe the total amount of foods recommended daily from each of the food groups.

Get Ready to WOW! 'Em

You will need the following:

- ▶ Colored boxes representing each of the six food groups in the MyPyramid. The larger the box, the more visual the experience for the students. You'll need at least eight boxes of each color that correspond to the colors on the pyramid: orange (grains), green (vegetables), red (fruits), yellow (oils), blue (milk), and purple (meats and beans).
- ▶ Worksheet 50.1, Stack 'Em Up! (one copy per student)
- ▶ Worksheet 49.1, MyPyramid (one copy per student from lesson 49)
- ▶ Examples of food portion sizes, such as 1 cup (240 ml) of milk, $1/2$ ounce (42 g) of hard cheese, 1 cup (40 g) of dry cereal, half a cup (87 g) of cooked rice, and half a cup (120 ml) of fruit juice

Background Information

The food choices that people make each day will affect their overall health and well-being. To be healthy and maintain a healthy body weight, people need to know what types of food to eat and how much of each food to eat. A tool was developed by the U.S. Department of Agriculture to illustrate the types of food as well as the **serving** size and **portions** that people should be consuming. This tool, called MyPyramid, provides these guidelines based on age, sex, and activity level. For more information on the types of foods and the amounts suggested in MyPyramid, refer to lesson 49 or visit www. MyPyramid.gov.

Now WOW! 'Em

1. Review the background information presented for this lesson with the class.

2. Using worksheet 49.1 on page 310, review with students the MyPyramid and the six food groups.

3. Ask for six volunteers from the class. Instruct each volunteer to pick one of the six food groups: grains, vegetables, fruits, oils, milk, or meat and beans.

4. Ask each volunteer to predict how many servings a person needs each day from the chosen food group. Using the colored blocks that correspond to the food groups, the students stack the boxes on top of each other based on their prediction (one colored box = one serving). Make sure the stacks of boxes are in the correct order corresponding to MyPyramid: orange, green, red, yellow, blue, and purple.

5. After each volunteer has completed the stacking, ask the rest of the class whether they think the predictions are correct. Make any changes they suggest.

6. Reveal to the class which food groups are correct and make any needed changes. The final stacking should look like this: six orange, three green, two red, three yellow, three blue, and five purple boxes.

7. Before moving on, make sure the students know the number of servings from each food group.

8. Next, hand out worksheet 50.1, Stack 'Em Up! Show the students examples of food serving sizes using typical foods and measuring utensils. Ask them to write down what they ate yesterday and their estimated totals for each meal based on the food equivalents listed on the handout. Students will need to add up their totals and place them in the blank in the right column.

Wrap It Up!

Once students have finished worksheet 50.1, ask them how they stacked up. If they didn't eat enough vegetables, ask them to write in the blank provided how they are going to improve their diet tomorrow.

Teaching Notes

Each lesson has suggested modifications, whenever possible, to adapt the concepts to younger or older students.

Modifications for Younger Students

Younger students may not be able to remember what they ate yesterday. To modify the lesson for them, ask them to list what they normally eat for breakfast. You can also let them use the school menu to complete the assignment.

Modifications for Older Students

None.

Concept Development

Ask the students to keep a food diary for three days to see how close they come to meeting the guidelines provided by the MyPyramid.

Assessment Options

Each lesson includes assessment options for the lesson and may include additional assessment options for the skills performed within a lesson.

For the Lesson

Students will demonstrate their knowledge of the MyPyramid through their participation in the class activity and completion of the Stack 'Em Up! worksheet.

Worksheet 50.1: Stack 'Em Up!

Name: _____

Instructions: How did your meals stack up yesterday? Can you stack 'em up higher tomorrow?

How did you stack up yesterday? In this column, list the food you ate for each meal yesterday.	Food group	Goal (based on 1,800 calories)	List each food you ate in its food group	Estimate your total for each food group
Breakfast: _____ _____ _____ _____	Grains	6 ounces (168 g) (1 ounce = • 1 slice bread, • 1 cup [40 g] cereal, or • 1/2 cup [87 g] cooked rice or pasta)		_____ ounces
Lunch: _____ _____ _____ _____	Vegetables	2 1/2 cups (450 g)		_____ cups
Snack: _____ _____ _____ _____ _____	Fruits	1 1/2 cups (375 g)		_____ cups
Dinner: _____ _____ _____ _____	Oils	3 teaspoons		_____ teaspoons

From C. Hopper, B. Fisher, and K.D. Munoz, 2008, *Physical Activity and Nutrition for Health* (Champaign, IL: Human Kinetics).

(continued)

(continued)

How did you stack up yesterday? In this column, list the food you ate for each meal yesterday.	Food group	Goal (based on 1,800 calories)	List each food you ate in its food group	Estimate your total for each food group
	Dairy	3 cups (1 c = 1 c yogurt [245 g] or milk [240 ml], or 1 1/2 oz [42 g] of cheese)		_____ cups
	Meat and beans	5 ounces (140 g) (1 ounce = • 1 ounce [28 g] meat, chicken, turkey, or fish; • 1 egg; • 1 tablespoon peanut butter; • 1/2 ounce [14 g] nuts; or • 1/4 cup [59 ml] dry beans)		_____ ounces

How did you stack up?   ❏ Tall   ❏ Average   ❏ Came up short

How can you improve tomorrow? _____

_____

_____

_____

_____

_____

_____

_____

From C. Hopper, B. Fisher, and K.D. Munoz, 2008, *Physical Activity and Nutrition for Health* (Champaign, IL: Human Kinetics).

Food Portions

One of the reasons people overeat is that they don't know how much food equals a portion. In the upcoming lessons, students will learn more about the recommendations for food portions listed in the MyPyramid.

Lesson 51: How Do You Measure Up?

Outcomes

At the end of this lesson, each student will be able to do the following:

▸ Identify the correct portion sizes for various foods.

▸ Plan a balanced breakfast.

Connections to Health Education Standards

▸ Health promotion and disease prevention

Connections to Other Standards

▸ Science standards: science in personal and social perspectives

Connections to WOW! Lessons

▸ Red level: lesson 12, "Food for Thought"

▸ Green level: lesson 10, "Tasty Tillie"

▸ Green level: lesson 11, "Soup and Salad?"

▸ Blue level: lesson 11, "Moderation"

▸ Purple level: lesson 11, "V Is for Variety"

WOW! Vocabulary

▸ serving size—The MyPyramid serving sizes specify the amount of a food that provides a designated amount of certain nutrients (e.g., 1 cup of milk, 1 slice of bread).

Get Ready to WOW! 'Em

You will need the following (solid measurements expressed in cups have metric equivalents expressed in grams in parentheses; where you see "measuring cup" in equipment lists, use a small coffee cup):

▸ Paper bowls, paper plates, and 10-ounce (~300 ml) paper cups (one each per group of students)

▸ Six instruction cards (one for each food group station; see figure 51.1)

▸ Worksheet 51.1, How Do You Measure Up? (one copy per student)

▸ Seven stations with the following items at each station:

1. Puzzle station—Measured foods, one from each food group, labeled A, B, C, D, E, and F. For example, this station could contain 3 cups (120 g) of breakfast cereal in a bowl, 1 banana, 1 egg, $^1/_2$ cup (270 g) of vegetables, 1 tablespoon of margarine, and 2 cups (480 ml) of milk in a glass. Some of these foods should be the correct serving size while others should not be. Indicate the amount of each food at the station.

2. Grains station—An empty box of cereal, a large bowl filled with cereal (at least 3 cups, or 120 g), a 1-cup measuring cup, and an instruction card.

3. Vegetable station—2 cups (~360 g) of any vegetable in a large bowl (frozen peas or corn works well for this station), a 1-cup measuring cup, and an instruction card.

4. Fruit station—Chopped fruit or canned fruit (drained) in a large bowl (fruit cocktail or chopped fresh fruit works well for this station), a half-cup measuring cup, and an instruction card.

5. Meat and beans station—5 or 6 ounces (140 to 168 g) of lunch meat or salami, a scale that weighs in ounces (or grams if you use metric), wax paper, and an instruction card.

6. Dairy station—A small pitcher of milk, a 1-cup measuring cup, and an instruction card.

7. Oils station—A bottle of oil, measuring spoons, and an instruction card.

▶ Transparency of MyPyramid from lesson 49

▶ Overhead projector and transparency pens

Background Information

MyPyramid is a guide designed to help people choose the right foods and the correct portion sizes in order to consume adequate calories and nutrients. Each food has an amount per serving based on weight or volume. Knowing the amount of each food that represents one serving is an important tool for maintaining a healthy lifestyle and a healthy weight. People need to understand **serving sizes** so they can eat the proper amounts from each food group. Here are some useful measurements when determining serving sizes within each food group:

1. Grains—Any of the following can count as a 1-ounce equivalent: 1 slice of bread; 1 cup (40 g) of ready-to-eat breakfast cereal; half a cup (~90 g) of cooked rice, pasta, or cooked cereal.

2. Vegetables—Any of the following can count as 1 cup: 1 cup (180 g) of raw or cooked vegetables, 1 cup (240 ml) of vegetable juice, or 2 cups (300 g) of raw leafy greens.

3. Fruits—Any of the following can count as 1 cup: 1 cup (250 g) of fruit or 100 percent fruit juice (240 ml), or half a cup of dried fruit.

4. Dairy—Any of the following can count as 1 cup: 1 cup of milk or yogurt, 1.5 ounces (42 g) of natural cheese, or 2 ounces (56 g) of processed cheese.

5. Meat and beans—Any of the following can count as a 1-ounce equivalent: 1 ounce (28 g) of meat, poultry, or fish; 1 egg; 1 tablespoon of peanut butter; a quarter cup of cooked dry beans; half an ounce (14 g) of nuts or seeds.

6. Oils—1 teaspoon of any oil counts as a serving.

Now WOW! 'Em

1. Before class, set up the seven stations as indicated in the "Get Ready to WOW! 'Em" section.

2. Begin the lesson by reviewing the background information presented for this lesson with the class. Use the transparency to describe the purpose of the MyPyramid. Ask students, *What does a serving size from the milk group look like?* (1 cup)

3. Instruct the students to observe the food at the puzzle station. Tell the students, *Predict which of the foods at the puzzle station represent a correct serving size.* Students should record their predictions on worksheet 51.1, How Do You Measure Up?

4. After making their predictions, students form groups of two or three students each. Explain the procedures they will follow: *Each group will be assigned to a station. Read and follow the instructions on the card at each table. After completing the task at the station, each group will move to the next station. This continues until each group has completed every station.*

5. After they have finished, ask the students to go back to the puzzle station and see if their earlier predictions were correct.

6. Go over the MyPyramid again and discuss the students' impressions. Ask students, *Were your predictions correct? Do you usually eat the amount suggested for each serving size?*

Wrap It Up!

To complete the lesson, ask each student to plan a breakfast with the correct serving size for each food they choose. Be sure to have them include at least one grain, one milk, and one fruit serving in their meal.

Teaching Notes

Each lesson has suggested modifications, whenever possible, to adapt the concepts to younger or older students.

Modifications for Younger Students

If students are too young to measure out the serving sizes, complete the activity as a class with the instructor doing the measuring.

Modifications for Older Students

None.

Concept Development

Assign the students to keep a food journal of the serving sizes they eat for one day. Then have them write a short paragraph about their dietary intake.

Assessment Options

Each lesson includes assessment options for the lesson and may include additional assessment options for the skills performed within a lesson.

For the Lesson

By completing the class activity and planning a breakfast, students will demonstrate their ability to recognize the correct serving size for each food group.

FIGURE 51.1   Instruction cards for food stations.

Dairy Station

Serving sizes of milk are measured in fluid ounces. One cup, or 8 fluid ounces (240 ml), of milk or 1 carton of yogurt equals one serving.

1. Measure one serving of milk using the measuring cup. Pour the serving of milk into the paper cup provided. Draw a line around the outside of the cup at the top of the milk line.
2. Write down examples of portion sizes for milk and yogurt on your handout.
3. Pour the serving of milk back into the pitcher and move to the next station.

From C. Hopper, B. Fisher, and K.D. Munoz, 2008, *Physical Activity and Nutrition for Health* (Champaign, IL: Human Kinetics).

Grain Station

Read the label on the cereal box. What are the two ways that the serving size is measured? (by volume and weight)

1. Using the measuring cup, measure out the amount of cereal that equals one serving size.
2. Pour this amount of cereal into the paper bowl provided.
3. Mark the level of cereal with a pencil or pen on the inside of the bowl.
4. After marking the paper bowl, pour the cereal back into the large bowl at the station.
5. Write on your handout the amount of food that equals a serving size for the following, then move to next station:
   - Bread = 1 slice
   - Cereal = 1 ounce (40 g)
   - Pasta or rice = half a cup (87 g)

From C. Hopper, B. Fisher, and K.D. Munoz, 2008, *Physical Activity and Nutrition for Health* (Champaign, IL: Human Kinetics).

(continued)

FIGURE 51.1   Instruction cards for food stations. *(continued)*

Fruit Station

Serving sizes of fruit vary. For example, half a banana, 10 grapes, 1 small apple or orange, or half a cup (125 g) of chopped fruit equals one serving size.

1. Measure one serving of the fruit at this station using the measuring cup provided.
2. Pour this measured amount onto a paper plate and draw an outline of the portion size.
3. Label the outline "fruit" and indicate the amount on the paper plate.
4. Write down examples of portion sizes for fruit on your handout.
5. Return the fruit to the large bowl at the station and move to the next station.

Oils Station

For oils, one teaspoon equals one serving size. Solid fats are considered discretionary or *extra* foods. For fat products such as margarine or butter, 1 teaspoon is a serving. Mayonnaise is not 100 percent fat, nor is peanut butter; therefore, 1 tablespoon is a serving.

1. Measure one serving of oil and place it on the paper plate. Draw a line around the oil on the paper plate. Label the oil and indicate the serving size.
2. Write down examples of portion sizes for oils on your worksheet.
3. Replace the lid on the oil and move to the next station.

FIGURE 51.1   Instruction cards for food stations. *(continued)*

Meat and Beans Station

The meat and beans group includes meat, poultry, fish, dried beans, eggs, and nuts. One serving is equal to 2 to 3 ounces (56 to 84 g) of cooked meat, poultry, or fish; a half cup of cooked dry beans; two tablespoons of peanut butter; two eggs; or a quarter cup (36 g) of nuts.

1. Measure one serving of meat using the scale provided.
2. Place it on the paper plate and draw an outline of the portion size. Label the outline "meat" and indicate the amount on the paper plate.
3. Write down examples of portion sizes for meat on your handout.
4. Replace the meat and move to the next station.

Vegetable Station

Half a cup (90 g) of cooked vegetables equals a serving. The exception is a vegetable such as lettuce, where 1 cup (150 g) equals one serving.

1. Measure out one serving of the vegetables using the measuring cup.
2. Pour this measured amount onto a paper plate and draw an outline of the portion size. Label the outline "vegetable" and write the amount on the plate.
3. Write down examples of portion sizes for vegetables on your handout.
4. Return the vegetables to the large bowl at the station and move to the next station.

Worksheet 51.1:
How Do You Measure Up?

Name: _____

Puzzle Station

List food	*Amount*	*Prediction (Y/N)*	*Actual (Y/N)*	*Difference*
A._____	_____	_____	_____	_____
B._____	_____	_____	_____	_____
C._____	_____	_____	_____	_____
D._____	_____	_____	_____	_____
E._____	_____	_____	_____	_____
F._____	_____	_____	_____	_____

List all possible servings.

Fruit station

Vegetable station

Meat and beans station

Oils station

Dairy station

Grains station

From C. Hopper, B. Fisher, and K.D. Munoz, 2008, *Physical Activity and Nutrition for Health* (Champaign, IL: Human Kinetics).

Lesson 52: Sizing Up Our Servings

Outcomes

At the end of this lesson, each student will be able to do the following:

▶ Choose common objects that represent serving sizes from MyPyramid.

Connections to Health Education Standards

▶ Health promotion and disease prevention

Connections to Other Standards

▶ Science standards: science in personal and social perspectives

Connections to WOW! Lessons

▶ Green level: lesson 10, "Tasty Tillies"
▶ Green level: lesson 11, "Soup and Salad"
▶ Green level: lesson 13, "Oodles of Noodles"
▶ Green level: lesson 14, "The Balancing Act"
▶ Blue level: lesson 11, "Moderation"
▶ Purple level: lesson 11, "V Is for Variety"

WOW! Vocabulary

None.

Get Ready to WOW! 'Em

You will need the following:

▶ Worksheet 52.1, Sizing Up Our Servings (one copy per student)
▶ A variety of common objects to represent serving sizes, such as the objects in the following list. Have the samples ready to show the students after they have completed the prediction activity.

- Golf ball = 2 tablespoons
- Tennis ball = 1/2 to 3/4 (115 g to 170 g) cup or 1 small fruit
- Fist = 1 cup (230 g)
- Baseball = 1 cup (230 g)
- Yo-yo = 1 standard-size bagel
- Deck of cards = 3 ounces (90 g) of meat
- Thumb = 1 ounce (30 g) of cheese
- Palm of the hand = 3 ounces (90 g) of meat
- Four stacked dice = 1 ounce (30 g) of cheese
- Computer zip disk = 1 slice of bread
- Computer mouse = 1/2 to 3/4 (115 g to 170 g) cup or 3 ounces (90 g) of meat
- Ice cream scoop = 1/2 cup (115 g)

Background Information

People should learn to recognize the correct serving size of different foods. This will help them plan healthier meals and maintain a healthy weight by eating the appropriate number of calories. Serving sizes can be compared to familiar objects to provide a convenient guide to eating. For example, a tennis ball is similar to a small piece of fruit or a measure of 1/2 to 3/4 cup; a computer mouse is similar to a 3-ounce (84 g) chicken breast or a measure of 1/2 to 3/4 cup.

Now WOW! 'Em

1. Before class, prepare a set of the common objects listed in the "Get Ready to WOW! 'Em" section along with their foods (such as 4 dice = 1 ounce [28 g] of cheese), as pictured on worksheet 52.1. Don't let the students see these items before you're ready.

2. Begin the lesson by reviewing the background information presented for this lesson with the class. Discuss the purpose of the MyPyramid and how important eating the correct serving sizes is to health.

3. Give each student a copy of worksheet 52.1, Sizing Up Our Servings. Instruct students to predict the serving size represented by each common object pictured. They should use the list of serving sizes provided.

4. After students are finished making their predictions, show the students the setup of common objects and the foods they represent. Go down the list on the worksheet and ask the students to check whether they were correct in their predictions. Ask students, *Were your predictions correct?*

Wrap It Up!

To complete the lesson, ask the students, *Can you think of any other common household objects that you could use to represent correct serving sizes?*

Teaching Notes

Each lesson has suggested modifications, whenever possible, to adapt the concepts to younger or older students.

Modifications for Younger Students

For younger students, go through the activity as a class rather than individually.

Modifications for Older Students

None.

Concept Development

Assign the students to bring at least one more object from home that represents a serving size. Place all the new objects and those used in this lesson on a display to remind students of the correct serving sizes.

Assessment Options

Each lesson includes assessment options for the lesson and may include additional assessment options for the skills performed within a lesson.

For the Lesson

By completing the class activity, students will demonstrate their ability to recognize the correct serving size for each food.

Worksheet 52.1: Sizing Up Our Servings

Name: _____

Instructions: Common household items can be used as a model for different portions of foods. Predict which serving size is represented by each of the following items. Use these serving sizes as a guide. Two of the serving sizes will be used more than once.

1 cup (230 g)

1/2 cup (115 g)

3/4 cup (170 g)

1 ounce (30 g)

1 teaspoon

1 tablespoon

1 piece of fruit

1 slice of bread

Household item	Predict the serving size	Actual serving size
Golf ball		
Tennis ball		
Closed fist		
Baseball		
Yo-yo		

From C. Hopper, B. Fisher, and K.D. Munoz, 2008, *Physical Activity and Nutrition for Health* (Champaign, IL: Human Kinetics).

(continued)

(continued)

Household item	Predict the serving size	Actual serving size
Deck of cards		
Thumb		
Open hand		
Four stacked dice		
Computer Zip disc		
Computer mouse		
Ice cream scoop		

From C. Hopper, B. Fisher, and K.D. Munoz, 2008, *Physical Activity and Nutrition for Health* (Champaign, IL: Human Kinetics).

Balanced Diets

In today's fast-paced society, people have very busy lives. This makes it more difficult to always follow the healthy eating guidelines covered earlier in this section. However, healthy choices can be found at restaurants and in packaged products. In the lessons in this part, students will learn how to evaluate restaurant menus. They will also gain additional experience in label reading to reinforce the skills they learned in previous lessons.

Lesson 53: Rate Your Plate

Outcomes

At the end of this lesson, each student will be able to do the following:

▶ Compare the carbohydrate, protein, fat, and calorie content of various foods from fast-food restaurants.

▶ Design a lunch menu that follows the recommendations for healthy eating based on selections from fast-food restaurants.

Connections to Health Education Standards

▶ Health promotion and disease prevention

▶ Access to valid health information, products, and services

Connections to Other Standards

▶ Science standards: science in personal and social perspectives

▶ Math standards: number and operations; measurement

Connections to WOW! Lessons

▶ Yellow level: lesson 14, "Tacos by Cody"

▶ Green level: lesson 10, "Tasty Tillies"

▶ Green level: lesson 11, "Soup and Salad?"

▶ Purple level: lesson 10, "The Balancing Act"

▶ Purple level: lesson 11, "V Is for Variety"

WOW! Vocabulary

▶ healthy eating—Following a balanced diet based on the recommendations of the MyPyramid.

Get Ready to WOW! 'Em

You will need the following:

▶ Menus and comparisons of the nutrient content from at least three fast-food restaurants, such as McDonald's, Burger King, and Taco Bell

▶ Worksheet 53.1, Rate Your Plate (one copy per pair of students)

▶ A cube of margarine or butter for the demonstration

▶ Family Activity 1 for Section 4, Good Snackin'

Background Information

In today's fast-paced society, it is often difficult to follow nutritional guidelines and consume heart-healthy meals. People are sometimes faced with the decision of eating at fast-food restaurants or not eating at all. Although fast food is usually not recommended, healthy choices are often available at these restaurants. The reason for discouraging frequent dining at fast-food restaurants is that many of the foods are high in fat and salt. The recommendations for **healthy eating** suggest a daily intake with less than 30 percent of the calories coming from fat. On a diet of 2,000 calories per day, that equals approximately no more than 66 grams of fat per day.

Now WOW! 'Em

1. Begin the class by asking students two questions:
   - *Do you ever eat at fast-food restaurants?*
   - *If you do, what are your favorite foods?*

2. Discuss the concerns about eating some of the foods offered at these restaurants and the effect these foods have on health. Be careful not to use the word *bad* for foods; instead, use the approach of presenting the healthy foods as *better choices.* Review the background information presented for this lesson with the class.

3. Put the students into pairs. Hand out the menus and comparison sheets to each pair. Ask them to design a healthy meal from the menu of one of the fast-food restaurants. After students have decided on the meal, instruct them to calculate the carbohydrate, protein, and fat content of the meal using worksheet 53.1, Rate Your Plate.

4. When everyone has finished, ask one pair of students to share the amount of fat they would have eaten in the meal.

5. Using the stick of butter or margarine, illustrate to the class how much fat would be represented by the meal. Tell students, *Every tablespoon of butter equals 12 grams of fat.* If they had 24 grams of fat in their meal, show them what 2 tablespoons looks like.

6. Ask if anyone chose a Burger King Double Whopper with cheese. Tell students, *This sandwich contains 70 grams of fat, which would equal almost six tablespoons of butter—that is, three quarters of a cube of butter (there are 8 tablespoons in one stick). This also represents more than a day's total intake of fat allowed on a healthy diet.*

Wrap It Up!

Ask the students to evaluate their meals as a class. If they did not choose foods that are low in fat, instruct the students to design a meal that would be healthier.

Teaching Notes

Each lesson has suggested modifications, whenever possible, to adapt the concepts to younger or older students.

Modifications for Younger Students

To modify the lesson for students who can't read, ask them to choose foods they think are low in fat from one local fast-food restaurant. Write these foods on the board. Record the fat content next to each food. Continue with the lesson, asking students to make changes to improve the meal.

Modifications for Older Students

None.

Concept Development

Assign the students to write a paragraph discussing their findings regarding the fast-food meals they planned. Ask students if they think fast food can be part of a healthy diet.

Assessment Options

Each lesson includes assessment options for the lesson and may include additional assessment options for the skills performed within a lesson.

For the Lesson

By completing the class activity, students will demonstrate their knowledge of the fat content of fast foods.

Worksheet 53.1: Rate Your Plate

Name: _____

Instructions: Using one of the fast-food menus, choose four foods that you think would make up a healthy meal. Once you've chosen your foods, record the food group that each food comes from. Also record the grams of carbohydrate, protein, and fat from the comparison sheet.

Food	*Food group*	*Carbohydrate (grams)*	*Protein (grams)*	*Fat (grams)*
1.				
2.				
3.				
4.				

Design a healthy, low-fat lunch from a fast-food restaurant. List the foods you've chosen here:

1.

2.

3.

4.

Section 4: Family Activity 1
Good Snackin'

Name: _____

When you feel a need to snack, use the following list of alternatives to choose a healthier option. As a family, plan three snacks for the week that are heart-healthy choices. Circle your choices and indicate the day you chose to snack healthy.

Instead of this	*Try this*
Potato chips or cheese puffs	Popcorn (no fat added) or pretzels
Doughnut	High-fiber muffin
Ice cream	Low-fat or nonfat yogurt
Soda	Fruit juice or sparkling mineral water
Beef burrito	Bean burrito
Chocolate chip cookies	Graham crackers
Chocolate cake	Angel food cake
Canned fruit in heavy syrup	Canned fruit in light juice
Mini pepperoni pizza	Mini cheese and veggie pizza

From C. Hopper, B. Fisher, and K.D. Munoz, 2008, *Physical Activity and Nutrition for Health* (Champaign, IL: Human Kinetics).

Lesson 54: The Case of the Label Connection

Outcomes

At the end of this lesson, each student will be able to do the following:

▸ Investigate cereal box labels for evidence of healthy ingredients.

▸ Make informed consumer choices when selecting breakfast cereals.

▸ Identify "hidden" fat in breakfast cereals.

Connections to Health Education Standards

▸ Health promotion and disease prevention

▸ Decision-making skills

Connections to Other Standards

▸ Science standards: science in personal and social perspectives

▸ Math standards: measurement

Connections to WOW! Lessons

▸ Red level: lesson 12, "Food for Thought"

▸ Yellow level: lesson 12, "Food for Thought"

▸ Blue level: lesson 12, "The Big Label Discovery"

▸ Purple level: lesson 11, "V Is for Variety"

▸ Purple level: lesson 13, "The High-Oc Mission"

WOW! Vocabulary

▸ hidden fat—Fat found in food that has not been added but is part of the food itself; an example of a food with hidden fat is peanut butter.

▸ hydrogenation—The chemical addition of hydrogen to a fatty acid, making the fatty acid more saturated.

▸ trans fatty acids—A type of unsaturated fat produced from liquid fat or oil that is turned into solid fat through a chemical process called hydrogenation. Eating a large amount of trans fatty acids raises blood cholesterol and the risk of heart disease.

Get Ready to WOW! 'Em

You will need the following:

▸ Worksheet 54.1, The Case of the Label Connection (one copy per student)

▸ Empty cereal boxes (at least two per group of students)

▸ An empty cereal box covered with blank paper so the package label can't be seen

▸ Family Activity 2 for Section 4, Label Search

Background Information

Understanding the coding on labels of packaged foods will help people make better-informed decisions about the foods they choose to eat and whether the food contains **hidden fat**. The USDA label requirements include important nutrition information about the amount of nutrients in a serving of the packaged food.

The labeling laws require the total fat, saturated fat, and cholesterol content of the food to be listed. These laws also require that labels include the amount of trans fatty acid in the food. **Trans fatty acids** are formed when oils have been changed to solid fats. This process, called **hydrogenation,** has been associated with increasing the risk of developing heart disease. For more information on the requirements for labels, visit www.cfsan.fda.gov/~acrobat/nutfacts.pdf.

Now WOW! 'Em

1. Show the class the cereal box with the label covered up. Ask students, *Do you know what's inside this box?* They will probably guess that it's cereal, but then you should ask them, *What kind of cereal? What type of grain? Is there any sugar? Salt? Nuts?* They will not know by looking at the blank label. Review with the class the background information presented for this lesson, and discuss why it's important for packaged foods to have nutrition labels.

2. Instruct each student to complete worksheet 54.1, The Case of the Label Connection. Go over the results of the worksheet to make sure the students are reading the label correctly.

3. Next, ask the students, *Which cereal do you like to eat and why?* Explain that some cereals contain more sugar and fat than others.

4. Organize the students into groups of two or three students, and provide at least two cereal boxes for each group to analyze. Ask them to examine and compare their cereals. Ask students, *Which one has more fiber? Which one has more fat? Does the cereal contain trans fat?*

Wrap It Up!

After the groups have examined their cereals, discuss their findings as a class. Ask students, *Which cereal do you think is the most nutritious?*

Teaching Notes

Each lesson has suggested modifications, whenever possible, to adapt the concepts to younger or older students.

Modifications for Younger Students

Younger students may not be able to read the labels. To modify the lesson for them, ask them to color their own cereal box with a nutrition label.

Modifications for Older Students

None.

Concept Development

▶ Assign the students to write a paragraph discussing their findings regarding the cereals they investigated.

▶ Ask the students to keep a record of the fat and sugar contents of the cereals they have at home.

Assessment Options

Each lesson includes assessment options for the lesson and may include additional assessment options for the skills performed within a lesson.

For the Lesson

By completing the worksheet and the class activity, students will demonstrate their knowledge of label reading.

Worksheet 54.1:
The Case of the Label Connection

Name: _____

Instructions: Inspector Smart is investigating Krispies cereal for healthy ingredients. Study the label and answer the questions to help him find the evidence. Then investigate two other cereal labels and compare them to the Krispies. Which cereal is the healthiest?

Krispies

1. First, check the nutrition information on the Krispies label. What's the serving size? _____

   How many grams of total fat are in each serving of Krispies cereal?

   _____

2. Next, check the ingredients list. Do you find extra fat or oil in the Krispies cereal?

   _____

   If yes, name it. _____

   Is the fat in the Krispies cereal saturated, monounsaturated, or polyunsaturated? How do you know?

   _____

   _____

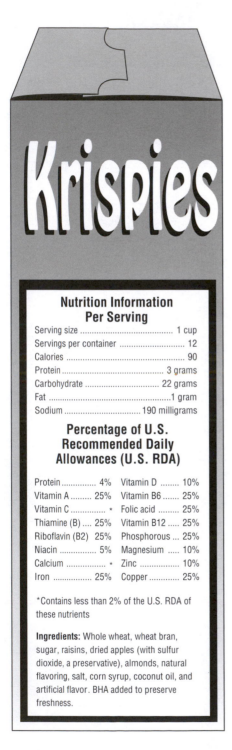

Nutrition Information Per Serving

Serving size .... 1 cup
Servings per container 12
Calories 90
Protein .... 3 grams
Carbohydrate .... 22 grams
Fat ....1 gram
Sodium .... 190 milligrams

Percentage of U.S. Recommended Daily Allowances (U.S. RDA)

Protein	4%	Vitamin D	10%
Vitamin A	25%	Vitamin B6	25%
Vitamin C	*	Folic acid	25%
Thiamine (B)	25%	Vitamin B12	25%
Riboflavin (B2)	25%	Phosphorous	25%
Niacin	5%	Magnesium	10%
Calcium	*	Zinc	10%
Iron	25%	Copper	25%

*Contains less than 2% of the U.S. RDA of these nutrients

Ingredients: Whole wheat, wheat bran, sugar, raisins, dried apples (with sulfur dioxide, a preservative), almonds, natural flavoring, salt, corn syrup, coconut oil, and artificial flavor. BHA added to preserve freshness.

(continued)

From C. Hopper, B. Fisher, and K.D. Munoz, 2008, *Physical Activity and Nutrition for Health* (Champaign, IL: Human Kinetics). Illustration reprinted, by permission, from C.A. Hopper, B.D. Fisher, and K.D. Munoz, 1997, *Health-Related Fitness for Grades 5 & 6* (Champaign, IL: Human Kinetics), 98.

3. The first item in the ingredients list is the one that makes up most (at least 60 percent) of the product. There's less of the second item, even less of the third, and so on. What's listed first on the Krispies label?

_____

4. Is the Krispies cereal cholesterol free? _____

Why or why not? _____

5. Does the Krispies cereal have any trans fat? _____

How do you know? _____

6. Do you think Inspector Smart will find Krispies to be a healthy cereal? _____

Why or why not? _____

_____

_____

_____

Fill in the blanks in the following table. Answer "Yes" or "No" to those phrases that end with a question mark.

	Krispies	Cereal B	Cereal C
Serving size			
Fat per serving			
Extra fat or oil?			
First ingredient			
Second ingredient			
Cholesterol?			
Trans fat?			
Healthy?			

From C. Hopper, B. Fisher, and K.D. Munoz, 2008, *Physical Activity and Nutrition for Health* (Champaign, IL: Human Kinetics).

Section 4: Family Activity 2
Label Search

Name: _____

Choose six packaged or canned foods from your cupboard. Write down the amount of fat (in grams) per serving for each food you choose. Then ask your parents if they can place the food in order (from highest to lowest in fat content) without looking at the labels. After they have finished ranking the foods, check to see how many they have right. Switch roles with your parents the second time around, using different foods. Write down the foods and their fat content on this form. Discuss the results with regard to planning family menus and shopping lists.

Parent

Food	Prediction	Fat per serving (in grams)	Ranking
1. _____	_____	_____	_____
2. _____	_____	_____	_____
3. _____	_____	_____	_____
4. _____	_____	_____	_____
5. _____	_____	_____	_____
6. _____	_____	_____	_____

From C. Hopper, B. Fisher, and K.D. Munoz, 2008, *Physical Activity and Nutrition for Health* (Champaign, IL: Human Kinetics).

(continued)

(continued)

Student

Food	Prediction	Fat per serving (in grams)	Ranking
1. _____	_____	_____	_____
2. _____	_____	_____	_____
3. _____	_____	_____	_____
4. _____	_____	_____	_____
5. _____	_____	_____	_____
6. _____	_____	_____	_____

Body Systems

Body systems help produce the energy necessary to perform daily activities. If these body systems function properly, this allows a person to lead a healthy, active lifestyle. In the upcoming lessons, students will learn to make the connection between the digestive, circulatory, and respiratory systems.

Lesson 55: Follow the Food

Outcomes

At the end of this lesson, each student will be able to do the following:

▶ Understand the connection between the cardiorespiratory, muscular, skeletal, and digestive systems in producing effective movement patterns.

Connections to Health Education Standards

▶ Health promotion and disease prevention

Connections to Other Standards

▶ Science standards: life science

Connections to WOW! Lessons

▶ Red level: lesson 18, "Busy Body"
▶ Blue level: lesson 19, "Body Systems"

WOW! Vocabulary

▶ cardiorespiratory system—The body system that includes the heart, the lungs, and the blood-transporting network of arteries and veins.
▶ digestion—The process by which food is converted into substances that can be absorbed by the body.
▶ digestive system—The body system that physically and chemically breaks down food so that nutrients can be used by the body.
▶ esophagus—A muscular tube for the passage of food from the mouth to the stomach.
▶ small intestine—The part of the digestive system that lies between the stomach and the colon and secretes digestive enzymes.

Get Ready to WOW! 'Em

You will need the following:

▶ Worksheet 55.1, Follow the Food, (one copy per student) 💿

Background Information

The human body is made up of several complex systems that enable the body to function as an integrated unit. Each of these systems depends on the health of the other systems. These systems include the **cardiorespiratory,** muscular, skeletal, and **digestive systems.**

Now WOW! 'Em

1. Use worksheet 55.1 to explain how the cardiorespiratory, muscular, skeletal, and digestive systems work. Students can follow the path and label the appropriate system function on the figure.

2. Review the background information presented for this lesson with the class. Explain how the digestive system provides nutrients for the cells in the muscles.

    a. *Food is taken in through the mouth and is broken down into smaller chunks through chewing.*

    b. *As food is reduced into smaller particles, saliva moistens the food, and enzymes in saliva start to break down the food.*

    c. *The food passes down the* **esophagus** *into the stomach.*

    d. *In the stomach, acids break down the food into a thick fluid.*

    e. *Food passes from the stomach to the* **small intestine.**

    f. *Undigested parts of the food pass into the large intestine or colon.*

3. Tell students the remaining steps of the digestive process:

    a. *The cardiorespiratory system transports oxygen and nutrients to the muscle cells and returns carbon dioxide to the lungs.*

    b. *Blood cells pumped to the small intestine pick up sugars, proteins, minerals, water, and vitamins. Blood transports these nutrients to the muscles and other parts of the body.*

    c. *Blood cells transport oxygen and nutrients to muscles so that they can contract and relax to enable the body to move.*

    d. *Carbon dioxide and other waste molecules are picked up by the blood, and this blood (with no oxygen) returns to the heart.*

    e. *The blood cells enter into the right atrium, and then the heart contracts and forces the blood into the right ventricle.*

    f. *As the heart contracts again, blood in the right ventricle passes into the pulmonary artery and to the lungs.*

    g. *In the lungs, blood transfers the carbon dioxide and picks up oxygen from the lungs.*

    h. *The oxygenated blood flows through the pulmonary vein to the left atrium. This chamber collects the blood from both lungs. When the heart contracts, blood passes into the left ventricle.*

    i. *From the left ventricle, blood is pumped into arteries that carry oxygen to all cells in the body, including the muscles.*

Wrap It Up!

Discuss the importance of a consistent and healthy eating plan. Regular meals, including breakfast, supply the body with energy and nutrients. Provide some examples of healthy breakfast selections, such as whole grain cereal with lowfat milk and bananas.

Teaching Notes

Each lesson has suggested modifications, whenever possible, to adapt the concepts to younger or older students.

Modifications for Younger Students

Emphasize the importance of eating fruits and vegetables for a healthy digestive system.

Modifications for Older Students

For older students, present more details on **digestion,** including how food is broken down and the role of specific enzymes. Also provide more details on how the lungs absorb oxygen.

Concept Development

1. Discuss how the body copes with strenuous exercise. Describe how the increased demands cause the body systems to use food and oxygen at increased rates.

2. Ask students to identify the effects of strenuous exercise (heart rate accelerates, breathing rate increases, food intake increases over a period of time).

Assessment Options

Each lesson includes assessment options for the lesson and may include additional assessment options for the skills performed within a lesson.

For the Lesson

Students will complete the "follow the food" pathway on the diagram.

Worksheet 55.1: **Follow the Food**

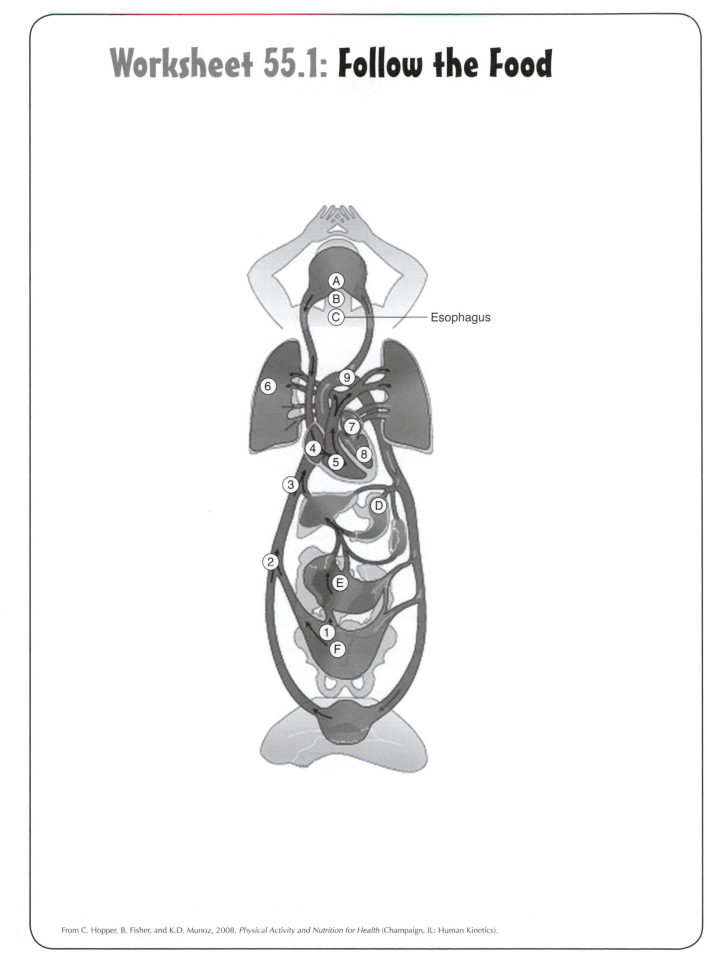

Esophagus

Lesson 56: Oxygen Grab

Outcomes

At the end of this lesson, each student will be able to do the following:

▶ Understand that muscles need oxygen to work effectively.

▶ Understand that blood cells provide oxygen to the muscles.

Connections to Health Education Standards

▶ Practice of health-enhancing behaviors

Connections to Other Standards

▶ Science standards: life science

▶ Physical education standards: understanding of movement concepts, principles, strategies, and tactics

Connections to WOW! Lessons

▶ Red level: lesson 18, "Busy Body"

▶ Blue level: lesson 19, "Body Systems"

WOW! Vocabulary

▶ capillaries—Tiny blood vessels that connect the smallest arteries and veins.

▶ cell—A basic unit of living matter.

▶ oxygen molecule—A small amount of oxygen.

Get Ready to WOW! 'Em

You will need the following:

▶ Five playground balls for outdoors or five balloons for indoors

▶ 20 cones to mark out an area representing a muscle

▶ Tennis balls for outdoors or foam balls for indoors (one ball for each pair of students); other types of balls can also be used depending on facilities.

▶ Two boxes, one labeled "heart" and one labeled "muscle"

▶ Watch

▶ Whistle

▶ One blindfold or one pair of sunglasses

Background Information

Activities such as running and jumping require the muscles to work harder compared to when sitting or standing. This places a demand on **cells** in the muscle. Because more oxygen is needed, the heart beats faster to pump more blood to the muscles of the body. Blood flows from arteries into **capillaries.** Capillaries come in contact with every cell in the body. Muscles need oxygen to complete movements. Oxygen is supplied to the muscle by the blood.

Now WOW! 'Em

1. Review the background information presented for this lesson with the class.

2. Mark out an area in the shape of a muscle (see figure 56.1).

3. Five students acting as muscle cells are positioned inside the muscle. Each of these students has a balloon (if inside) or a playground ball (if outside).

4. The remaining students pair up, with one member of the pair on each side of the muscle. These pairs act as blood cells with **oxygen molecules** (tennis or foam balls).

5. The pairs try to roll tennis balls (underhand) or throw foam balls (overhand) across the muscle area. Their task is to make sure the ball does not get intercepted.

6. The muscle cells try to intercept the oxygen molecule (tennis or foam ball) while keeping the balloon in the air. If playing this game outside, the students can bounce the playground ball on the ground.

7. If the oxygen molecule is intercepted, it is placed in the muscle box. The blood cells must then run to get a new ball from the heart box.

8. If the muscle cells let the balloon or playground ball touch the ground, they give back one of the tennis or foam balls from the muscle box.

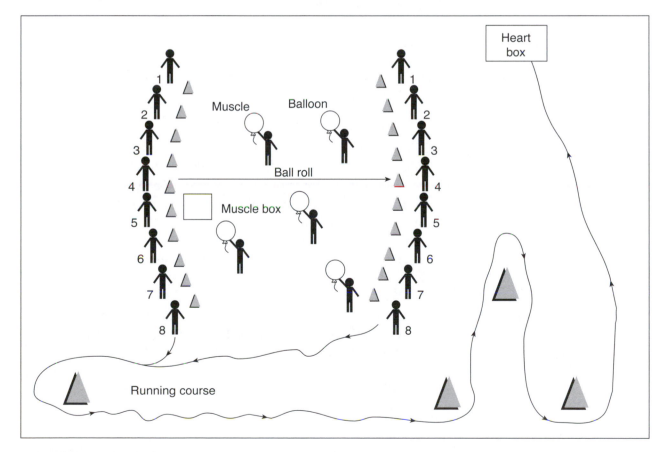

FIGURE 56.1   Oxygen grab.

Adapted, by permission, from C.A. Hopper, B.D. Fisher, and K.D. Munoz, 1997, *Health-Related Fitness for Grades 3 & 4* (Champaign, IL: Human Kinetics), 8.

9. Play for a three-minute period. Muscle cells try to intercept as many balls as possible in the time period. Blood cells try to make sure their ball is not intercepted. Rotate students into the muscle area.

10. The number of students in the muscle area can be reduced or increased to make the task of rolling the ball across the muscle easier or more difficult. Similarly, the size of the muscle area can be increased or decreased. Students can practice using right and left hands.

11. To help ensure safety, do not allow students to roll balls directly at other students to hit them.

Wrap It Up!

Ask students to explain how capillaries are connected to arteries and veins. Reinforce the concept that muscles need oxygen to work effectively and that daily exercise improves the efficiency of the body in providing oxygen to muscles.

Teaching Notes

Each lesson has suggested modifications, whenever possible, to adapt the concepts to younger or older students.

Modifications for Younger Students

Younger students should be limited to rolling the balls so they do not get hit by a thrown ball.

Modifications for Older Students

Older students can kick larger foam balls across the muscle area, but they must kick the ball low and be careful not to hit each other.

Modifications for Students With Vision Difficulties

At least 80 percent of children who are blind have some residual vision. When starting an interaction with a student who has vision difficulties, you should always state your name. Do not expect to be recognized by the sound of your voice. Always ask if help is needed with mobility, and do not grab the student's arm. The student with poor vision can grasp your upper arm. Give verbal cues, such as "move right" or "move left." Ball handling can present a real challenge. Use balls that are orange or yellow. Another way to simulate poor vision is to put petroleum jelly on a pair of sunglasses.

Concept Development

To help students understand how individuals who have poor vision (or individuals who are blind) experience movement, organize the blood cells into groups of two for the oxygen grab game. One student wears a blindfold and is assisted by another student in the group of three. The two students work together to roll the ball across the muscle. The mentor gives directions for when to roll the ball. Students take turns wearing the blindfold.

Assessment Options

Each lesson includes assessment options for the lesson and may include additional assessment options for the skills performed within a lesson.

For the Lesson

By participating in the oxygen grab game, students will demonstrate an understanding that muscles need oxygen to function effectively.

For Throwing

- A downward arc of the throwing arm initiates the windup.
- The hip and shoulder rotate to a point where the nondominant side faces an imaginary target.
- Weight is transferred by stepping with the foot opposite the throwing hand.
- The throwing arm follows through beyond the ball release, moving diagonally across the body toward the side opposite the throwing arm.

Goal Setting

In this part, students will learn about how a person's height and weight are measured, and they will track changes in their height and weight over time. They will also learn about setting short- and long-term goals focused on improving and maintaining physical fitness levels. These lessons focus on activities that can be performed throughout a person's lifetime. Students will participate in challenges that enable them to track their activity and improvement. They will also participate in cooperative games. These activities encourage students to establish healthy and active lifestyles.

Lesson 57: Checking In on Height and Weight

Outcomes

At the end of this lesson, each student will be able to do the following:

▶ Use the correct techniques for measuring height and weight.

▶ Understand how body types are different and that growth and development take place at varying rates.

Connections to Health Education Standards

▶ Health promotion and disease prevention

Connections to Other Standards

▶ Physical education standards: health-enhancing level of physical fitness

Connections to WOW! Lessons

▶ Red level: lesson 8, "Sturdy, Strong, and Stretchy"

▶ Orange level: lesson 7, "Sturdy, Strong, and Stretchy"

WOW! Vocabulary

▶ body mass index—A formula used to estimate how much body fat a person has based on height and weight.

▶ height—How tall a person is.

▶ weight—How heavy a person is.

Get Ready to WOW! 'Em

You will need the following:

▶ A setting for height and weight measurements. In some cases, the school nurse's office may be the best location. Measurement stations can also be set up in the classroom.

▶ A scale to weigh students (balance beam scale or electronic or digital scale)

▶ A portable or wall-mounted stadiometer or a tape measure attached to a wall

▶ Worksheet 57.1, Height and Weight (one copy per student)

Background Information

Height and **weight** measurements are used to assess growth patterns and to determine if a person is overweight or underweight. Many factors go into determining the right weight for a person, and there is no single technique for doing so. Children grow and develop at different rates. Heredity plays a role in body shape and what a person will weigh. People from different ethnic groups tend to have different body fat distributions or body compositions (amounts of bone and muscle versus fat). As children grow up, hormones spark physical changes, such as muscle growth. The onset of these changes can vary in age from 8 to 14, so there will be great variations in height and weight in children of the same chronological age.

Now WOW! 'Em

1. Review the background information presented for this lesson with the class.

2. Have students measure their height and weight:
   - Height: Students should remove their shoes and any heavy coats and hair ornaments or braids. Regardless of the measurement device used, students should stand with legs together, arms at the side, and shoulders relaxed. The back of the body should touch either the stadiometer or the wall. The headpiece or a flat object is placed on top of the head (with sufficient pressure to press the hair down) when taking the measurement.
   - Weight: Weight measurements require some privacy and should be completed in a private setting. Students should remove their shoes and coats.

3. Students record their scores on worksheet 57.1, Height and Weight. They should use this chart to track their height and weight measurements throughout the year. Changes from the previous measurement can be tracked in the height and weight change columns.

4. Discuss the importance of privacy regarding weight. A person's weight is personal information and should not be shared with others.

Wrap It Up!

Explain that a student's weight consists of muscles, bones, organs, and body fat. Maintaining an appropriate body composition is important for health. Too much body fat (25 percent or more for boys and 30 percent or more for girls) can cause health problems. Skinfold measurements can provide a more direct estimate of body fat than does the **body mass index**.

Teaching Notes

Each lesson has suggested modifications, whenever possible, to adapt the concepts to younger or older students.

Modifications for Younger Students

Use height and weight to introduce the use of inches and pound (meters & kilograms) as measurement techniques.

Modifications for Older Students

Students can calculate their body mass index (BMI), which refers to the ratio of the body's weight to the square of its height. BMI is an indication of the appropriateness of weight relative to height. This can help students determine if they weigh too much for their height. Use measurements with height in whole numbers (e.g., 4 feet 5 inches) and weight in pounds (e.g., 95 pounds). Then convert those measures to meters (e.g., 4 feet 5 inches = 1.4 meters) and kilograms (e.g., 95 pounds = 42.9 kilograms). Here is the formula used to determine BMI:

Body weight (kg*) divided by height squared (in meters**)

*1 kilogram = 2.216 pounds
**1 meter = 39.37 inches
For more information, refer to the healthy fitness zone standards in the *Fitnessgram Test Administration Manual,* by M.D. Meredith and G.J. Welk (Champaign, IL: Human Kinetics, 2007).

Concept Development

Using the protocols described in the *Fitnessgram* manual, skinfold measurements can be taken to estimate each student's percentage of body fat. Measurements should be taken at two sites, the triceps (back of arm) and the calf (inside of lower leg). Calipers are used to determine the size of the skinfolds.

Assessment Options

Each lesson includes assessment options for the lesson and may include additional assessment options for the skills performed within a lesson.

For the Lesson

Students will demonstrate their understanding of how height and weight are measured, and they will track their changes in height and weight.

Worksheet 57.1: Height and Weight

Name: _____

Instructions: Record your height and weight scores and calculate the change throughout the year.

Date	Height	Height change	Weight	Weight change

From C. Hopper, B. Fisher, and K.D. Munoz, 2008, *Physical Activity and Nutrition for Health* (Champaign, IL: Human Kinetics).

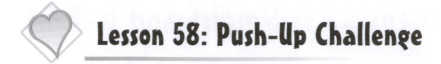

Lesson 58: Push-Up Challenge

Outcomes

At the end of this lesson, each student will be able to do the following:

▶ Complete a practical goal-setting exercise using push-ups.

▶ Distinguish between outcome and process goals.

▶ Describe and interpret Fitnessgram scores for personal goal setting.

Connections to Health Education Standards

▶ Goal-setting skills

Connections to Other Standards

▶ Physical education standards: regular participation in physical activity; health-enhancing level of physical fitness

Connections to WOW! Lessons

▶ Red level: lesson 8, "Sturdy, Strong, and Stretchy"

▶ Orange level: lesson 7, "Sturdy, Strong, and Stretchy"

WOW! Vocabulary

▶ outcome goals—Goals that focus on an outcome, such as the number of repetitions of an exercise.

▶ parallel—Two lines an equal distance apart.

▶ process goals—Goals that focus on the experience of performing the activity.

Get Ready to WOW! 'Em

You will need the following:

▶ An activity area of approximately 25 by 25 yards (23 by 23 m) where students can complete push-ups

Background Information

Establishing specific short- and long-term goals is critical to improving and maintaining physical fitness levels. Being healthy is not a meaningful objective for most elementary students. They need objectives that are relevant to their daily lives, such as achieving goals, improving scores, and feeling good about their body. Short-term goals can be either **outcome goals** (e.g., being able to perform a certain number of push-ups) or **process goals** (e.g., performing a variety of activities to strengthen the upper body). Although increasing the number of repetitions is important, focusing on the score does not provide variety and interest for students. Performing a range of activities in addition to push-ups is beneficial and more interesting for students. Repetitions of push-ups should be included in the general plan in order to provide specific practice that is essential to improvement. Students should be encouraged to try hard and should be praised for effort, which is under the students' control.

Now WOW! 'Em

1. Review the background information presented for this lesson with the class.

2. Each student will complete push-ups, an exercise that can be used throughout life as a conditioning activity and for self-testing of upper body strength and endurance. Before they begin, ask students to estimate what their best performance will be (highest number of repetitions for push-ups). Each student should record this number in class. Make sure that students estimate on their own without discussion among classmates.

3. Describe the correct form for completing push-ups. See the "Assessment Options" section later in this lesson for information on the correct form for push-ups.

4. Once each student has performed push-ups and established a score, the process of goal setting can begin. This process will help students improve or maintain their scores. In most cases, improvement will be necessary. Students record their actual performance in relation to their original estimate. To determine if students are in the "healthy fitness zone," use the health fitness standards from *Fitnessgram/Activitygram Test Administration Manual, Fourth Edition,* by M.D. Meredith and G.J. Welk (Champaign, IL: Human Kinetics, 2007).

Wrap It Up!

Challenge students to keep performing push-ups on a systematic basis. Refer to previous lessons that have introduced the specificity of exercise (see lesson 29, "Target Practice"). Remind students that push-ups can be done at home, on the beach, in a hotel room when on vacation, and many other places. Students can keep track of their scores.

Teaching Notes

Each lesson has suggested modifications, whenever possible, to adapt the concepts to younger or older students.

Modifications for Younger Students

Younger students without upper body strength can complete knee push-ups until they build up greater strength. Another developmental option is for students to start in the up position and let the body weight down slowly. Students can also do wall push-ups, standing with the feet about 2 to 3 feet (61 to 91 cm) from the wall, with the feet shoulder-width apart and the hands against the wall.

Modifications for Older Students

Older students can challenge themselves by completing push-ups with their feet on a low bench. They can also have a partner place hands on their shoulder blades to offer slight resistance to the upward movement. This increases the difficulty of the exercise.

Modifications for Students With Limited Arm and Shoulder Strength

For students with limited arm and shoulder strength, the isometric push-up is one option. In an isometric push-up, the student maintains the up position as long as possible. Using the crab walk movement can help build strength. Light soup cans may be used as weights for exercises.

Concept Development

1. The emphasis on lower body activities often results in students having limited upper body strength and achieving low scores for push-ups and pull-ups. Activities that use similar muscle groups can be used as part of the program, including the flexed arm hang, pull-ups, knee push-ups, chair push-ups, horizontal ladder activities, climbing a rope, and crab walks. The same goal-setting approach can be used for these other exercises.

2. The main muscles used in the push-up are the pectoralis, deltoids, and triceps. These muscles cross the elbow and shoulder joints. The action is very similar to a bench press but requires no equipment.

Assessment Options

Each lesson includes assessment options for the lesson and may include additional assessment options for the skills performed within a lesson.

For the Lesson

Students will complete push-ups and learn how to set goals for future performances with a focus on individual self-improvement.

For Push-Ups

- The student starts in a prone position with the hands under the shoulders.
- The legs are straight back, slightly apart.
- The student pushes up off the mat until the arms are locked straight.
- The legs and back remain straight.
- The student lowers the body with the arms until a 90-degree angle is reached.
- The upper arms remain **parallel** to the floor.
- The recommended rate is to complete 20 push-ups per minute, or 1 push-up every three seconds.

Lesson 59: Cooperative Games

Outcomes

At the end of this lesson, each student will be able to do the following:

- ▶ Participate in active games.
- ▶ Practice teamwork and cooperation.

Connections to Health Education Standards

- ▶ Interpersonal communication skills

Connections to Other Standards

- ▶ Physical education standards: responsible personal and social behavior

Connections to WOW! Lessons

- ▶ Red level: lesson 9, "Family Fitness Fun"
- ▶ Yellow level: lesson 9, "Family Fitness Fun"
- ▶ Orange level: lesson 9, "Family Fitness Fun"

WOW! Vocabulary

- ▶ cooperation—Working or acting together for a common goal or purpose.
- ▶ support—To assist someone in achieving a goal.

Get Ready to WOW! 'Em

You will need the following:

- ▶ 10 balls or beanbags
- ▶ 10 hoops
- ▶ Music and CD or tape player

Background Information

In cooperative games, students interact with each other to achieve common goals or to overcome challenges. Students work with and **support** each other rather than compete against each other. All students are actively involved in the game regardless of their personal skill level, and students are not eliminated based on performance.

Now WOW! 'Em

1. Review the background information presented for this lesson with the class.
2. Group juggling
   - Organize students into groups of five or six in a circle with one ball. The circle should be fairly small, about 10 yards (9 m) in diameter.
   - Students pass the ball underhand across the circle, with the ball being passed to a new person each time. The passing continues until each person has caught and thrown the

ball. The same sequence of passing is repeated; students must remember who passes the ball to them and whom they pass to next.

- The objective is to keep the ball in the air, moving around the circle.
- Variations can include adding another ball or increasing the size of the circle.

3. Thread the hoop
   - Groups of five or six students form a circle and join hands.
   - A hoop is placed over one student's wrist (similar to a bracelet).
   - The objective is to move the hoop around the circle as quickly as possible by stepping, bending, and twisting through the hoop.
   - Students keep holding hands throughout the game.
   - Variations can include changing the direction of the hoop (clockwise versus counter-clockwise), using more than one hoop, and using timed movements of the hoop around the group.

4. Beanbag up
   - Divide students into groups of four to six.
   - Each group should have the same number of beanbags as the number of students in the group. To begin, one student in the group is holding a beanbag.
   - Students form a small circle and crouch down toward the ground.
   - One student counts out aloud, "1, 2, 3, jump."
   - On this cue, the student who has the beanbag throws it up into the air. The objective is for another member of the group to catch the beanbag.
   - If the beanbag is successfully caught by another student, another beanbag is added, and two beanbags are thrown upward.
   - If the group catches the two beanbags, another one is added. For every beanbag not caught, the number is reduced for the next throw.
   - At first, beanbags should be thrown a few feet (meters) above the heads of the students, and the height of the throw can gradually be increased. Beanbags must be thrown on the cue.

5. Musical hoops
   - Each student has a hoop.
   - Students move around the area using specified jogging, skipping, or hopping movements.
   - Music is played, and every time the music stops, a hoop is removed. As hoops are removed, students must start sharing hoops with others.
   - Keep going until only one hoop is left, with all students getting part of their body in the hoop (or specify 10 students to a hoop).
   - Add balls or beanbags to the activity. Students can walk while tossing a ball or beanbag into the air and catching it. Start with very small tosses, gradually increasing the height of the toss.

Wrap It Up!

Encourage students to support each other with positive comments. Remind students to give praise to each other for trying hard and producing effective performances. Encourage students to talk to each other and develop strategies for success. Ask students to present successful strategies to the class. Explain how the concept of working together and supporting the efforts of each individual can be applied to health issues such as nutrition. Encourage students to support each other in making healthy food choices. Ask them to discuss the benefits and drawbacks of eating specific foods.

Teaching Notes

Each lesson has suggested modifications, whenever possible, to adapt the concepts to younger or older students.

Modifications for Younger Students

With younger students, use smaller groups (three or four students each) to simplify the activity. Gradually increase the group size as skill and understanding of the game increase.

Modifications for Older Students

Provide challenges by adding more equipment (such as balls and hoops) and by increasing the speed of the activity. Add additional movement requirements to challenge students.

Modifications for Students With Juvenile Rheumatoid Arthritis

Students with juvenile rheumatoid arthritis (JRA) may have severe joint pain that limits their mobility. JRA affects five times as many girls as boys. In JRA, one joint (usually the knee) or several joints may be involved. Joint swelling causes pain, and the knees and hips are often in a flexed position. Students may be able to participate in activities but with limited movements. Prolonged inactivity increases joint stiffness; therefore, flexibility exercises are encouraged. Exercise in a pool with warm water is strongly recommended.

Concept Development

1. Encourage students to play these games at recess to promote a cooperative playground climate.
2. These games can also be played at home with family and friends (e.g., at parties and family gatherings).

Assessment Options

Each lesson includes assessment options for the lesson and may include additional assessment options for the skills performed within a lesson.

For the Lesson

Students will demonstrate **cooperation** by working in a constructive and positive way with each other. They will focus on working together during the games.

For Catching

▶ In the preparation phase, the elbows are flexed and the hands are out in front of the body.

▶ The arms extend in preparation for ball contact.

▶ The ball is caught and controlled by the hands only.

▶ The elbows bend to absorb force.

▶ The body bends at the knees to assist in absorbing force.

Lesson 60: Keep on Walking

Outcomes

At the end of this lesson, each student will be able to do the following:

- ▶ Walk a mile (1.6 km).
- ▶ Develop a five-week walking program to complete with friends and family.

Connections to Health Education Standards

- ▶ Practice of health-enhancing behaviors

Connections to Other Standards

- ▶ Math standards: number and operations
- ▶ Physical education standards: regular participation in physical activity; health-enhancing level of physical fitness

Connections to WOW! Lessons

- ▶ Red level: lesson 7, "Heart Healthy"
- ▶ Red level: lesson 9, "Family Fitness Fun"
- ▶ Orange level: lesson 9, "Family Fitness Fun"
- ▶ Yellow level: lesson 9, "Family Fitness Fun"
- ▶ Green level: lesson 8, "Physical Education"
- ▶ Purple level: lesson 6, "Health-Related Fitness"
- ▶ Green level: lesson 23, "A Walking Club"

WOW! Vocabulary

- ▶ briskly—Moving with speed and vigor.
- ▶ rhythmic—Smooth, coordinated movements performed in sequences.
- ▶ sustained—Maintaining movements over a period of time.

Get Ready to WOW! 'Em

You will need the following:

- ▶ Popsicle sticks, poker chips, or coffee stir sticks (four per student)
- ▶ Worksheet 60.1, Walking Is Super Healthy (WISH; one per student)
- ▶ Maps of the local region or the United States to chart journeys

Background Information

Walking has considerable value as a lifetime activity. Therefore, walking is an excellent activity to introduce to students. Walking is an easy-to-organize activity that students can participate in with family members to stay active. **Sustained** walking for 20 to 30 minutes per day contributes to an effective exercise program.

Walking uses muscle groups in the upper and lower body in a **rhythmic** action. Although it may take longer to achieve aerobic benefits through walking than through other more strenuous activities, walking is an excellent lifetime activity. Walking **briskly** at a fast pace makes the heart beat faster and increases the breathing rate.

Now WOW! 'Em

1. Review the background information presented for this lesson with the class.
2. Map out a mile (1.6 km) for a class walk. You can use a track or a specific walking course in your school. Students can participate in calculating a mile course.
3. The objective for this lesson is for everyone to walk one mile. If using a track, you can use popsicle sticks or chips to help students keep track of their laps. Clearly explain that this activity is a walk, not a run. Tell the class that you will ask them to run in another lesson. Invite parents to walk with the class.
4. Use the class walk to establish a five-week walking program for your class.
5. Students can form small groups in class. Each group decides on a distant place in the United States that they would like to visit. Use a map to determine how far away that destination is.
6. Divide the number of miles to the selected destination by 15 walking sessions to determine how many miles each 1-mile walk session represents. For example, a person living in San Francisco who decides to take an imaginary trip to New York would divide the 2,500-mile (4,023 km) distance by 15 walking sessions. This person would determine that each walking session represents 167 miles (269 km).
7. Students complete the 15 walking sessions over a five-week period. They chart their progress on the map after each session.
8. Students should fill out worksheet 60.1, Walking Is Super Healthy (WISH), as they complete the program.

Wrap It Up!

Encourage students to walk at recess. Set up a walking course. This may be helpful for students whose parents do not participate.

Teaching Notes

Each lesson has suggested modifications, whenever possible, to adapt the concepts to younger or older students.

Modifications for Younger Students

Younger students can walk a shorter distance, such as half a mile (0.8 km).

Modifications for Older Students

Challenge older students to walk faster. Depending on the destination of the walk, class lessons can review the geography and history of the areas passed through on the journey.

Concept Development

1. If the walking course is on campus, students can complete their walking activities during recess, breaks, and lunch hour.

2. Ask students to share their selected destinations and why these places had special appeal. Then turn your walkers into researchers by having them read about their destinations and report on tourist attractions and other points of interest. Encourage them to provide additional information about some of the locations they could visit en route to their selected destinations.

3. Parent and school permission is needed for any course off the school grounds.

4. In ordinary or everyday walking, the feet step forward in two parallel tracks. When fitness walking at a faster pace, the footsteps fall in one nearly straight line. The heel of the forward foot should land in line with the toes of the back foot. The hips are rotated from front to back.

Assessment Options

Each lesson includes assessment options for the lesson and may include additional assessment options for the skills performed within a lesson.

For the Lesson

Students will demonstrate the ability to complete a walk in class and transfer information to a map to chart their progress.

For Walking

- In the starting posture, the shoulders are pulled back, the head and neck are erect, the abdomen is pulled in, and the buttocks are tucked in.
- In the walking stride, the heel contacts the ground first, and the foot rolls forward, keeping weight toward the outer edge of the foot until the toes touch the ground.
- The feet and knees point straight ahead.
- The arms are bent at 90 degrees at the elbow joint.
- The hands are in a relaxed fist position.
- The arms swing in a straight path and remain close to the body.
- In the forward phase, the hands can swing to chest level.
- The upper body relaxes, especially the shoulders

Worksheet 60.1:
Walking Is Super Healthy (WISH)

Name: _____

Instructions: Use this worksheet to track 15 one-mile walking sessions over a five-week period. Decide on a place you would like to visit. Use a map to find out how far away that destination is. Then divide the number of miles to the destination by 15 walking sessions to determine how many miles each of your one-mile walks will represent. For example, a person living in San Francisco who decides to take an imaginary trip to New York City would divide the 2,500-mile distance by 15 walking sessions. This person would determine that each walking session represents 167 miles.

Destination:

Miles to destination:

"Selected journey miles" per workout (divide miles to destination by 15):

Week #	Walk 1	Walk 2	Walk 3	Weekly total
1				
2				
3				
4				
5				
Total miles				

From C. Hopper, B. Fisher, and K.D. Munoz, 2008, *Physical Activity and Nutrition for Health* (Champaign, IL: Human Kinetics).

About the Authors

Chris Hopper, PhD, is associate dean for teacher preparation and credentialing and a professor of kinesiology at Humboldt State University in Arcata, California. He has degrees from the University of Exeter in England and the University of Oregon. Dr. Hopper is a specialist in adapted physical education and has helped promote active lifestyles for children with disabilities. He has played and coached soccer at the high school and college levels. Dr. Hopper has authored six other books and has served on numerous curriculum and advisory committees for Humboldt State University and has written dozens of articles and chapters in books. He has served as a consultant to school districts on promoting health and physical activity.

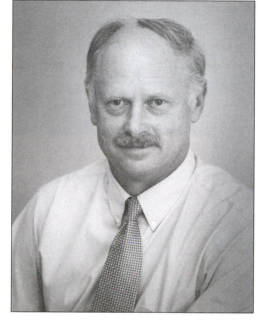

Bruce Fisher, BA, is an instructor at Humboldt State University focusing on teaching math and science in the elementary curriculum. He has also served as a fieldwork coordinator, supervisor of student teachers, and seminar instructor. He was a distinguished teacher in residence at Humboldt State from 1997 to 2000. Mr. Fisher is coordinator and trainer for Humboldt County Beginning Teacher Support and has been an elementary teacher, instructional services teacher, and teacher of the severely disabled. He has written three other books with the coauthors of this book, has written and published many articles, and has received numerous professional honors, including the Lifetime Achievement Award from the Humboldt County Office of Education and a National Educator Award. He has been a member of Computer-Using Educators, the National Teacher of the Year Association, the California Science Teachers Association, and the Association of Supervision and Curriculum Development.

Kathy D. Munoz, EdD, RD, is a professor of nutrition and chair of the department of kinesiology and recreation administration at Humboldt State University. She is a member of the American Dietetic Association (ADA) and the California Dietetic Association (CDA) and has completed the certification in Adult Weight Management. She has published in *Research Quarterly for Exercise and Sport, Children's Health Care, Journal of Nutrition Education,* and *International Journal of Sport Nutrition and Exercise.* With the coauthors of this book, she has written a series of curriculum guides for elementary teachers, which is published by Human Kinetics. She is currently coauthoring a college-level textbook for beginning nutrition majors. Dr. Munoz has been recognized for her research in and development of asynchronous learning with an award from the Bbionic Course Contest, an international competition sponsored by Blackboard, Inc., which helps universities host classes online.

DATE DUE

GAYLORD   PRINTED IN U.S.A.